DESCARTES

PHILOSOPHICAL WRITINGS

Descartes

PHILOSOPHICAL WRITINGS

Selected and Translated

by

NORMAN KEMP SMITH

Emeritus Professor of Logic and Metaphysics
in the University of Edinburgh

Author of *Studies in the Cartesian Philosophy*
and of *New Studies in the Philosophy of Descartes*

THE MODERN LIBRARY · NEW YORK

ABBREVIATIONS

A.T.	C. Adam and P. Tannery (eds.), *Oeuvres de Descartes*, 1897-1910
Com.	E. Gilson, *Discours de la Méthode, Texte et Commentaire*, 1925
New Studies	N. Kemp Smith, *New Studies in the Philosophy of Descartes*, 1952

CONTENTS

INTRODUCTION

WITH Descartes philosophy made a fresh start. A new set of problems had arisen, and it is owing to the manner in which he faced these problems that he has been called "the father of modern philosophy." If we seek to characterize the point of view of the Greek and medieval philosophers, especially of those who came under the influence of Aristotle, it would on the whole be true to assert that for them man and nature are inwardly related. The soul, Aristotle teaches, realizes itself in and through the body. Matter and form, the material and the immaterial, are two aspects involved in all natural existences, and are separable only artificially by abstraction. Descartes' attitude is very different. Those aspects which Aristotle in distinguishing reconciles are by Descartes held apart as contrasted opposites.

Speaking very roughly, it was in the writings of the Stoics and through Christianity, that the contrasting features in man and nature came to be felt. Through the Christian conception of the value of each human soul, the individual was separated out from the cosmic whole, and given an independent reality and worth. The kind of problems upon which Augustine wrote treatises—predestination and the freedom of the will, divine grace and original sin—shows how complete has been the break with Greek modes of thought. His treatment of our human knowledge, in his emphasis on its subjectivity, is no less modern, and again closely akin to that of Descartes.

There are two problems which Augustine recognized as being for him especially puzzling, and indeed insoluble. The first of these is how the unextended mind can contain images of an extended world. "There is in the mind a certain wonderful power (*mira quaedam vis*) by which it can contain *tanta coeli, terrae, marisque spatia.*"[1] Knowledge, he asks us to agree, is a subjective process going on separately in the mind of each individual. "Each sees one thing in himself such that another person may believe what he says of it, yet may not see it."[2]

And it is as a consequence of this that he formulates the *cogito ergo sum*. "We both are, and know that we are, and delight in our being and have knowledge of it. . . . In respect of these truths I am not at all afraid of the Academicians, who say, What if you are deceived? For if I am deceived, I am. For he who is not cannot be deceived; and if I am deceived, by this same token I am."[3]

The second mystery is how the mind can know external objects, and yet be ignorant of those internal parts of the body with which it is in immediate connection. "This is a very important question which I now ask, Why have I no need of science to know that there is a sun in the heavens and a moon, and all the other stars, but must have the aid of science to know, on moving my finger, whence the act begins—with my heart, or my brain, or with both, or with neither. . . . How is it that while we can count our limbs externally, even in the dark and with closed eyes, by the bodily sense which is called 'the touch,' we know nothing of our internal functions in the very central region of the soul itself, where that power is present which imparts life [and sensation to the body]—a mystery this, which, I apprehend, no medical man of any kind . . . or any man living, has any knowledge of."[4]

The advance from Augustine to Descartes, and in Descartes the deepening of the problems, consists in this, that while these two problems remain, and remain at bottom as insoluble

[1] *De Quanto.*

[2] *De Trinitate,* lib. IX, VI, M. Dods' edition, p. 231. Augustine also however—here again agreeing with Descartes—allows (cf. pp. 230-33) that common to all minds is the immediate awareness of eternal, unchanging essences which yield knowledge of the non-creaturely and of God.

[3] *De Civitate Dei,* lib. XI, cap. XXVI, Dods' transl. pp. 468-69.

[4] *De Anima et ejus Origine,* lib. IV, cap. VII, p. 305.

for Descartes as for Augustine, there has arisen, through the rise of the physical sciences the further problem, how soul and body can possibly interact, and how, therefore, the latter can produce sensations in the mind. Augustine depreciated the physical sciences as of no use for the attaining of the soul's salvation. What he alone sought was knowledge of God and of the self. *"Deum et animam scire cupio? Nihilne plus? Nihil omnino."*[5] And it was not until some eight centuries later, when nature, through love of her in the arts and study of her in the sciences, had come to be recognized as being at once the opposite and the complement of the self, that further steps could be made toward solution of the problems of knowledge. The Renaissance philosophers, however, in their reaction against the view of nature as the principle of evil, went to the other extreme, and blurred its features by spiritualizing it. It was a return to the Greek point, and so far a gain, a gain too in the restored respect for natural science; but it had, through Galileo and Descartes, to speak more clearly before the specifically modern formulation of the problems could be possible. In the sharply outlined dualism of Descartes there is a plastic clearness which is in as great contrast to the mystic pantheism, all things interfused, of the Renaissance thinkers, as to the Aristotelian physics of the Schools.

Descartes' Early Life

René Descartes was born in Touraine, March 31, 1596. His paternal grandfather was a medical practitioner, and married the daughter of a medical colleague. René's father, on becoming a Councillor of the Brittany Parliament, ranked as belonging to the *petite noblesse.* René, his second son, shared in the family fortune—a share sufficient to secure his independence—and following his father's example he adopted the dignified two-worded signature Des Cartes. In Latin writings he came to be referred to as Renatus Cartesius: hence the adjective Cartesian.

[5] *Soliloquiorum,* lib. I, cap. II.

In 1606, at the age of ten, he was entered as a pupil in the Royal Jesuit College of La Flèche. The course of study lasted nine years, six years of the humanities and three of philosophy. The philosophy, not then distinguished from the special sciences, was in three parts, the first year being devoted to morals and logic, the second to mathematics and physics, with metaphysics in the final year. Descartes, at the close of his school life, was therefore in his nineteenth year; and having been instructed in all that was then known in the fields of mathematics and physics was quite adequately equipped for further independent work. His Jesuit schooling in the field of theology was also a continuing influence. His theological views, as later modified to meet the requirements of his own new physics, are in the main a variation on those of Aquinas.

Descartes' critical comments on these various studies, in his *Discourse on Method,* are directed, it should be noted, not against the College or his teachers, but against the general state of the studies and sciences of the time. They represent his first impressions of them, but as meantime reinforced and made clearer to him in the course of his own later work. Some of them may, quite possibly, have been suggested to him by the teachers themselves. While still at La Flèche he knew of the enthusiasm aroused among them by the newly invented telescope and of the revolutionary discoveries Galileo had made by means of it.

On leaving La Flèche, Descartes proceeded to Poitiers, graduating there as Bachelor in Law in 1616. Probably, however, he spent most of the four years 1614-18 in Paris, and throughout this period was (we have grounds for conjecturing) in a detached and skeptical mood, reinforced, and perhaps induced, by an absorbed reading of Montaigne's *Essays.*

Critical Turning-Points in Descartes' Later Life

In 1618 he joined the army of Maurice of Nassau, serving, at his own expense, as a volunteer. Peace, however, was then prevailing; and more decisive for him than the military duties was his accidental meeting with Isaac Beeckman, a student of the sciences, several years his senior. On April 23, 1619, Descartes writes him: "I shall cherish you as the promoter and first author of my studies. In truth, it is you who have shaken me out of my indolence, and have made me recall my almost forgotten learning." Also, already on March 26 of the same year he had written: "It is now six days since I returned here [i.e., to Breda] and I have set myself to cultivate the Muses with more zeal than I have done at any time in the past. In this short term I have found . . . four demonstrations of no little importance, and completely new. . . . To conceal nothing from you regarding my labors, I propose to give the public . . . an entirely new science . . . so that almost nothing will remain to be discovered in geometry. It is an *opus infinitum,* and is not to be achieved by any one man. How incredibly ambitious! And yet in the obscure chaos of this science I have discovered I know not what light, by the aid of which I expect to be able to dissipate darkness however dense." Then a month later, in the letter of April 23rd above quoted: "But for almost a month I have done no serious study. These inventions have so exhausted my mind that when I proposed to inquire into other questions awaiting answer it had no sufficient strength left."

The mental tensions induced by these mathematical discoveries were increased by his growing conviction that the *opus infinitum* must indeed be carried out by some one man. "Among the first of the thoughts that came to me was this, that often there is less perfection in works composed of several parts and the product of several different hands than in those due to a single master-workman."[6] Could it be, he found himself asking, that he, René Descartes, was predestined for this tremendous task? Alternately enthusiastic and diffident, already more or less convinced of the feasibility of the task, and yet dismayed at the magnitude of it, he was still on the night of November 10, 1619, excitedly bewildered; and on

6 *Discourse,* II. Cf. below, p. 101.

his retiring to rest, the inner debate, still continuing, took the form of a three-fold dream. In it nothing was disclosed to him beyond what he had been thinking out in the preceding six months; what gives it biographical and historical importance is solely that it helped to convince him that it was indeed the "Spirit of Truth" which had been inspiring him, and that he could confidently count on divine approval. The following nine years 1619-28 Descartes spent in the leisurely testing of his new principles, and in the defining of them in a treatise which he entitled *Regulae ad Directionem Ingenii*.

The next turning-point came nine years later, in November, 1628. A Sieur de Chandoux, who professed medicine and was versed in chemistry, held a conference in Paris, under the patronage of the Papal Nuncio and before a distinguished audience including Cardinal de Bérulle, Mersenne and other notables. After he had delivered a lengthy discourse in refutation of the philosophical teaching current in the Schools, to the great acceptance—so Baillet declares—of his hearers, Descartes, who was observed to have abstained from any outward signs of approval, was so pressed to speak, that he had no option save to yield. With polite compliments to Chandoux, and after approving also his desire to revise the Aristotelian teaching then dominant in the Schools, he proceeded to propound his own counter-thesis, that certainty, and not, as Chandoux had argued, probability, is alone the basis on which knowledge worthy the name can be made to rest. His own method, as "drawn from the mathematical sciences," had two essential requirements: (1) that we start from what is so simple and evident as to be indubitable; and (2) that in advancing from the simple to the complex, no step be taken which is not similarly indubitable. So impressed was Cardinal de Bérulle (himself, like the congregation of the Oratory which he founded, Augustinian in his sympathies and outlook) that he entreated Descartes to give him the opportunity of hearing him once again on these matters in private; and on Descartes' affording him glimpses of the benefits which must result should his philosophy be employed in improvement of the mechanical crafts and medicine, the Cardinal reproved him for his dilatoriness in the promulgation of it.

This was what Descartes' own conscience had long been requiring of him; and that he might be the better enabled to do so, he decided to take up residence in Holland, where, as he believed, he could best secure the necessary quiet and leisure.

As we learn from the unfinished *Regulae,* Descartes had already, before 1628, concluded that his physical principles could suffice to account for animate as well as for inanimate nature, and that animals (with the sole exception of man) are non-conscious automata. This, in turn, had led him to believe that it would be in medicine, even more than in mechanics, that his most important and beneficent discoveries would be made. For if all bodily processes are mechanistically caused, bodily diseases, once their causes have been determined, should be remediable with the same precision and certainty as the disorders of a clock.

Save for three brief visits to Paris, and his final ill-starred journey to Sweden, Descartes remained in Holland all the rest of his life; and to avoid becoming entangled by social and other ties, he moved, at intervals, from one town to another. In each of these residences, when at all possible, he had a laboratory in which he practiced anatomy (on specimens supplied by the slaughterhouses), with a garden in which he studied plant-life. And being thus ever-increasingly absorbed by the promising vistas opening out before him, in the twin fields of mechanics and "medicine," he left the *Regulae* unfinished, and instead started a new treatise, entitled *Le Monde.* Revising such notes as he already had in hand, he combined them to form a comprehensive account of physical nature, inclusive of man's animal organism.

The year 1633 opened for Descartes very auspiciously. The completion of his *Le Monde* being then well in sight, he could, he believed, joyfully look forward to spending the remainder of his life in reaping the rich harvest which, in Baconian fashion, he foresaw as following upon the technical application of his mechanistic principles, and more especially upon their application in the "medical" domains (vegetable and animal) to which they had hitherto been supposed to be inapplicable. We can understand, therefore, how bitter was his disappointment when, in November of this very year, word reached him that the Inquisition had condemned as heretical Galileo's advocacy of the Earth's motion round the Sun—an integral part of his own teaching, and one which, in his cosmology, involved consequences still less likely to be approved by the Inquisition. At once he decided to suppress his *Le Monde*. Meantime, in the hope of an early reversal of Church policy, he would prepare the way for the ultimate acceptance of his teaching, doing so in three stages. First, by way of three lengthy *Essais, La Dioptrique, Les Météores,* and *La Géometrie,* he would report on some of the discoveries his new method had already enabled him to make. Also, he would preface these "Essays" by a brief *Discours* in which, in place of the projected thirty-six rules of the *Regulae,* he would dwell, in quite general semi-popular terms, on the nature of his method, and of his hopes of making by its means yet further discoveries. Then, in a further work to be entitled *Meditationes de Prima Philosophia*—aimed at enlisting the sympathetic support of the Church Authorities, and more especially of the teachers in the Jesuit Colleges, and composed this time in Latin—he would treat of the two questions in regard to which there need be no quarrel between him and the Church: the existence of God and the immortality of the soul. Should he succeed in converting his readers to his manner of establishing these two central doctrines, they would, he believed, be the more ready to accept his teaching in its entirety, including his physics. Then, in another work, also in Latin, entitled *Principia Philosophiae,* he would venture to give a detailed account of his physics, doing so in the manner most likely to gain general acceptance—as, for instance, by adopting the approved deductive method of exposition, and by leaving unrevised his early, purely relativist, teaching in regard to motion and using it to camouflage his continuing advocacy of the Earth's motion round the Sun.

The *Essays* (his first published work, issued in 1637, when he was already forty-one years of age) served Descartes' purposes well—the brief preface to them becoming the most famous and widely read of all his writings. The *Meditations,* issued in 1641, with six series of *Objections* appended, proved, however, only very doubtfully helpful, while the *Principles,* issued in 1644, had so negative a reception as to convince Descartes, once and for all, that he could no longer hope to obtain entry for his teaching in the Jesuit Colleges. Accordingly, from then on, we find him speaking his mind much more freely, especially in his letters. All along he had recognized that the self is not externally related to the body in the manner of a pilot to his ship or of a workman to his tools. Now, however, taking at last due account of the experiences which hitherto he had left more or less unconsidered, viz., the sensations of light, heat, sound, etc., and the feelings and passions, he had no option save to question several of the assumptions upon which he had hitherto been proceeding. If these sensuous experiences cannot be accounted for in terms either of body alone or of mind alone, and if further the occasionalist mode of explanation be ruled out, the only remaining alternative is to ascribe them to the action of mind and body in *joint* co-operation—this, in turn, involving the admission, as recognized by Descartes[7] (and emphasized by Locke and by Spinoza, each in his own very different manner), that in both matter and mind there are "several properties of which we have no idea," an admission which, in view of his earlier utterances, was for Descartes a most embarrassing confession to have to make.

We can only conjecture how far, and in what particular respects, he would have proceeded in the further revision of his earlier doctrines. In any attempt to do so, we have to rely,

[7] Cf. his letter to his Oratorian friend, Father Gibieuf, Jan. 19, 1642.

in addition to surviving letters, on the two works on which he was engaged in the years between the publication of the *Principles* and his premature death on February 11, 1650— *Les Passions de l'Âme* and *La Description du Corps Humain,* posthumously published with the subtitle, *La Formation du Foetus.* They at least suffice to show that at no time in his life was he more awake to the need for assistance in the making of observations and of thereby supplementing his high *a priori* method of reasoning. We know too[8] that he was planning a School of the Arts and Crafts—what we should now call an Institute of Technology—in which theorists and manual workers would co-operate, one of their first fruits being perhaps— so at least Descartes would seem to have been hoping—the construction of an instrument which would do for the sensibly apprehended objects we can handle what the telescope has done for bodies in the heavens, and so give access to precisely the kind of observations of which he stood most in need.

It is now customary to distinguish between Descartes' teaching and that of the "Cartesians." The adjective Cartesian is taken as applying to all those various types of philosophy over which Descartes has exercised a determining influence. But how divergent they are, each rejecting certain of his central doctrines, and modifying, often quite radically, those they have retained—the occasionalism of Geulincx and Malebranche, the pantheism of Spinoza, the monadism of Leibniz, the sensationalism and carefully qualified rationalism of Locke! And, as V. Vartanian has very convincingly shown,[9] when the term Cartesian is used in this wide sense, the above list has also to include those eighteenth-century Enlightenment thinkers—Diderot, La Mettrie and d'Holbach—for whom the mechanistic treatment of physical nature and of the animal and human body was all-important. Clerselier (with others of lesser note) seems to have remained unquestioningly faithful to all of Descartes' publicly recorded doctrines; but Clerselier was a minor figure compared with any one of the above.

[8] Cf. *New Studies,* pp. 360-62.
[9] *Diderot et Descartes* (Princeton University Press), 1953.

For justification of the terms used in my translations I must refer readers to my *New Studies in the Philosophy of Descartes;* and in doing so I may give warning that in three main respects I have departed from the views generally held in authoritative circles, viz., (1) in the emphasis I have laid on Descartes' manner of differentiating between the "clear" and the "distinct," and on the role it plays in the argument of the *Meditations;*[10] (2) in my interpretation of Descartes' statements regarding the *corporeal* imagination—a doctrine common to Descartes and to Newton; and (3) in my insistence on Descartes' view of conscious awareness as being always sheerly immediate, and of our thinking as being therefore exclusively determined by what is at the moment being attended to, with no power of actively forming mental images or of constructing concepts. For the former it has to wait upon their formation as patterns in the pineal gland; for the latter it has to rely on finding them in the mind, as having been deposited in it at its creation. The many difficulties with which he was thereupon faced, and his manner of dealing with them —especially in respect of the relations holding between this type of awareness and our fallible acts of interpretative judgment, and more generally as to the relations holding between the understanding and the will—are, however, much too complicated to be dealt with, even briefly, in this Introduction.

N. K. S.

[10] Even Gilson has dealt with it only quite casually, in his commentary on the *Discourse* (pp. 200-04); Laporte and Alcuié ignore it, using the two terms as if they were synonymous.

RULES FOR THE GUIDANCE OF OUR NATIVE POWERS[1]

[PART I. THE RULES OF METHOD, AS REQUIRED IN DEALING
WITH THE DATA OF EXPERIENCE AND AS THEREBY
SAFEGUARDING THE MIND'S NATIVE POWERS
OF INTUITION AND DEDUCTION]

RULE I

The aim of our studies should be that of so guiding our mental powers that they are made capable of passing sound and true judgments on all that presents itself to us.

WHEN men observe two things to be in some respect similar, they are wont to ascribe to each what they have found to be true of the other, to the neglect of that in which they differ. Thus they draw a wrong comparison between the sciences which exercise exclusively the mind's cognitive capacities, and the arts which call for the use and trained skill of the body. The arts, they see, cannot all be acquired by the same man. Observing, too, that he who exercises one only is the more likely to become a really good executant, since the same hands cannot be suitably adapted both to agricultural pursuits and to harp-playing, or to a variety of such differing

---

[1] *Regulae ad directionem ingenii.* Composed, it would seem, prior to 1629, it remained unpublished until 1701. A MS. copy of it had, however, been shown by Clerselier to Arnauld, Leibniz and others. It was planned to be in three Parts, cf. below, pp. 71, each of twelve Rules. Part I is complete; Part II treats of perfectly understood questions, and Part III was to treat of imperfectly understood questions. Part II is incomplete; Part III is entirely lacking. On Descartes' use of the term *ingenium,* cf. below, pp. 14, 49, 55.

employments as to one alone, they have believed that this must also be true of the sciences. Distinguishing the sciences, one from another, according to the diversity of their objects, they have come to think that they ought to be studied separately, each science independently of all the others. In this they are indeed deceived. No one of the sciences is ever other than [the outcome of] human discernment,[2] which remains always one and the same, however different be the things to which it is directed, being no more altered by them than is the light of the sun by the variety of the things it illumines. There is, therefore, no need for our mental powers to be narrowly restricted. So far is the knowledge of one truth from hindering us, on the analogy of the arts, in the discovery of other truths, that on the contrary it is helpful to us. Indeed, it seems strange to me that while so many men are concerned to inquire with the utmost diligence into human customs, the virtues of plants, the motions of the stars, the transmutations of metals, and the objects of other such disciplines, hardly any give thought to right understanding,[3] i.e., to that universal Wisdom[4] which I have in view and in the furtherance of which, and not by their own separate claims, all other studies are to be esteemed.

For these reasons this rule has good claims to be ranked as first among the rules. Nothing is so likely to divert us from adopting the true path in our pursuit of truth as the directing of our studies not to this comprehensive end but to particular topics. I am not referring to perverse and censurable pursuits, such as empty glory or base gain; quite evidently counterfeit reasonings and absurdities, suited to vulgar minds, provide a much more direct road to such ends than the well-grounded knowledge of truth. I am speaking of pursuits which are in themselves honorable and praiseworthy. For often the manner in which these influence us is the more subtly misleading. Con-

---

[2] *Humana sapientia*, i.e., that type of discernment which is made possible by the *natural* light of reason. Cf. below, p. 3.

[3] *de bona mente*.

[4] *Sapientia* (this time with a capital S).

sider, for instance, those sciences which contribute to the conveniences of life, or which yield the pleasure found in the contemplation of truth, almost the only one of our earthly delights that is blameless and free from all vexations. These legitimate fruits the sciences carry in their train, and we can indeed count on them; but if, in the midst of our studies, we allow ourselves to think of them, the effect of our so doing is that we are then apt to omit many matters that are necessary for the further extension of our knowledge—things that on first acquaintance may well seem to be of little utility and of no particular interest. We ought to bear in mind that all the sciences are so closely interconnected that it is much easier to study them together than to isolate one from the others. If, therefore, anyone genuinely desires to investigate the truth of things, he should not select some one particular science; all of them stand together and are interdependent. What he should alone consider is how best to augment the natural light of reason, not however with a view to resolving this or that difficulty, as propounded in the Schools, but in order that his understanding may guide his will in the choices he has to make on all the various issues by which he is faced throughout life. Soon he will be amazed to find that he has made far greater progress than those who devote themselves to special studies, and that he has not only obtained all that the others desire but also something far exceeding anything they can have hoped for.

RULE II

Only those objects should engage our attention, to the sure and indubitable knowledge of which our native powers seem to be adequate.

ALL science consists in sure and evident knowledge. He who entertains doubts on many matters is no wiser than he who has never thought of such matters; rather he would appear to be the more unschooled of the two, should he in respect of any of them have adopted a false opinion. It is better, therefore, not to study at all than to occupy ourselves with objects so difficult that, owing to inability to distinguish true from false, we may be obliged to accept the doubtful as certain. In such inquiries there is more risk of diminishing our knowledge than of increasing it. Thus, in conformity with the above rule, we reject all modes of knowledge that are merely probable,[5] and resolve to believe only that which is perfectly known, and in respect of which doubt is not possible. The learned may perchance have brought themselves to think that there are very few such certainties; owing to a common failing prevalent among men, they have scorned to take notice of such certainties, as being too easy and within everyone's reach. I warn them that there are many more such truths than they think, and that these enable us to prove with certainty innumerable propositions which hitherto they have been able to argue about in a merely probable manner. Believing, as they do, that it is unbecoming in a man of learning to be ignorant of anything, they have so accustomed themselves to have elaborate reasonings ready at hand, that they

[5] *tantum probabiles.* The *tantum* makes the phrase equivalent to "merely plausible." The modern theory of probability had not yet taken shape.

4

have ended by imposing on themselves, and have cried up those [merely plausible] reasonings as being true.

Assuredly, if we adhere faithfully to this rule, there will be only very few things which we shall be able to study. There is in the sciences scarce any question about which men of ability have not disagreed. Now whenever two such men are carried to opposite conclusions regarding one and the same matter, one at least must be in error; indeed, neither of them, it would seem, has the required knowledge. For if the reasoning of either of them were certain and evident, he would be in a position to propound it to the other in such wise as to convince him also of its truth. In all such matters of probable opinion, we would seem, therefore, to be ruled out from acquiring knowledge that is genuinely knowledge: it would indeed be rashness in us to hope for success where those others have failed. Accordingly, if we are representing the situation correctly, observation of this rule confines us to arithmetic and geometry, as being the only sciences yet discovered.

We are not, on this account, meaning to condemn the manner of philosophizing to which others have hitherto resorted, nor those weapons of war, so well suited for bellicose controversies, the probable syllogisms favored by the Scholastics. They afford mental exercise for the young, awakening a certain emulation among them, which is certainly better than leaving them entirely to their own devices. Thereby too they become acquainted with those opinions which, however uncertain, are the current subjects of controversy among the learned. Left without guidance, they might wander disastrously; whereas, so long as they follow in the steps of their teachers, though they may at times diverge from the truth, they can yet be certain of holding to a course which is more trustworthy, at least in this respect, that it has had the approval of those more prudent than themselves. We rejoice that we ourselves, in our early school years, were trained in this way. But now, freed from the sacred obligation which subjects us to the teacher's orders, and of sufficiently mature years to be independent of the master's rod, if we wish in all seriousness to formulate for ourselves rules which will enable us to ascend to the heights of human knowledge, we must allow as one of the first of these rules this special warning: namely, that we must not abuse our leisure, as so many do, neglecting what is easy, and engaging only in loftier matters. The conjectures which the many then devise are certainly very subtle, and their reasonings exceedingly plausible;[6] but after much labor they at last discover, too late, that they have only increased the number of their doubts, and this without having made any addition to their knowledge.

We were saying that of all the disciplines yet known, arithmetic and geometry alone are free from any taint of falsity or uncertainty; let us now consider more carefully the reason why this is so. First we must note that there are two ways by which we arrive at the knowledge of things, viz., either by experience or by deduction, i.e., the pure illation of one thing from another. We must further note that while our experiences of things are often fallacious, deduction, though it may, through failure to take advantage of it, be omitted, can never be wrongly performed by an understanding that is in the least degree rational. Those fetters by which the dialecticians prefer to regulate human reason seem to me far from helpful in the drawing of these deductions, though I am not denying that they may be excellent for other purposes. For none of the deceptions which can befall men are due to faulty inference; they are due solely (I am referring to men, not to the brutes) to our relying on certain imperfectly understood experiences, or to our venturing on judgments which are hasty and groundless.

From these considerations it is evident why arithmetic and geometry far surpass all the other known disciplines in certitude. They alone treat of an object so pure and simple as to admit of nothing that experience can render uncertain; they entirely consist in a sequence of consequences which are rationally deduced.[7] They are therefore the easiest and clear-

6 *valde probabiles.*
7 I.e., intuited through the *natural* light of reason.

est of all the disciplines; and since to err in their regard, save through inattention, is scarce humanly possible, their object is precisely of the kind that our rule requires. We need not, however, be surprised if many find themselves more attracted by other studies or by philosophy. The reasons for this are obvious. On matters which are obscure, they can (as they may not do in matters which are evident) boldly indulge themselves, freely advancing their own conjectures. It is so much easier to have some vague notions about any and every subject than to arrive at the precise truth about some one question, however simple the question may be.

From all this we have to conclude, not that arithmetic and geometry are alone to be studied, but that in our search for the direct road to truth we should not occupy ourselves with any object about which we are unable to have a certitude equal to that of arithmetical and geometrical demonstrations.

RULE III

In treating of the objects proposed for investigation what we have to examine is not what others have opined, nor what we ourselves may conjecture, but what we can clearly and evidently intuit, or can deduce with certainty: knowledge is not obtainable in any other way.

WE should read the writings of the ancients, since it is an immense help to be able to avail ourselves of the labors of so many other men; and we should do so both in order to learn what has already, in the past, been correctly established, and also that we may be apprised as to what, in all those disciplines, still remains to be thought out. Should we, however, occupy ourselves too exclusively with these writings, there is great danger of our being infected with their errors, however contrary this may be to our intention and however we guard ourselves against it. For writers, once they have incautiously or inadvisedly committed themselves in some matter on which contrary opinions are upheld, are usually disposed to endeavor, by means of the most subtly devised arguments, to carry us along with them. On the other hand, should they, by good fortune, have come upon something at once certain and evident, they never exhibit it in this light, but only in association with various irrelevant accompaniments, fearing, forsooth, that the simplicity of their reasoning may have the effect of lessening our appreciation of the merit of their discovery, or because they grudge us frank knowledge of the truth.

But even supposing that all writers were open and candid, never passing off the doubtful as being true, but expounding to us everything in entire good faith, yet since scarcely anything is said by any writer that is not directly challenged by some other writer, we should still always be left uncertain which of the two should be believed. Nor would it in the least avail to count heads, following that opinion which has the greater number of supporters. For if the question be a difficult one, the truth is more likely to have been discovered by few than by many. But even should the authors, one and all, agree among themselves, their teaching would still not meet our need. Thus, for instance, no matter how completely we may hold in memory all the demonstrations discovered by others, we shall never thereby qualify as mathematicians; we must ourselves acquire the power of resolving any and every such problem. Nor shall we be philosophers, even should we have read all the arguments of Plato and Aristotle. So long as we are unable to arrive at a firm judgment of our own on the matters of which they are treating, what we are thereby learning is not science, but history.

We further require that no conjectures of any kind be allowed into the judgments we pass on the truth of things. This warning is of no little importance. Neglect of it is the main reason why in the current philosophy we find nothing which is so evident and certain as not to allow of being called in question. The learned, not content with the knowledge of what is perspicuous and certain, have ventured to propound assertions which are obscure and uncomprehended, and which have been reached by merely plausible conjectures. Thereafter, in due course, they come to rely on them with complete confidence, mingling them promiscuously with the true and the evident; and, in the end, therefore, the only conclusions they are in a position to draw, rest, it would seem, on propositions of this questionable kind, and are therefore themselves uncertain.

Lest we in turn yield to this same error, let us now more closely examine all those actions of our understanding by which we are able to arrive, without fear of deception, at the knowledge of things. We recognize only two, viz., intuition and induction.[8]

By intuition I understand, not the fluctuating testimony of the senses, nor the misleading judgment of a wrongly combining imagination, but the apprehension[9] which the mind, pure and attentive, gives us so easily and so distinctly that we are thereby freed from all doubt as to what it is that we are apprehending. In other words, intuition is that non-dubious apprehension of a pure and attentive mind which is born in the sole light of reason; and it is surer than deduction (though, as we have already noted,[10] deduction also can never be wrongly performed by us) in virtue of its being simpler. Thus each of us can see by intuition that he exists, that he thinks, that the triangle is bounded by three lines only, the sphere by a single surface, and the like. Such intuitions are more numerous than most people are prepared to recognize, disdaining, as they do, to occupy their minds with things so simple.

[8] "Induction" would seem, on first reading, to be a misprint for "deduction," since, as the immediately following paragraphs show, Descartes is here referring to the "illative" process involved in all *demonstrative* reasoning, and not to what we now understand by induction. Adam and Tannery would, however, seem to be right in keeping to the original text. It is uniform in both the A. and the H. MSS., though in the latter the two concluding words, "et inductio," after being written, have been crossed out. It is not unlikely—I venture the conjecture—that at the time of writing, Descartes was hesitating as to how he should distinguish his view of deduction, as being intuition, from the traditional syllogistic view, and that for a time he inclined to use *inductio* in the sense of *illatio*. (As he assures us, in the immediately following paragraph, it was "the meaning proper to the Latin of each word" that guided him in his readaptation of current terms; and in that regard *inductio* and *illatio* are indistinguishable.) In the end, however, he seems to have decided that this departure from current usage would be more misleading than helpful to his readers. Induction is a term that from now on he rarely uses, and almost invariably as synonymous with "enumeration," and therewith as meaning not a generalization from particular instances to a universal, but in its Aristotelian sense as valid only when the induction is exhaustive, *per enumerationem simplicem.*

[9] *conceptum*. Cf. below, p. 55.

[10] Above, Rule II, p. 6.

As readers may perhaps be troubled by this novel use of the term intuition, and of other terms which I am constrained in similar fashion to dissociate from their current meaning, I here give a general warning that I have no thought of keeping to the meaning with which those terms have of late been employed in the Schools. For it would have been difficult for me so to employ them, while still maintaining my own differing standpoint. When appropriate terms are lacking, I convert to my own use those which seem to me most suitable. I shall pay no attention save to the meaning proper to the Latin of each word.[11]

To proceed, this evidence and certitude, proper to intuition, is required not only in single affirmations but also in all discourse. Consider, for example, this consequence: 2 and 2 amount to the same as 3 and 1. Not only do we have to intuit that 2 and 2 amount to 4 and that 3 and 1 also amount to 4, but also that the first-mentioned proposition is a necessary conclusion from these two.

The question may therefore be raised, why do we place alongside intuition this other mode of knowing, viz., by way of *deduction*—by which we understand all that is necessarily concluded from other certainly known data. Could we, however, have done otherwise? Many things are known with certainty, though not by themselves evident, but only as they are deduced from true and known primary data[12] by a continuous and uninterrupted movement of thought in the perspicuous intuiting of the several items. This is how we are in a position to know that the last link in a long chain is connected with its first link, even though we cannot include

[11] This proviso bears specially on Descartes' manner of employing the Latin terms *principia* (= primary data), *propositio* and *propositum* (= datum), *subjectum* (= substance, both bodily and mental), *objectum* (= any and every entity that presents itself to the mind, i.e., used, like *res*, Fr. *chose*, in the widest possible sense).

[12] *principiis*. When Descartes in his later writings ceased to use the expression "naturae simplices," the term which he adopted in its place was *principia* (Fr. *principes*), used in its etymological sense as meaning the first item in any duly ordered series. Cf. *New Studies*, p. 60.

all the intermediate links, on which that connection depends, in one and the same intuitive glance, and instead have to survey them successively, and thereby to obtain assurance that each link, from the first to the last, connects with that which is next to it. We therefore distinguish intuition from the certitude yielded by deduction in this respect, that we have to conceive deduction as calling for a certain movement or succession not required in the case of intuition; and also, therefore, in this further respect, that inasmuch as immediately present evidence, such as is required for intuition, is not indispensably required by deduction, its certitude rests in some way on memory. To sum up, we can therefore say that those propositions which are immediately gathered[13] from primary data[14] are, according to our differing manner of arriving at them, known sometimes by intuition and sometimes by deduction—the primary data themselves by intuition alone, the remote conclusions not otherwise than by deduction.

These two paths are the most certain of the paths to knowledge, and in respect of powers native to us[15] no others should be admitted. All other paths should be regarded as dangerous and liable to error. This does not, however, hinder us from believing that what has been divinely revealed to us is more certain than all we otherwise know, inasmuch as this faith of ours, like all faith that bears on things obscure, is an act not of our cognitive powers[16] but of the will. In so far, however, as our beliefs rest on intellectual foundations, they can and ought to be, more than all things else, reached by one or other of the two above-mentioned paths, as we may perhaps elsewhere find opportunity to explain more at length.

[13] *concluduntur*.

[14] *ex primis principiis*.

[15] *ex parte ingenii*.

[16] *non ingenii*—an unusually narrow use of the term, which elsewhere is taken as including the will.

RULE IV

In the search for the truth of things method is indispensable.

So blind is the curiosity with which mortals are obsessed that they often direct their energies along unexplored paths, with no reasoned ground for hope, but merely making trial whether what they seek may by happy chance be thereby found. As well might a man, fired with a senseless desire to find treasure, spend his time roaming the streets, in the hope of perhaps finding something dropped by a passer-by. This is the manner in which almost all chemists, most geometers, and not a few philosophers pursue their studies. I am not denying that in their wanderings they sometimes happen on what is true. I cannot, however, allow that this is due to greater address on their part, but only to their being more favored by fortune. Indeed it were far better never to have so much as thought of seeking after truth than to do so without method. For what is quite certain is that such unregulated studies and confused meditations tend only to confound the natural light, blinding the mind. Those who thus accustom themselves to walk in darkness so weaken their eyesight that they cannot afterwards bear the light of day. And as experience similarly testifies, those who have never occupied themselves with letters, are, as we often find, able to judge of whatever presents itself to them far more soundly and clearly than those who have spent all their time in the Schools. Now by method I intend to signify rules which are certain and easy and such that whosoever will observe them accurately will never assume what is false as true, or uselessly waste his mental efforts, but gradually and steadily advancing in knowledge will attain to a true understanding of all those things which lie within his powers.

Here there are two requirements which have to be met: (1) never to assume as true that which is false; and (2) to arrive at a knowledge that takes in all things. [To take the second first], if we are in ignorance of any one of the things we are capable of knowing, this can only be because we have not yet discovered a path which will lead us to this knowledge, or because we have fallen into the contrary error [that of assuming what is false]. But if our method rightly explains how by making use of intuition we can avoid falling into the contrary error, and how by way of deduction we can reach to a knowledge that takes in all things, nothing else, it seems to me, is needed to render our knowledge complete, since, as already remarked, no knowledge can be acquired save by way either of intuition or of deduction. There can be no question of extending the method so as to show how these two operations ought to be performed, since they are the simplest of all mental operations, and primary. If our understanding were not of itself qualified to perform them, it would be unable to comprehend any of the precepts prescribed by the method, however easy.[17] As to those other [syllogistic] mental

[17] This is one of Descartes' most distinctive doctrines. Intuition is, he holds, a mode of direct face-to-face awareness, i.e., is sheerly contemplative, "patiently" acceptive of whatever comes within its field. Either it operates or it does not operate; but if it operates at all, it does so in an infallible manner. Accordingly, for its guidance, no rules are required. This view Descartes extends to cover deduction, i.e., inference, or as he likewise entitles it "illation." These are titles for this same power of intuition when considered not as static, i.e., as directed exclusively on this or that exhaustively known "simple nature," but as operating in and through "acts of comparison" (cf. below, p. 81) and as thereby enabling us, on variation in the factors constituting this or that "simple nature" (e.g., of the lines and angles constituting the complex, triangularity), to discover relations not previously known (e.g., that the three angles of a triangle are always equal to two right angles). Thus intuition and deduction are not processes which call for, or for their correct use depend on, rules of method. On the contrary, being native to the mind they are presupposed by the rules; and it is solely because of their essential trustworthiness that success can be looked for by way of method. The question as to how this implicit reliance on intuition—on intuition of relations as well as of terms, and therewith on inference—can be justified and what, if any, are the limits within which it thus operates,

operations, which dialectic (relying on the aid of these prior ones) labors to direct, they are here useless or rather positively harmful; for nothing can be added to the pure light of reason[18] which does not in some way obscure it.

Since, then, the usefulness of this method is so great that without it our labors are more likely to be harmful than profitable, I am inclined to believe that already in ancient times it must have been in some fashion evident to those of outstanding mental powers, nature itself guiding them to it. For the human mind has in it a something divine, wherein are scattered the first seeds of useful modes of knowledge. Consequently it often happens that, however neglected and however stifled by distracting studies, they spontaneously bear fruit. Arithmetic and geometry, the easiest of the sciences, are instances of this. We have sufficient evidence that the ancient geometers made use of a certain "analysis" which they applied in the resolution of all their problems, although, as we find, they grudged to their successors knowledge of this method.[19] There is now flourishing a certain kind of arithmetic, called algebra, which endeavors to determine in regard to numbers what the ancients achieved in respect of geometrical shapes. These two sciences are no other than the spontaneous fruits above mentioned; they are products of the innate principles[20] of the method here in question; and I do not wonder that these sciences, dealing as they do with such objects, the simplest of all objects, should have yielded a harvest so much more rewarding than the other sciences in which greater obstructions tend to choke all growth. But

is in Descartes' view a metaphysical, not a logical issue; and it was not until after his treatise on the *Regulae,* as we now have it, was completed, that he arrived at a definitive answer to it.

[18] The function of *natural* reason, Descartes holds, is solely that of enabling us to have a direct immediate face-to-face awareness of the sheerly given, i.e., of those data which as primary are both simple and fruitful, "the things on which the mind's attention has to be concentrated, if any truth bearing on them is to be discovered." Cf. Rule V.

[19] Cf. below, p. 18.

[20] *ingenitis principiis.*

certainly these other sciences, if only we cultivate them with due care, can also be brought to full maturity.

This, indeed, is what I have chiefly had in view in preparing this treatise. For I should not ascribe much value to these rules, if they sufficed only for the solution of those unprofitable problems with which logicians and geometers are wont to beguile their leisure. I should then only be claiming for myself the power to argue about trifles more subtly than others. Though I shall often have to speak about geometrical shapes and numbers, that is only because no other disciplines can furnish us with examples so evident and so certain. Whoever, therefore, pays due regard to what I have in view will easily see that nothing is less intended by me than ordinary mathematics, and that I am indeed engaged in expounding quite another discipline, of which these examples are rather the outer covering than the constituents. For this discipline claims to contain the primary rudiments of human reason, and to extend to the eliciting of truths in every field whatsoever. To speak freely, I am convinced that it is a more powerful method of knowing than any handed down to us by human agency, and that it is indeed the source from which those older disciplines have sprung. In dwelling, as I have done, on the outer [mathematical] integument, my purpose has not been to cover over and conceal this discipline, with a view to warding off the vulgar, but rather to clothe and adorn it, that it may thereby be the more suitably conformed to our human powers.

When first I applied my mind to the mathematical disciplines, I read through most of what writers on these subjects are wont to teach; and I paid special attention to arithmetic and geometry, because they were said to be the simplest, and as it were, a path leading to all the rest. But in neither field did I meet with authors who fully satisfied me. I did indeed read in them many things regarding numbers which on calculation I found to be true; and in respect of geometrical shapes they exhibited things in a certain manner to the eyes, and from them drew consequent conclusions. But to the mind itself they failed to submit evidence why these things are so or how they have been discovered. Accordingly I am not surprised that many people, even among the talented and learned, on sampling these sciences, very soon set them aside as being idle and puerile; or else, judging them to be exceedingly difficult and intricate, they have stopped short at the very threshold. For truly there is nothing more futile than to occupy ourselves with bare numbers and imaginary shapes, as if we could be content to rest in the knowledge of such trifles. Nothing, too, is more futile than to accustom ourselves to those superficial demonstrations which are discovered more often by chance than by skill, and which address themselves so much more to the eyes and to the imagination than to the understanding that we in a manner disaccustom ourselves to the use of our reason. Moreover, there can be no more perplexing task than to tackle by any such manner of proof new difficulties bearing on unordered numbers.[21] When, however, I afterwards bethought myself how it could be that the first practitioners of philosophy refused to admit to the study of wisdom anyone not previously versed in mathematics, i.e., viewed mathematics as being the easiest of all disciplines, and as altogether indispensable for training our human powers and for preparing them to lay hold of the other more important sciences, I could not but suspect that they were acquainted with a mathematics very different from that which is commonly cultivated in our day. Not that I imagined that they had full knowledge of it. Their extravagant exultations, and the sacrifices they offered for what are minor discoveries, suffice to show how rudimentary their knowledge must have been. Nor am I shaken in this opinion by those machines of theirs, which historians have eulogized. The machines may have been quite simple and may well have been lauded as miraculous by the ignorant and wonder-loving multitude. I am convinced that certain primary seeds of truth implanted by nature in our human minds—seeds which in us are stifled owing to our reading and hearing, day

[21] *confusis numeris.* Cf. below, p. 43.

by day, so many diverse errors—had such vitality in that rude and unsophisticated ancient world, that the mental light by which they discerned virtue to be preferable to pleasure and honor to utility, although they knew not why this should be so, likewise enabled them to recognize true ideas[22] in philosophy and mathematics, although they were not yet able to obtain complete mastery of them. Certain vestiges of this true mathematics I seem to find in Pappus and Diophantus,[23] who, though not belonging to that first age, yet lived many centuries before our time. These writers, I am inclined to believe, by a certain baneful craftiness, kept the secrets of this mathematics to themselves.[24] Acting as many inventors are known to have done in the case of their discoveries, they have perhaps feared that their method being so very easy and simple, would, if made public, diminish, not increase the public esteem. Instead they have chosen to propound, as being the fruits of their skill, a number of sterile truths, deductively demonstrated with great show of logical subtlety, with a view to winning an amazed admiration, thus dwelling indeed on the results obtained by way of their method, but without disclosing the method itself—a disclosure which would have completely undermined that amazement. Lastly, in the present

[22] First use in the *Rules* of the term "idea." Cf. below, pp. 54-55, 59, 84.

[23] Two Alexandrian mathematicians, probably of the fourth century A.D. Pappus' *Mathematicae Collectiones* was first printed in 1588. Diophantus is credited with the invention of algebra. His treatise, the *Arithmetica,* has survived only in part.

[24] Descartes is here interpreting the past in the light of tactics practiced in his own day, and in one notable instance, as he frankly confesses, practiced by himself; namely in his manner of composing the essay on geometry appended to the Discourse, "Ma Géométrie est comme elle doit être pour empêcher que le Rob[erval] et ses semblables n'en puissent médire sans que cela tourne à leur confusion, car ils ne sont pas capables de l'entendre, et je l'ay composée ainsi tout à dessein" (letter to Mersenne). Cf. L. Roth, *The Discourse on Method,* p. 21: "The *Geometry* is an essay in defiance as well as in the "method," and its spirit is that of the then prevailing fashion of calling attention to one's discoveries by publishing a challenge announcing a problem only to be solved by the unique method of the discoverer."

age there have been certain very able men who have attempted to revive this mathematics. For it seems to be no other than this very science which has been given the barbarous name, algebra—provided, that is to say, that it can be extricated from the tortuous array of numbers and from the complicated geometrical shapes by which it is overwhelmed, and that it be no longer lacking in the transparency and unsurpassable clarity which, in our view, are proper to a rightly ordered mathematics.

These were the thoughts which recalled me from the particular studies of arithmetic and geometry to a general investigation of mathematics; and my first inquiry was as to what precisely has been intended by this widely used name, and why not only the sciences above mentioned, but also astronomy, music, optics, mechanics and the several other sciences are spoken of as being parts of mathematics. It does not here suffice to consider the etymology of the word; for since the term mathematics simply signifies [in Latin] *disciplina* [i.e., science], all the other sciences can, with as much right as geometry, be so entitled. Yet, as we see, there is almost no one, with the least tincture of letters, who does not easily distinguish, in the matters under question, between what relates to mathematics and what relates to the other disciplines. What, on more attentive consideration, I at length came to see is that those things only were referred to mathematics in which order or measure is examined, and that in respect of measure it makes no difference whether it be in numbers, shapes, stars, sounds or any other object that such measure is sought, and that there must therefore be some general science which explains all that can be inquired into respecting order and measure, without application to any one special subject-matter, and that this is what is called "universal mathematics"—no specially devised designation, but one already of long standing, and of current use as covering everything on account of which the other sciences are called parts of mathematics. How greatly it excels in utility and power the sciences which depend on it, is evident from this, that it can extend to all the things of which those other sciences take cognizance, and many more besides. Such difficulties as it may contain are also found in those other sciences, while these, on their part, owing to the particularity of their objects, exhibit yet other difficulties peculiar to themselves. Everyone knows the name of this discipline, and understands with what it deals, however inattentive he may be to it. How then is it that so many men laboriously pursue those other disciplines, and yet that no one is concerned to inform himself regarding this universal discipline upon which they depend? Assuredly I should marvel, were I not well aware that everyone thinks it to be the easiest of all disciplines, and had I not long since observed that we leave aside what we consider ourselves easily able to comprehend, hastily reaching out to what is new and more imposing.

For my part, conscious as I am how slender are my powers, I have resolved, in my search after knowledge of things, perseveringly to follow such an order as will require that I begin always with the things which are simplest and easiest, and that I never step beyond them until in their regard there remains, it would seem, nothing more to be done. This is why, hitherto,[25] I have to the best of my ability concentrated on universal mathematics, so that when in due course I may judge myself to be qualified to treat of the more advanced sciences, my labors will not be premature. But before I embark on these further inquiries I shall endeavor to bring together and to arrange in an orderly manner all that in these preceding studies I have found to be specially worthy of attention, so that, when increasing age has weakened my memory, I shall still, if need arises, have the convenience of being able to recall them as required, on consulting this written record, and that meantime having disburdened my mind of them I may be the better able to advance in my inquiries with a mind free and undivided.

[25] Up to 1627-28?

RULE V

Method consists entirely in the orderly handling of the things upon which the mind's attention has to be concentrated, if any truth bearing on them is to be discovered. We shall comply with it exactly, if we resolve involved and obscure data[26] step by step into those which are simpler, and then starting from the intuition of those which are simplest, endeavor to ascend to the knowledge of all the others, doing so by corresponding steps [taken in reverse order].

IN this one requirement we have the sum of all human endeavor; whoever enters on the pursuit of knowledge must rely on this as implicitly as he who entered the labyrinth had to rely on the thread that guided Theseus. But many seekers either do not reflect on what it prescribes, or simply ignore it, presuming that they themselves are in no need of it, setting themselves to examine the most difficult questions with so little thought of due order, that, as it seems to me, they act like a man who would attempt to spring at a bound from the base to the summit of a house, spurning the ladders provided for the ascent, or not noticing them. This is how the astrologers behave. Though ignorant of the nature of the heavens, and having made no proper observations even of their motions, they yet expect to be able to declare their effects. This, too, is what many do who study mechanics apart from physics, rashly engaging in the devising of new instruments for producing motion. This also is how those philosophers proceed, who to the neglect of experience,[27] imagine that truth will

[26] *propositiones.*

[27] *neglectis experimentis.* As this passage clearly shows, Descartes takes due account of those "empirical" data to which we have access solely in and through sense-experience; they too have to be recognized as being *principia*, i.e., *initial, primary* data. They are indeed *sensuously* experienced, but are not for that reason any the less open to the mind's direct inspection.

spring from their brain like Pallas from the head of Zeus.

Obviously all of these sin against this rule. But since the order which it requires is often so obscure and intricate that not everyone can detect it, it is scarcely possible to guard adequately against error save by diligent observation of the next following rule.

RULE VI

For the distinguishing of the simplest things from those that are complex, and in the arranging of them in order, we require to note, in each and every series of things in which we directly deduce truths from other truths, which thing is simplest, and then to note how all the others stand at greater or lesser or equal distance from it.

THOUGH this rule may seem to teach nothing really new, it yet contains the chief secret of the method, and in all this treatise there is none more useful. For it admonishes us that all things can be arranged in certain series, not indeed in so far as they are referred to some ontological genus,[28] in the manner in which philosophers classify them according to the categories,[29] but in the order in which each item contributes to the knowledge of those that follow upon it; so that, when a difficulty presents itself, we are at once able to decide whether it will be helpful to consider certain other difficulties first, and which, and in what order.

To be able to do this correctly, we have first to note that all things in so far as they can be serviceable for our purposes, i.e., as having natures not isolated but comparable one with another, can be said to be either absolute or relative.

I entitle absolute whatever possesses in itself the pure and simple nature that we have under consideration, i.e., whatever is viewed as being independent, cause,[30] simple, universal,[31]

[28] *genus entis.*
[29] *sicut illas Philosophi in categorias,* i.e., as in the Tree of Porphyry, determining things *per genus et differentiam.*
[30] I.e., "cause" as being what, as coming first, *initiates* a series. For Descartes' use of "cause" as meaning "ground" or "reason," cf. *New Studies,* pp. 61 n., 309 ff.
[31] I.e., "universal" because disclosing itself to us in each and every

one, equal, like, straight and such like. This "absolute," this *"primum,"* is the simplest and easiest [of apprehension], and so is of service in our further inquiries.

The relative, on the other hand, while participating in the same absolute nature, or at least having some such share in it as permits of its being brought into relation to this absolute, and of its being thereby deduced from it in a certain serial order, yet also involves in its concept, over and above the absolute nature, certain other characters which I entitle the relatives,[32] e.g., whatever is said to be dependent, effect, composite, particular, multiple, unequal, unlike, oblique, etc. These relatives are further removed from the absolutes in proportion as they contain more relatives of this kind in [continued] subordination one to another. The above rule requires that these relatives be all distinguished from one another, and the linkage[33] and the natural order of their interrelations be so observed, that we may be able, starting from that which is nearest to us [as empirically given], to reach to that which is completely absolute, by passing through all the intermediate relatives.

The secret of this whole method is, therefore, this: that in all things we carefully take note of that which is most completely absolute. . . .

Secondly, we must note that the pure and simple natures

experience that is relevant to the question asked: as thus disclosing itself to us in this immediate face-to-face manner, our knowledge of it is "adequate" not abstract. As he explains in Rule XII (below, p. 57), what distinguishes the merely abstract from the "simple," and therefore from all "absolutes," is that it is "obtained from a plurality of natures wholly diverse, and to which therefore it cannot be applied save ambiguously." Cf. *New Studies,* pp. 312-13.

[32] *respectus.* These relatives, as being thus additional, can be apprehensible by us only as *given,* i.e., must no less than their absolutes be apprehended by us in *self-evidencing intuition,* and, if they are to serve in "deduction" must prove "comparable," i.e., must be found to stand to their absolutes and to one another in relations likewise given and similarly intuited. Thus, in Descartes' view, even in the process of "illation," of "deduction," the mind is non-creative and sheerly contemplative.

[33] *nexus.*

which we are in a position to intuit *primo et per se*,[34] i.e., as not [in our knowing of them] dependent on any others, but as immediately disclosed to us either in this and that sense-experience, or by a light that is native in us, are few in number; and as we have been saying, it is these which should be carefully observed; for they are those natures which we have spoken of as being the simplest in each of the series. None of the other [given] natures [making up the series] can be apprehended save as deduced from them [i.e., as standing in intuitively apprehended relation to them] either immediately, or proximately by the mediation of two, three, or more different steps. The number of these steps should be noted, that we may know whether the relatives are separated from the primary and completely simple datum by a greater or smaller number of intermediates. These series of the things under inquiry, series of the kind to which every question should be reduced, owe their origin to the connections which thus hold throughout between the terms in sequence; and it is these connections [these relations as being intuited and therefore directly known] which enable us to examine the series methodically and with certainty. But because it is not easy to keep in view all these connections, and also because our task is not so much that of retaining them in memory as of discerning them with a certain precision, we must cultivate whatever will so discipline our mental powers as to enable us to apprehend such connections instantly when we have need to do so. For this purpose, as experience has taught me, nothing assuredly is so effectual as the accustoming ourselves to attend with a concentrated awareness to the least recondite of those connections which are already familiarly known to us.[35]

[34] Cf. below, Rule XII, p. 68: "Simple data must come before the mind of themselves; they cannot be reached by way of inquiry." Cf. also Rule XIII, p. 73.

[35] I.e., we shall thereby so familiarize the mind with the genuinely, indubitably evident, that it will be the more sensitive to its presence in any and every context, and the less liable to rest content with any lesser misleading substitute. Not only, Descartes contends, is no one truth more difficult than another, no truth is in itself difficult, provided our approach to it is duly ordered. Cf. below, p. 40.

Thirdly, and finally, we must note that our studies ought not to start with the investigation of difficult matters. Before tackling any specific question we ought first to ponder at length and impartially those truths which have of themselves presented themselves to us, and starting from them to inquire whether others can be reached by way of them, and again others from these, and so on in orderly sequence. This done, we should then reflectively attend to the truths thus discovered, and diligently inquire why it is that we have been able to discover some of them prior to and more easily than others, and what these are. Then, when we come to deal with some specific question, we shall be in position to judge what prior questions ought first to be attended to and answered. . . .

RULE VII

For the completing of our knowledge, the things which bear on what we have in view must one and all be surveyed by a movement of thought which is continuous and nowhere interrupted, and embraced in an enumeration which is sufficient and orderly.

OBSERVANCE of these requirements is necessary, if we are to admit as being certain those truths which we have been speaking of as not being immediately deduced from the primary self-evidencing data.[36] For this deduction sometimes involves so long a series of connected terms in sequence, that when we come to our final conclusion we do not easily retain in mind the whole of the route which has conducted us to it; and this is why a certain continuous movement of thought is, as I say, required to remedy this weakness of the memory. Thus, e.g., if I have found, by way of separate operations, what the relation is, first, between the magnitudes A and B, then between B and C, and finally between D and E, I do not, in so doing, thereby see what is the relation between A and E, nor am I able to learn of it from the truths antecedently known unless I recall all of them. This is why I have to run them over several times, the imagination operating with a motion so continuous, that while it is intuiting each step it is simultaneously passing on to the next, until I have learned to pass from the first to the last so quickly, that almost none of the steps are left to the care of memory, and that it then seems as if I were intuiting the series simultaneously as a whole. And not only is the memory thus strengthened, the sluggishness of our mental powers is diminished and their capacity extended.

This movement, we add, should nowhere be interrupted.

[36] *a primis et per se notis principiis.*

27

For frequently those who seek to deduce something too quickly and from remote starting-points do not trace the whole chain of intermediate conclusions with accuracy sufficient to prevent their inconsiderately omitting many of the steps. And assuredly, when even the smallest link is missing, the chain is instantly broken, and the certainty of the conclusion entirely escapes us.

We further declare that for the completion of our knowledge, enumeration [or induction] is required. The other precepts do indeed aid us in resolving a great number of questions, but only by means of enumeration can we be assured of always passing a true and certain judgment on whatever is under investigation, in such wise that nothing entirely escapes us and that in all questions there is something [however minute or however negative] of which we may judge ourselves to have knowledge.

This enumeration or induction is therefore the seeking out of all the things which have a bearing on the question that is being asked, a search so careful and accurate that in the light of it we can conclude, with certitude and evidence, that nothing can inadvertently have escaped us. Provided, therefore, we have employed this [sufficient] type of enumeration,[37] should what we are seeking still elude us, we shall at all events be wiser in this respect, namely, in now having the certain knowledge that there is no path available to us by which we could have discovered it. For if perchance, as often happens,[38] we have been able to explore all the paths to it which lie open to men, we shall be entitled boldly to assert that the knowledge of it transcends our human powers.[39]

Further, we should note that by a sufficient enumeration or induction is meant that enumeration by which we may reach truth with more certainty than by any other kind of proof,

[37] I.e., an enumeration which, as unbroken, is self-evidencingly complete.

[38] Namely as happens in the case of those questions which involve only such data as are experienced by all men, even by the rustic.

[39] Cf. below, pp. 33, 38.

excepting only simple intuition. When our knowledge of some matter cannot be reduced to simple intuition—rejecting, as we do, all syllogistic devices—this enumeration is the sole path remaining open to us, and we should hold to it with complete confidence. When we have deduced one [intuited] thing from another immediately, then, if the illation has been evident, each [step] has thereby been found to rest on a true intuition. When, however, we have to infer by way of many separate steps, our intellectual capacity is often not sufficiently great to be able to embrace them in a single intuition, and the certainty afforded by the enumeration should then suffice. This is how we proceed when unable to distinguish in one comprehensive glance all the links of a lengthy chain; having seen the connection which unites each link with the next in order, we are justified in saying that we have seen how the last link is connected with the first.

I have said that this operation [i.e., this "enumeration or induction"] *ought* to be sufficient, because often it can be defective, and in consequence subject to error. For sometimes, although in our enumeration we may pass in review much that is completely evident, should we yet omit a single link, however small, the chain is broken and the certainty of the conclusion is entirely lost. Sometimes also, even though all the things [bearing on our question] are indeed embraced in the enumeration, they are not distinguished one by one from one another, and so are known by us only confusedly.

Again, though the enumeration ought sometimes to be complete, and sometimes to be distinct, there are cases in which neither is called for; and this is why in the rule I have required only sufficiency. Thus should I seek to prove by enumeration[40] how many kinds there are of corporeal things, or how they are accessible to the senses, I shall not indeed assert that they are just so many and no more, unless I have previously made certain that the enumeration, as including all

---

[40] Here the enumeration is not of the members in a linked series, and the above intuitively guaranteed test of completeness, i.e., of an unbroken continuity, is therefore not available.

the relevant items, is duly complete, and as distinguishing between them is also distinct. But should I by this same path seek to show that the rational soul is not corporeal, there is no need for the enumeration [of the corporeal genera] to be complete; the enumeration will be sufficient if all bodies are grasped by me together in certain collections, in such fashion that it enables me to demonstrate that the rational soul cannot be referred to any of the collections. If, to give a last instance, I seek to show by enumeration that the area of the circle is greater than the area of all geometrical figures which can be enclosed in the circle, there is no need to review all geometrical figures. If I demonstrate this in particular cases, that will suffice for concluding by induction[41] that this holds of all the others.

I have likewise required that the enumeration be methodical, partly as being the most effective remedy for the defects above-mentioned, and partly because, as often happens, should each single thing bearing on the issue under question

[41] Here, too, the precise meaning given to the term induction is not explained. In this paragraph, as already in the preceding paragraphs, and still more in the next following paragraphs, Descartes would seem to be tentatively feeling his way toward his final, very definite manner of differentiating between the clear and the distinct (cf. New Studies, p. 55 ff.), and in doing so to be asking himself whether perhaps his new method may not call for not unimportant modifications in treating of specific problems in the physical sphere, or when applied metaphysically, in demonstrating that the rational soul is not corporeal. The references to Rule V (in the two concluding paragraphs) are in this last regard of special significance. In other words, he is already not unaware that the method, in all its strictness, is available only in treating of quantitative relations, and that in all other fields the emphasis has to be exclusively on "order," not on "measure," and further, that the discernible order is far from being invariable in type. As Descartes himself insists (cf. below, pp. 35, 39 ff.) he has "in these preliminaries . . . discovered only certain rough precepts," and as he proceeds to explain in Rules IX and X, they can be made effective only in proportion as we exercise ourselves in the art of right thinking. Thereby only can we hope to acquire "perspicacity" in the distinguishing of the things dealt with and "sagacity" in the ordering of them. Neither of these aptitudes can be acquired save by prolonged practice in the application of the rules. Cf. New Studies, p. 86 ff.

have to be separately examined, no man's life would suffice, either because these things would be too numerous or because the same things would be returning upon us over and over again. But if they are all arranged in the best order and are thereby reduced to certain classes, it will, for the most part, be sufficient to take one instance of each class, or some one feature of the single instances, or certain of the instances rather than the others; and we shall at least never have to waste time in considering the same instance twice. The advantages of this procedure are so great that often, thanks to a well-devised order, a multiplicity of things can be gone over quickly and easily, though on first view it seemed immeasurable.

In such cases, the order of enumeration allows, however, of variation, and what this order should be depends on each man's judgment. This is why for the more accurate employment of our judgment it behooves us to bear in mind what has been said in the fifth rule.[42] Often, too, in the solution of our more trivial, artificial questions, the deciding of this order is the whole of method. Thus if we seek to construct a perfect anagram by the transposition of the letters of a name there is no need to pass from the easiest things to the more difficult, or to distinguish those which are absolute from those which are relative. There is here no place for these processes. It will suffice, if in examining the combinations of letters we adopt an order such that we have never to cover the same combinations twice, and that their number be, e.g., so divided into fixed classes that it may be immediately apparent in which of them there is the better prospect of finding what is sought. In this way the task will often be so shortened as to be almost childishly simple.

For the rest, these last three prescriptions [Rules V, VI and VII] should not be separated. All three contribute to the perfection of the method, and should therefore be simultaneously kept in mind. There has indeed been no imperative reason for expounding one of them prior to the others. And if we have

[42] I.e., on the need of "experiences."

hitherto explained them only briefly, the reason is that there is almost nothing [in respect of doctrine] which needs to be added. The more detailed treatment of what has been outlined in a general manner in the above rules has therefore been reserved for the remaining sections of this treatise.[43]

[43] Cf. opening of Rule XII, below, p. 50.

RULE VIII

If in any series of things into which we may be inquiring we come upon something which our understanding is unable to intuit sufficiently well, there we must stop short. What follows thereupon is not to be studied; that would be useless labor, and from it we should abstain.

. . . For whoever, in the treatment of any difficulty, has faithfully conformed to the preceding rules, and yet by this eighth rule is commanded to stop short at a certain point, may then rest assured that no further labors will enable him to obtain the knowledge he is seeking; and this not owing to any failure in the use of his mental powers, but because the very nature of the difficulty, or at least his being humanly conditioned, cuts him off from it. This knowledge [of our necessary ignorance] is no less truly science than that which reveals the nature of the thing itself; to attempt to carry our curiosity further is to betray lack of sound judgment.[44]

[So to cite another question, outside the field of mathematics] let us take the noblest of all examples. If a man set himself the problem of examining *all* truths, i.e., all those the knowledge of which is within the competence of human reason—and this seems to me to be a task which should be undertaken once in his life by everyone who seriously strives to attain wisdom—he will assuredly find, in conformity with the above given rules, that nothing can be known prior to the understanding, since the knowledge of all things else depends

[44] Cf. Montaigne III, 2 (Florio's translation): "Yea but there is some kinde of ignorance strong and generous, that for honor and courage is nothing beholding to knowledge: An ignorance which to conceive rightly there is required no lesse learning, than to conceive true learning."

on this knowledge,[45] and not contrariwise. Then, when he has clearly apprehended all those things which follow proximately on knowledge of the pure understanding, he will enumerate whatever [native] instruments of knowledge we have in addition to the understanding, and of these there are two only, phantasy and sense. He will therefore devote all his energies to the distinguishing and examining of these three modes of knowing; and recognizing that while truth and falsity, rightly regarded, cannot be save in the understanding alone, they often derive their origin from those other two modes of knowing, he will direct his attention diligently to the sources of deception resulting therefrom, that he may guard himself against them. Also he will carefully enumerate all the paths to truth which lie open to men, that he may follow the path which leads to certainty. Not being numerous, these paths can all of them be easily discovered and adequately enumerated. This may seem surprising and incredible to the inexpert; but our inquirer, should he, in respect of each single object, distinguish, as he may easily do, those cognitions which occupy and embellish only the memory from those on account of which he can be truly said to be better instructed . . .[46] he will assuredly discover that absence of further knowledge is in no wise due to lack of mental power or skill, and that nothing can be known by any other man which he is not himself capable of knowing, provided only that he directs his

[45] What Descartes intends to mean by this assertion is more explicitly stated below, p. 35 ff. He has in mind the two-fold inquiry: (1) as to the *cognitive* powers of the human *ingenium*, viz., as to the intuitive powers of the pure understanding, and as to what are the roles rightly assignable to the other cognitive faculties, sense, imagination and memory; (2) as to what are the *objects* to which our human understanding has direct intuitive access, thus recognizing that the only adequate method of defining these various faculties is by reference to the *objects* proper to each. While the two inquiries supplement one another, enabling Descartes to define more precisely "the rough precepts" (cf. below, p. 35) outlined in the preceding rules, in the second of the two inquiries he raises and answers the question as to the limits of knowledge, the limits beyond which we can never, by our human powers, hope to pass.

[46] As the 1701 Amsterdam edition notes, something is here missing.

mind to it with the needful application. Many questions which this rule prohibits him from treating may indeed continue to force themselves on his attention, yet since he will clearly apprehend that they transcend the scope of the human mind he will not regard himself as being the more ignorant on that account. On the contrary, this very knowledge, viz., that the matters in question cannot possibly be known by us, will, if he is reasonable, amply suffice to abate his curiosity.

That we may not, therefore, remain always uncertain as to the powers of the mind, and that we may not labor mistakenly and at random, we ought, before setting ourselves to the detailed treatment of things, to inquire, once in our lives, of what things, in the way of knowledge, the human reason is capable; and that this may be the better done, we should, in respect of such questions as are equally easy of treatment, always give priority to those which are the more immediately helpful.

There is here a resemblance between our method and the procedure of those mechanical arts which are independent of outside aids, and which themselves teach how to fabricate the tools they need. For instance, should a man wish to practice any one of these crafts, such as that of the smith, and be lacking in all tools, he will at the start be constrained to use as an anvil a hard stone or some rude piece of iron, a stone in place of a hammer, a shaped piece of wood as tongs, and collect other such tools as his necessities require. Equipped with these he will not then forthwith attempt to forge swords or helmets or anything made of iron for the use of others, but will first fabricate hammers, anvil, tongs and other tools for his own use. From this example we may learn that since in the above preliminaries we have thus far been able to discover only certain rough precepts, dictated, it would appear, by our native mental endowments, but not yet artfully elaborated, we should not forthwith attempt with their aid to settle philosophical disputes, or to find the solution of difficulties in mathematics. We must first make use of them in seeking to determine with the utmost care such other things as, in the search for truth, are more immediately necessary—the more so as there is no reason why these should prove more difficult of solution than some of the questions commonly propounded in geometry or in physics or in the other disciplines.

Now, there is assuredly nothing that can, at this stage, be more usefully chosen for prior treatment than the question what human knowledge is and how far it extends; and so we are brought back to the question which [as above stated] we consider should be examined prior to all others, with the aid of the above [roughly shaped] rules. This is a task which [as also already said][47] should be undertaken once in his life by everyone who has any love of truth, since it is by way of this inquiry that the true instruments of knowing and the whole of method disclose themselves to us. Nothing, indeed, seems to me more foolish than boldly to dispute, as many have done, about the secrets of nature, the influence of the heavens on sub-lunar happenings, the predicting of future events and suchlike, without ever having inquired whether our human reason is equipped for answering such questions as these. If thus often we do not hesitate to pass judgment on things which are outside us and quite foreign to us, why should the task of determining the limits of that *ingenium* which we experience in ourselves be regarded as arduous and difficult? Nor is it an excessive task to seek to embrace in thought all things contained in the Universe, provided our purpose be that of determining how [and whether] they may severally be subject to our mental scrutiny. Nothing can be so complex or so wide-ranging that we need fail, on applying our prescribed method of enumeration, to confine it within limits and to order it under a few headings. To test whether this be so in the case of the question before us, we start by dividing all that pertains to it into two parts: the question ought to relate either to us who are capable of knowing or to the things which can be known. These two parts we will discuss separately.

In ourselves we observe that while the understanding alone is capable of scientific knowledge, it may yet be helped or

[47] Above, p. 20.

hindered by three other faculties, namely, imagination, sense and memory. We must therefore consider in an orderly manner these three faculties with a view to determining where each may prove to be a hindrance, so that we may be on our guard; or how each may assist us, that we may take full advantage of their powers. This part of our task will be discussed in the light of an adequate enumeration, as will be shown in the next following rule.[48]

Secondly, we have to deal with the things themselves, though only in so far as they can come within the reach of the understanding. So taken, we divide them into those natures which are completely simple and those which are complex or composite. There are no simple natures which are not either spiritual or corporeal or pertaining to both. Among the composite natures are some which the understanding experiences to be such, before it attempts by way of judgment to determine anything regarding them; but there are others which it itself composes. All this will be explained at greater length in the twelfth rule, where it will be shown that there can be no falsity save in this last group, that of the composites made by the understanding itself. This is why we have to distinguish the two species of composite ideas, viz., those composites which are deducible from natures completely simple and known *per se* (these we shall deal with in the next Part), and those which presuppose [i.e., are explicable only by reference to] other natures which experience shows us to be composite *a parte rei*. The whole of the third Part we reserve for these last.[49]

Throughout the treatise as a whole our aim will be to follow so carefully the paths which lie open to man and which lead

---

[48] Descartes ought rather to have said in subsequent rules. Rules IX, X and XI treat only of the part played by the pure understanding, amplifying the account already given of intuition and deduction in Rules III and VII. He then proceeds in Rules XII and XIV to treat of the aids afforded to the understanding by the other faculties— imagination, sense and memory.

[49] This part Descartes has not succeeded in sketching, even in outline. Cf. above, p. 1 n.

to truth, and to render them so easy that anyone who has perfectly mastered this whole method, however ordinary his mental powers, may be enabled to see that no path is closed to him which is not also closed to all others, and that his ignorance is therefore not due to any defect in his native powers or in his method of procedure.[50] As often as he applies his mind to the knowing of anything he will either be entirely successful, or he will realize that success depends on some experience[51] which he has [thus far] been unable to obtain, and accordingly will not blame his mental powers for his being thus perforce halted. Or he will succeed in showing that the thing sought altogether exceeds the range of our mental powers, and accordingly will recognize that he is not on this account the more ignorant; for this kind of knowledge is as truly knowledge as any other.

[50] *ingenii defectu vel artis.*
[51] *experimento.*

RULE IX

We ought [for the training of the mind in perspicacity] to concentrate our native powers on those things which are simplest and easiest, and to dwell on them at such length that we thereby confirm ourselves in the habit of intuiting truth distinctly and perspicuously.

HAVING treated of those two operations of our understanding, intuition and deduction, which alone, as we have said, can be employed in the acquisition of scientific knowledge, we proceed, in this and the next following rule, to explain how we can render ourselves more skilful in the exercise of them, and in so doing cultivate two special mental aptitudes, *perspicacity* in the intuiting of each single thing distinctly,[52] and *sagacity* in the artful deducing of these single things one from another.[53]

How the mind's intuiting powers may best be employed can be learned from the manner in which we use the eyes. For he who endeavors to view a multitude of objects all at once in a single glance sees none of them distinctly; and similarly anyone who is wont to attend to many things at once in a single act of thought does so with a confused mind. But just as workmen who engage in tasks calling for delicate manipulation, and are thereby accustomed to direct their eyes attentively to single points, by practice acquire a capacity adequately to distinguish things which are subtly minute, so likewise is it with those inquirers who refuse to have their thought distracted by a variety of simultaneous objects. Occupying themselves with the things that are simplest and easiest, these too become perspicuous.

But it is a common failing of mortals to be unduly impressed

52 Dealt with throughout the remainder of this rule.
53 Dealt with separately in the next following rule.

39

with the difficult. The great majority of men on finding the cause of a thing to be quite perspicuous and simple consider that they are learning nothing. Their admiration is reserved for the sublime and loftily conceived theories of the philosophers, based it may be, as indeed these usually are, on foundations which no one has ever satisfactorily surveyed. Truly, they are deranged in mind, thus to prize darkness above the light! Instead, as we ought to recognize, those who truly know, discern truth with equal facility, be the subject-matter from which they have derived it simple or be it recondite. Each truth, once they have reached it, they comprehend by an act which, while being in itself distinct, is yet similar to all other intuitive acts. The sole diversity is in the path leading to it, which has to be longer in proportion as the truth in question is more remotely related to what is primary and altogether absolute.

Everyone ought, therefore, to accustom himself to grasp in thought things so simple, and at any one moment so few, that he will never thereafter be tempted to think that he is knowing anything, save when he has an intuition of it no less distinct than the intuition he has of that which he knows most distinctly of all. Some are indeed born with much greater aptitude than others for such intuitive discernment. But by art and exercise our [native] mental powers can be immensely improved. The point upon which, as it seems to me, I ought to insist above all others is therefore this: that everyone should confirm in himself the conviction that it is not from things lofty and obscure, but solely from what is easy and readily accessible, that sciences, however recondite,[54] have to be deduced.

For example, if I wish to examine whether it is possible for a natural power[55] to pass instantaneously from a distant place, while yet traversing the whole intervening space, I shall not forthwith direct my mind to the power of the magnet, or to the influence of the stars, or even to the speed

[54] *occultas.*
[55] *potentia naturalis.* Cf. above, p. 39 n.

of light, inquiring whether perchance these actions take place instantaneously. The solution of these questions would be more difficult than the question proposed. I should rather devote my attention to the local movements of bodies, as being of all motions[56] the most manifest.[57] A stone, as being a body, is indeed, as I observe, unable to pass instantaneously from one place to another distant place. If, on the other hand, a power similar to that which moves the stone is to pass from one subject[58] to another, and does so nakedly [i.e., unsupported by a body that requires to be conceived as "carrying" it], it must do so instantaneously. For instance, if I move one end of a staff of whatever length, I easily conceive the power by which that part of the staff is moved as necessarily moving at one and the same instant all its other parts, because the power is then communicated nakedly, and not as existing in some body (such as the stone) which carries it along.

In the same way, if I wish to understand how one and the same cause can give rise at one and the same instant to contrary effects, I shall not cite the remedies of the physicians, which expel certain humors and retain others, nor shall I romance about the moon as warming by its light and chilling by some occult quality. Instead I shall gain instruction from the balance, the weight raising one arm at the instant at which it depresses the other, and from other like examples.

[56] *in toto hoc genere,* i.e., taken in the wider Scholastic sense of the term "motion."
[57] *sensibile.*
[58] *subjecto.* Cf. below, p. 81 n.

RULE X

To train ourselves in sagacity [i.e., in the required power of proceeding in an orderly manner, and not at random] we should exercise our mental powers on those questions which have already been solved by others, and in doing so, we should, in a methodical manner, take account even of the least important of the traditional handicrafts, paying special attention to those arts in which order is brought out or imposed.

My own natural disposition, I confess, is such that my chief pleasure has never consisted in attending to the reasonings of others, but in making discoveries by my own personal efforts.[59] This was what especially attracted me, while still young, to the study of the sciences. Whenever a book by its title held promise of a new discovery, before reading further I made trial whether I might not myself perhaps, by means of a certain inborn sagacity, attain to something similar, and was careful lest the hasty reading of the book might deprive me of this innocent pleasure. So often did I succeed in this, that at length I came to realize that I was no longer working my way to the truth of things in the manner in which others were wont to do, by way of vague and blind searchings, relying on good fortune rather than on skilled address, but that my protracted tentative efforts have enabled me to detect rules which are of no little help in such inquiries and which I have since been using in the discovery of several other rules. It was in this way that I diligently elaborated this whole method, confirming myself in the conviction that the manner of study which I had indeed been following from the very start is the most serviceable.

[59] Cf. *Discourse,* below, p. 94.

42

But because not everyone is by nature thus strongly disposed to rely on his own exertions, the above rule teaches
that we ought not at the start to occupy ourselves with the
more difficult and arduous inquiries, but should first study
those arts which are easiest and simplest, and, above all,
those in which order is dominant, e.g., the arts of those
craftsmen who weave cloth and tapestry, or of those women
who embroider, intermingling the threads in infinite diversity
of varied texture. Again, there are the games that involve
the use of numbers, and indeed all employments that call
for arithmetic, and the like. It is amazing how greatly such
arts discipline our mental powers, always provided we do
not learn the procedure from others, but discover it ourselves.
For since there is nothing occult in them, and since they are
thus entirely within the capacity of our cognitive powers, they
exhibit to us in the most distinct possible manner innumerable instances of order, all different one from another, and
yet none the less all of them conforming to rule; and it is
precisely in the due observance of such order that human
sagacity almost entirely consists.

This is why we maintain that in our inquiries we must
proceed methodically. In the lesser arts this method is for
the most part found to consist in the steady observance of
the order prescribed either by the thing itself or by ingenious
human devising. Thus if we wish to read something dis-
guised in cipher, there is indeed in it, we find, no appearance of order. On starting, we imagine a certain order, for
the purpose of testing all conjectures[60] that can be made
regarding the single letters, words or sentences, and for the
arranging of them in such wise that by an enumeration of
them we may know what may be deduced from them. What
we have chiefly to guard against is the wasting of our time
in guessing unmethodically, at random. For although the
answer can often be obtained without method, and sometimes, if fortune favors, more quickly than by method, yet

[60] *praeiudicia.*

in so proceeding we are bound to weaken the mind's powers of insight, accustoming ourselves to what is puerile and trifling, and acquiring the habit of attending always only to the surface-appearance of things, unable to penetrate more deeply. We must not, however, fall into the counter-error of those who occupy themselves only with things lofty and momentous; they reap as the reward of their manifold labors nothing but confusion of mind, not the profound knowledge to which they are aspiring. This is why we ought to train ourselves first in those easier matters, but methodically. Thereby we shall accustom ourselves to proceed always by easy and familiar paths, and so, as easily as though we were at play, to penetrate ever more deeply into the truth of things. By this procedure we shall gradually, in a much shorter time than we could have foreseen, find ourselves in a position to deduce from evident primary data[61] many propositions which have the appearance of being exceedingly difficult and intricate.

It may perhaps seem surprising that in this inquiry as to how we may improve our powers of deducing truths from other truths, we make no reference to any of those precepts by which the dialecticians propose to regulate the human reason. They prescribe certain [syllogistic] forms of argument which are, they declare, so necessarily conclusive that reason, even while disinteresting itself in the clear and attentive consideration of that particular illation, may yet, in virtue solely of its form, be in position to draw a conclusion, and to do so with certainty. But as we find, the truth often fails to be held fast by these fetters, and those who so rely on the syllogistic forms are then left behind in bondage. Those who dispense with those forms are less frequently betrayed into error. As experience testifies, sophisms, however ingenious, hardly ever deceive those who rely on pure reason [i.e., on the *natural* light of reason]; it is the sophists themselves who fall victims to them.

What we have chiefly to guard against is, therefore, lest

61 *ex evidentibus principiis.*

our reason disinterest[62] itself in examining the things, the truth of which is under question. This is why we reject all those [syllogistic] forms as being at variance with this requirement. Instead we look around for all available means that may aid us in keeping our thought attentive, as will be shown in what follows. But meantime, to make my point even clearer, viz., that the [syllogistic] mode of procedure contributes nothing whatsoever to knowledge of the truth, we may note that the dialecticians are unable to construct a syllogism that leads to a true conclusion, save in so far as they already have the matter of which it is composed, i.e., unless they have previously known the very truth which the syllogism is deducing. It is evident, therefore, that from such a syllogistic form nothing new can be learned. The currently used dialectic, that is to say, is entirely useless for those who are desirous of inquiring into the truth of things. Its only use is in enabling us to explain to others more easily, as is now and then the case, the truths already known; and it should therefore be transferred from philosophy to rhetoric.

[62] *feriatur:* literally, "take holiday from."

RULE XI

If we have intuited several simple propositions, and propose to deduce something else from them, it is useful to run through them in a continuous and uninterrupted act of thought, to reflect on their relation to one another, and so far as is practicable, to apprehend distinctly several of them, all at once. For in this way our knowledge is rendered much more certain and the mind's capacity very greatly increased.

HERE we find the opportunity of explaining more clearly what has already been said regarding the mind's intuiting, in Rules III and VII. In one passage[63] we opposed it to deduction; in another[64] we opposed it only to enumeration, which we defined as being an illation gathered from several separate things, while also at the same time declaring that simple deduction of one thing from another is effected by intuition.

This double mode of distinction has to be employed, because for *intuition* we require two things: (1) that the intuited[65] be apprehended clearly and distinctly, and (2) that it be apprehended all at once, and not successively. *Deduction,* if, as in Rule III, we are thinking of how it comes about, does not indeed seem to be executed as a whole at the same instant; it involves, in the process of the inferring of one thing from another, a certain movement of our mind. This is why we have there found good cause to distinguish it from intuition. If, however, we are attending to it as already drawn, then as we have said in Rule VII it no longer signifies a movement, but the completion of a movement; and that is why we have there spoken of the deduction as

[63] In Rule III, cf. p. 10 ff.
[64] In Rule VII, cf. p. 28 ff.
[65] *propositio.*

being intuited when it is simple and perspicuous, but not
when it is multiple and involved. In the latter case, we assign to it the title "enumeration" or [as marking illation]
"induction." For we are not then able to apprehend it by
the understanding as a whole and all at once, and its certainty
is therefore to some extent dependent upon memory, in which
our judgments[66] regarding the single parts enumerated have
to be retained, if from these parts taken together some one
conclusion is to be drawn.

All of these distinctions are required for the understanding of the above rule. Rule IX has treated only of the mind's
intuiting [i.e., of methods for improving the mind's perspi-
cacity] and Rule X only of enumeration[67] [i.e., of methods
for improving the mind's sagacity]. The present rule explains
the manner in which these two operations aid and complete
one another. In so doing, they can be seen as coalescing into
one single operation by way of a certain movement of thought
which, while attentively intuiting [in a perspicuous manner]
each single item, at the very same instant passes on [in a
sagacious manner] to the others.

In this we mark a two-fold advantage: (1) that it affords
a more certain knowledge of the conclusion we have in view;
and (2) that it renders the mind more apt in the discovery
of yet other truths. Since memory (on which, as we have
just said, depends the certainty of the conclusions which
embrace more than we can grasp in one single intuition)
is weak and apt to fail us, we are called upon to refresh and
confirm it by repetition of this continuous act of thought.
Thus if by separate acts I have learned first what the relation
is between the first and the second of a series of magnitudes,
then in sequence the relation between the second and the
third, between the third and the fourth, and finally between
the fourth and the fifth, I do not thereby intuit what the
relation is between the first and the fifth, nor can I deduce it
from the relations already known, unless by remembering

[66] *judicia.*
[67] There enumeration is being equated with deduction.

all of them. What is necessary is that I should run over them all repeatedly in thought, until I pass so rapidly from the first to the last that almost none of the parts is left to memory, and I seem to be intuiting the whole [series] at one and the same instant.

By this device, as everyone will see, the slowness of our mental powers is quickened and their capacity enlarged. But that is not all. The chief advantage of this rule, as we should further note, consists in this, that by reflection on the mutual dependence of the simple data[68] we acquire the habit of distinguishing at a glance[69] what is more and what is less relative, and through what steps the relative stands related to what is absolute. . . .

[68] *simplicium propositionum.*
[69] *subito.*

RULE XII

Finally, we have to make use of all the aids afforded by understanding, imagination, sense and memory; first, for the purpose of intuiting distinctly the simples which come before the mind; secondly, in comparing the things into which we are inquiring with those we already know, in such fashion that they may thereby come to be likewise known; and thirdly, in finding the things which allow of being thus compared, in order that, so far as our human powers allow, nothing be omitted. [The distinction between simple data and questions.]

THIS rule summarizes all that has been said in the preceding rules, which have expounded in a general manner what has now to be explained in more detail as follows.

In treating of knowledge, two factors have to be considered, ourselves who know [ourselves *quâ* embodied][70] and the things we are engaged in knowing. In us there are but four faculties of which we can make use, namely, understanding, imagination, sense and memory.[71] The understand-

---

[70] Cf. below, p. 50 ff.

[71] Cf. above, p. 34. Descartes is not, it may be noted, declaring these to be strictly *mental* faculties: sensings and the imagings which make imagination and memory possible rest on bodily conditions. The four faculties are proper not to the *vis cognoscens*, but to the mind-body complex, the *ingenium*. In the *Principles*, pt. i, § 12, in an addition made in the French translation (presumably on Descartes' own suggestion) it is emphasized that it is only when the "self" is *metaphysically* considered that we have to understand by it the mind alone: "We then clearly apprehend that neither extension, nor shape, nor local motion [in French version, in place of "local motion" existence in any place] nor anything similar that can be attributed to body, pertain to our nature, and nothing, indeed, save thought alone." To the very last, Descartes' modes of expression continue to be highly ambiguous. Cf. *Principles*, pt. i, § 53. "He cannot conceive imagination or sense . . . unless in a thinking thing." For his teaching, when more consistently formulated, cf. *New Studies*, pp. 30 ff., 74 ff., 147 ff.

49

ing is indeed alone capable of apprehending truth; none the less it has to be assisted by the imagination, sense and memory. This is necessary in order to guard ourselves against omitting perchance what may yet be within our reach. As to the things to be known, it is enough to carry out three inquiries [as already done above, but not in sufficient detail]: (1) as to what it is that of itself presents itself to us; (2) how we may know one thing by way of another; and, finally, (3) what the conclusions thus deduced are and from what things they are deduced.[72] The above enumeration seems to me to be complete, omitting nothing which can come within the reach of our human powers.

As to the first of the two above-mentioned factors [ourselves who know], I should have liked to explain here what the mind of man is, what the body of man is, and in what manner the body is "informed"[73] by the mind, what precisely are the faculties in the composite whole [the mind-body complex, the *ingenium*] which serve in the knowing of things, and how each faculty operates. But the present discussion I find to be too narrowly circumscribed to allow of my dwelling on all that must be granted, if truth in these matters is to become evident to all my readers. For in all I write regarding such issues as are of current controversy, I should prefer to make no assertion until I have stated what the evidence is which has led me to it, and by which I am judging that others also may be persuaded.

But since that is not here possible, I shall have to be content to explain in the briefest terms, and in the manner most helpful for my purposes, how we may view everything in us which is contributory to the knowing of things. Do not, unless you like, believe that this is how things are. There can, however, be no objection to our following these suppositions, if, as would appear, they in no way obscure the truth of things, and serve indeed to render them all much clearer to us. That is how we proceed in geometry, making

---

[72] Treatment of these three last questions follows below, p. 57.
[73] *informetur*.

in regard to some quantity suppositions which do not in any way weaken the force of the demonstrations, though in physical inquiry the quantity may often have to be judged to be otherwise constituted.

Let us therefore represent the constitution of the human *ingenium* as follows:[74] first, that all the external senses, in so far as they are parts of the body, and despite the fact that we actively direct them on objects (namely, by local movements of the sense-organs), none the less, properly regarded, serve in a purely passive way, precisely in the manner in which wax receives shape from a seal. It must not be thought that what I am here suggesting is an analogy merely. We have to think of the external shape of the sentient body as being really altered by the object precisely in the manner in which the shape of the surface of the wax is altered by the seal. This has to be admitted as happening, not only when we touch a body which has shape, hardness, roughness, etc., but also when by touch we apprehend heat and cold and the like. Similarly in the case of the other senses. The first opaque structure in the eye receives the shape impressed upon it by the light with its various colors, and the first surface[75] in the ears, the nose and the tongue, which is impervious to the object, similarly borrows a new shape from the sound, the odor and the flavor.

To represent all these occurrences in this way is very helpful. For nothing falls more readily under sense than shape. It is both touched and seen. Nothing false follows

[74] As Descartes has here been careful to point out, he does not, in what follows, make any profession of having shown that the positions for which he is arguing can be established in accordance with the strict requirements of his method. Instead he argues only that the assumptions which he is asking us to accept justify themselves by their "helpfulness," i.e., by the fruitful manner in which they enable us to interpret and to co-ordinate a multiplicity of "sensibles." This is the first of many admissions tacitly made in the *Regulae,* and throughout his later writings, of his inability to make good the claim that his rules of method are as strictly applicable in the fields of physics and metaphysics as in the purely mathematical disciplines.

[75] *cutis.*

from this supposition [at least not] more than from any other; and the reason why this is so is that the apprehension of shape is so common and simple, that it is involved in all sensibles whatsoever [i.e., even in the case of the "secondary" qualities]. To take, for instance, color; whatever you may suppose color to be, you yet will not deny that it is extended, and in consequence shaped. Does any serious difficulty follow if—taking care not to admit and rashly to postulate any needless new entity, and also not denying what others may be pleased to assert regarding color, but merely abstracting from every other feature save only its having the nature of shape—we think of the diversity existing between white, blue, red, etc., as being that which exists between the following similar shapes?[76]

The same can be said of all other sensibles; for it is certain that the infinite multiplicity of shapes suffices for the expression of all the differences in sensible things [i.e., of all the various qualities, secondary as well as primary].

Secondly, we must hold that when an external sense is set in motion by the object, the shape which it thereupon receives is conveyed to a certain other part of the body (called the *sensus communis*) in the very instant, and without any entity really passing from the one place to the other. Exactly in the manner in which, while I am now writing, I comprehend that at the very instant at which the various characters are formed on the paper, not only is the lower part of the pen moved, but that no motion, not even the smallest, can occur in it which is not simultaneously shared by the

[76] For his later manner of representing the differences of color as due to differences of motion, and thereby of shape, cf. *Dioptric*, below, pp. 147-50; *New Studies*, pp. 104-06.

whole pen. All these diversities in the pen's motions are being traced in the air by its upper end, and this without our having to think of anything real as passing from the one end of the pencil to the other. Now who believes that the connection between the parts of the human body is less close than that between the parts of the pen; and in what simpler way can this connection be envisaged?

Thirdly, we have to think of the part of the body which is the *sensus communis*[77] as in its turn functioning in place of the seal [i.e., in place of the bodies which act on the senses] for the forming in the phantasy or imagination,[78] just as if in wax, of those very shapes or ideas[79] which come pure and without body[80] from the external senses. And this phantasy [this imagination] has to be conceived as a genuine part of the body, of sufficient magnitude to allow of its different parts assuming shapes in distinctness from each other, and to enable those parts to acquire the habit of retaining those shapes for some time—this being what we entitle the memory.

Fourthly, we have to think of the moving force [by which we move the limbs] as deriving its origin from the brain, in which the phantasy is located, and that the phantasy moves the nerves [and thereby the muscles] in diverse ways, just as the *common sense* is moved by an external sense, or the pen as a whole by its lower end. This example also shows how the phantasy can be the cause of many movements in the nerves, of which, however, it does not have the images

[77] How precisely Descartes distinguishes between the *sensus communis* and the region of the brain which receives the imprints, i.e., between the parts of the brain which serve as seal and the pineal gland on which they act, is far from clear. (Cf. *Meditation* VI, below, p. 245: "The mind is immediately affected, not by all parts of the body, but only by the brain, or rather perhaps only by one quite small part of it, viz., that in which the *sensus communis* is said to be.") What is alone clear is that both are being conceived as genuine parts of the body. Cf. *New Studies,* pp. 76 ff., 143 ff.

[78] *phantasia vel imaginatione.* Descartes uses the term "phantasy" as equivalent to "imagination."

[79] *figuras vel ideas.*

[80] *puras et sine corpore,* i.e., "naked."

stamped upon it, but certain other images which enable the movements to come about. This lets us understand how all the movements of the brute animals can be brought about, though no knowledge of things can be allowed to them, but only a purely corporeal phantasy.[81] It also enables us to understand how in ourselves all those operations are brought about which we accomplish without any assistance from reason.

Finally, in the fifth place, we have to think of the power[82] by which we are properly said to know things as being purely spiritual, and no less distinct from the whole body than blood is from bone, or hand from eye. We have likewise to think of this power as one and the same whether it receives, coincidently with the [corporeal] phantasy, shapes from the *sensus communis,* or applies itself to those which are present in the [corporeal] memory, or forms new ones. Often these latter shapes so preoccupy the [corporeal] imagination that it is not in a position to receive ideas[83] from the *sensus communis* [i.e., those resulting from actual present affection of the outer senses] or to transmit them in the usual purely bodily manner to the motor mechanism. In all these operations the cognitive power is at one time passive, at another active, resembling now the seal and now the wax.[84] This, however, is to be taken as an analogy merely; for nothing altogether similar to this cognitive power is to be met with in corporeal things. Moreover it is, throughout, one and the same power. If, in co-operation with the [corporeal] imagination, it occupies itself with the [shapes due to] the *sensus communis,* it is said to see, touch, etc.; if, on addressing itself to the [corporeal] imagination, it is concerned with it solely in so far as this is decked out with diverse shapes, it is said to remember; if it

---

[81] This shows that already, prior to 1629, Descartes had arrived at his automatist view of animal behavior.

[82] *vim.*

[83] *ideas,* again employed as a term synonymous with *figuras.*

[84] Passive when sensing, active when reviving in the pineal gland shapes previously sensed, or when (as in imaging a centaur) it also calls for rearrangement of these brain-patterns.

applies itself to the [corporeal] imagination in order to create new shapes, it is said to imagine or cognize;[85] and finally if it acts alone it is said to understand.[86] In what manner this last is carried out, I shall explain more at length in its proper context.[87] According as it discharges these diverse functions the agency is entitled either pure understanding, or imagination, or memory, or sense. When, however, it is forming new ideas [i.e., shapes, *figuras*] in the phantasy, or attends to those already formed there, strictly speaking its proper name is *ingenium*.[88] [Viewed thus as the mind-body complex] we consider it to be capable of all the above operations; and the distinction in the names applicable to the several operations must be kept in view in what follows. If all these matters be thus conceived, the attentive reader will have no difficulty in gathering what are the aids to be obtained from each faculty, and how far human address can avail to supplement the defects of our *ingenium*.

[85] *concipere,* i.e., in Descartes' usage of the term, any and every mode of cognitive awareness. Since Descartes uses *percipere* and *concipere* as virtually synonymous terms, they have been translated by a neutral term, such as "awareness" or "cognizing."

[86] *intelligere.* Thus "understanding" is for Descartes an alternative title for "the natural light of reason," or, in other words, for the mind's specifically *cognitive* power. But though in itself single and uniform, it can yet be entitled either sensing, remembering, imaging or understanding, according to the nature of the "objects" which it is then disclosing to us. When it is pure understanding it is "unaided by any corporeal image" (cf. below, pp. 58-60) and instead has as its "objects" the self and its states, knowing, doubting, willing, etc. In his later teaching, on formulating his doctrine of innate ideas (cf. *New Studies,* p. 226 ff.), Descartes adds to this list of the "objects" of pure understanding, the idea of God and certain archetypal ideas, required by the *aliquid amplius* involved in all judgments. The ideas common to both the mental and the corporeal (inclusive of "relations," so cursorily dealt with in the *Regulae*) have an ambiguous status, not further defined. They can be apprehended, Descartes discloses (below, p. 60), "either by the pure understanding, or by the understanding in its intuiting of the images of material things." The tentative exploratory character of his teaching in the *Rules* is here especially in evidence.

[87] Cf. below, pp. 58-60.

[88] *Ingenium* is here, as in the title of the treatise, taken as signifying man's entire cognitive mind-body equipment.

For since the understanding [when not acting alone, but in collaboration with the imagination][89] can be moved by the [corporeal] imagination or on the contrary act upon it, and since the imagination can by its motor power act on the senses [i.e., on the sense-organs] directing them to objects, while they in their turn act on it, that is to say, can depict on it images of the objects, and since the memory—that memory at least which is corporeal and similar to that of the brutes—is in no respect distinct from the imagination, we are brought to the assured conclusion, that if the understanding be dealing with matters in which there is nothing corporeal or similar to the corporeal, it cannot be aided by those powers, and that if it is not to be hampered by them, the senses must be held off from it, and the imagination [i.e., the corporeal imagination], in so far as that is at all possible, emptied of every distinct impression. If, on the other hand, the understanding sets itself to examine something which can be referred to body, its idea [i.e., its *figura,* shape] must be fashioned as distinctly as possible in the [corporeal] imagination; and that this may be done the more effectively,[90] the thing itself which this idea [this shape] is to represent should be exhibited to the external senses. A multiple thing cannot be of assistance to the understanding in the distinct intuiting of single things. If, as has often to be done, one thing be deduced from a number of things, we must remove from the ideas of the things [i.e., from the shapes of the things] whatever does not require present attention, so that the remaining features may be the more readily retained in memory. For the same reason, it is not the things themselves which should be exhibited to the external senses, but preferably certain reduced shapes which abbreviate them; and provided they suffice in guarding against failures of the memory, they are

[89] When, as here, Descartes is speaking of understanding as aided (or hampered) by the imagination, he is identifying it with the *vis cognoscens,* i.e., with the natural light of reason, the light that discloses to us the true nature not only of the self and its states but also —when directed on the brain patterns—of extension and its modes.

[90] I.e., more effectively than in relying on *revived* corporeal images.

the more helpful in proportion as they are simple. Whoever will observe all these prescriptions will, in my view, have omitted nothing that bears on this first part of the rule [i.e., the distinct intuiting of simples].

We now come to the second part of our task,[91] that of distinguishing accurately the notions of simple things from those which are composed of them, and of seeing in respect of both where falsity may come in, so that we may be on our guard, and concern ourselves only with those matters which can be known with certainty. But here again, as in the preceding inquiries, we must make certain assumptions as to which all are not perhaps agreed. But even should they have to be viewed as being no more real than the imaginary circles which astronomers employ in describing their phenomena, that matters little, provided they in fact do enable us in each given case to distinguish true knowledge from false.

First, then, we declare that *in the order of our knowledge* single things[92] should be viewed otherwise than if we were speaking of them as they indeed exist. Thus, for instance, if we consider an extended and shaped body, we shall indeed admit in respect of the thing itself, that it is one and simple. We cannot in that regard treat it as a composite of corporeity, extension and shape, since these parts have never existed separately from each other. But since we have to think of them separately, before we can be in position to judge that the three are to be found together in one and the same subject, we pronounce it, *in respect of our understanding,* to be a composite of those three natures. For this reason, since we are here treating of things only in so far as they are apprehended by the understanding [as aided by the imagination], we call only those simple, the cognition of which is so perspicuous and distinct that they cannot be divided by the mind into others more distinctly known. Such are shape,[93]

---

[91] I.e., the three questions cited above, p. 50: in what follows the three are treated conjointly, under eight headings, ending p. 65.

[92] *res singulas.*

[93] Here (and again on p. 59) it may be noted, Descartes, contrary to his usual custom, cites *figura* prior to *extensio,* and proceeds

extension, motion, etc. All others we conceive to be in some way composed of these; and this is to be understood in a manner so general that we make no exception in favor even of those notions which we sometimes abstract from these simples, as, for instance, where we say that shape is the limit of an extended thing, conceiving by the term limit something more general than the term shape, since we can speak of a limit of duration, a limit of motion, etc. For even although limit, as thus understood, is abstracted from shape, it should not for that reason be regarded as simpler than shape. Since it is also attributed to other things, such as the outer boundary of duration or of motion,[94] etc., things which differ from shape *toto genere,* it has to be abstracted from these natures also; and accordingly, is something composite, obtained from a plurality of natures wholly diverse, and to which therefore it cannot be applied save ambiguously.[95]

Secondly, we declare that those things which in respect of our understanding are called simple are either purely mental,[96] or purely material, or common to the two. Those are purely mental which are known by the understanding through a certain inborn light[97] unaided by any corporeal image.[98] That a number of such things exist is certain. It is certain also that we are unable to construct any corporeal

to dwell on the simplicity and ultimacy of shape, notwithstanding its being dependent on, i.e., its being a "mode" of extension. His thesis would seem to be that extension, like all other universals, when apprehended *in genere,* is known only in and through its instances, i.e., only as a "dimension" common to all shapes.

[94] Here, as in so many of Descartes' references to motion, his meaning is left imprecise.

[95] This ambiguity of meaning is one of the features which in Descartes' view distinguishes such *abstract* notions from other simples, even from those simples which are common to both the physical and the mental. The simples in his third group, like all other simples, are, Descartes is maintaining, adequate, not abstract. Cf. *New Studies,* pp. 312-13.

[96] *pure intellectuales.*

[97] *per lumen quoddam ingenitum,* i.e., by what Descartes elsewhere entitles the natural light of reason.

[98] Cf. above, p. 56.

idea[99] [i.e., any *figura,* shape] which shall represent to us what knowledge[100] is, what doubt is, what ignorance is, or what that action of the will is which allows of its being called volition, and the like.[101] All those things we know as they indeed are; and we know them so easily that for doing so it suffices that we be endowed with [the natural light of] reason. Purely material simples are those which are apprehended only in bodies, such as shape,[102] extension, motion, etc. Lastly those simples are to be entitled common which are attributable now to corporeal things, now to spirits, without distinction [i.e., unambiguously],[103] such as existence, unity, duration and the like. To this last group we must also assign these common notions which are, as it were, links[104] for the connecting together of the other simple natures[105] and on the evidence of which rests all that we conclude by way of reasoning.[106] Such, for instance, are: things which are the

---

[99] *idea corporea. Imago* and *idea* are, it will be observed, taken here as in *Meditation* III (cf. below, p. 195) as being possibly interchangeable terms. The term "idea" does not occur in the *Regulae,* save once in Rule IV (above, p. 18), in this twelfth Rule and in Rule XIV, and even there never with the wider sense given to it in the *Meditations and Principles.* Cf. *New Studies,* pp. 223 ff., 261 ff.

[100] *cognitio.*

[101] "Knowledge, doubt or ignorance, volition and the like." This is one of the few attempts which Descartes has made to give a list of the simples which are mental, not physical; and he is ranking them with the latter as being intuited no less easily, and no less immediately.

[102] Descartes again gives priority of mention to "shape."

[103] Cf. above, p. 58.

[104] *vincula.*

[105] Among the links for the connecting of the "simple natures" Descartes here reckons not only the intuitively apprehended *relations* in which they stood to one another, but also *axioms.* In thus grouping together relations and axioms as forming a class by themselves, he is by implication admitting that they call for separate treatment, which yet is nowhere forthcoming in any of his writings; and this notwithstanding his having himself drawn attention to the all-important part played by relations in the field of knowledge. (Cf. below, pp. 65, 81.)

[106] This last statement, followed as it is by the mention of *axioms,* is dangerously misleading; it holds, on Descartes' teaching, only if

same as a third thing are the same as one another; or again, things which do not bear the same relation to a third thing, are in some respect different from one another. These common notions can be known either by the pure understanding [in its intuiting of the purely mental things] or by the understanding in its intuiting of the [corporeal] images of material things.

Further, among the simples, in turn, we must also find place for the privatives and negatives[107] of them, in so far as these are understood by us. For the cognition through which I intuit what nothing is, or an instant, or rest, is as genuine as that by which I apprehend what existence is, or duration, or motion. This way of classing them will be helpful in enabling us to maintain that all other things known to us are composed of these simple natures. If, for instance, I judge that some shape is not in motion, I shall say that my thought is in some fashion composed of shape and rest, and so in other cases.

Thirdly, we declare that these simple natures are one and all known *per se,* and never contain any falsity. This is easily seen, provided we distinguish the faculty by which the understanding intuits and knows things from that by which it judges through affirmation or negation.[108] For it can happen that we consider ourselves to be ignorant of things we really know, as for instance when we conjecture that in the

the common notions be taken as including intuitively apprehended relations. Descartes' thesis, consistently held to, is that relations are intuited *in specie* as *self-*validating and do not, therefore, require to be justified by reference to axioms. The axioms, he holds, are merely those same relations considered *in genere.* Cf. *New Studies,* p. 313 ff.

[107] Here again Descartes' manner of classing privatives and negatives apart by themselves, while yet admitting that they are genuine "simples," allows of his passing lightly over them, without further comment.

[108] Descartes, it may be noted, is already (writing in or prior to 1628) viewing the understanding and the will as separate faculties —the one sheerly contemplative, the other sheerly active—with no attempt made to explain how, in *true* judgments (cf. above, p. 2), i.e., in the judgments of "the wise" (cf. below, p. 63), the will is yet submissive to, and "guided by" the understanding.

things which we intuit, or attain by [intuitive] thinking, there is something further which is hidden from us, even though this conjecture is false. It is evident, therefore, that we are in error, should we judge that any one of these simple natures is not completely known by us. For if our mind attains to any apprehension of it whatsoever, however minimal—and this we must necessarily have done, since we are supposed to pass some judgment upon it—we can at once conclude that we know it completely. Otherwise it could not be said to be simple; it would have to be a composite of that which we apprehend in it and that of which we judge ourselves to be ignorant.

Fourthly, we declare that the conjunction of these simple natures one with another is either necessary or contingent. It is necessary when one is so implicated in some inexplicit manner[109] in the concept of another that we could not conceive either distinctly, should we judge that the two are really apart from each other. Thus shape is united with extension, motion with duration or time, etc., because we are not free to cognize a shape lacking in all extension, or a motion lacking in all duration. Similarly, if I say that 4 and 3 are 7, this combination is a necessary combination. For we do not conceive the number 7 distinctly, unless we include in it in some inexplicit manner the numbers 3 and 4. And in the same way, whatever is demonstrated regarding shapes or numbers necessarily holds of that of which it is affirmed.[110] Nor is it merely in things sensible that we are faced with this necessity.[111] If, for instance, Socrates says that he doubts all things, it necessarily follows that at least he knows this, that

---

[109] *confusa quadam ratione.* Cf. Descartes' argument in the next following paragraph.

[110] I.e., in respect of all such things as stand in *quantitative* relations to one another and therefore allow of a common measure.

[111] Here Descartes is making the far-reaching, highly questionable assertion that his method, formulated by study of the mathematical disciplines, i.e., of the sciences which treat of the quantitatively measurable, will be found to be no less valid, and to be fruitful, in general philosophy and in metaphysics.

he doubts; and it likewise further follows that he knows that there is something which can be true or false, etc. For all these consequences are necessarily annexed to the nature of doubt. That union is, on the other hand, contingent, when the relation uniting them is not indissoluble, as when we say that a body is animate, that a man is clothed, etc. Again, it happens that many things which are necessarily conjoined are often reckoned among those that are contingent, namely by those who fail to discern what the relation is that holds between them, as in the case of the proposition: I am, therefore God is; or, again, I know, therefore I have a mind distinct from the body. Lastly we have to note that necessary propositions, when converted, are most of them contingent. Thus, for instance, from the fact that I exist, I conclude with certainty that God exists; but it is not for that reason permissible to affirm that because God exists, I also exist.

Fifthly, we declare that nothing can ever be understood by us beyond these simple natures and a certain mixture or composition[112] of them. Often, indeed, it is easier to be aware of several of them joined together than to separate one of them from the others. For instance, I am able to know what a triangle is, although I have never taken thought that in that knowledge is contained also the knowledge of the angle, the line, the number 3, shape, extension, etc. But this does not conflict with our declaring that the nature of the triangle is composed of all those natures, and that they are better known than the triangle, since they are the natures which are understood in the understanding of the triangle. It may be also that in the triangle other natures are involved which escape our notice, e.g., the magnitude of the angles as being equal to two right angles, and the innumerable [other] relations which hold between the sides and the angles, the size of the area, etc.

Sixthly, we declare that those natures which we name composite are known by us either because we experience them as they are, or because we ourselves compose them. We experi-

112 Cf. below, p. 80.

ence whatever we perceive by sense, whatever we learn from others, and in general whatever reaches our understanding, be it from without, or be it from the self's reflex contemplation of itself. And here we must note that the understanding can never be deceived by anything experienced if it limits itself to intuiting the thing presented to it precisely as given, i.e., either as it is in itself [i.e., as apprehended non-spatially, through the mind's direct contemplation of it] or in some image[113] [i.e., as apprehended spatially, in the corporeal organ of the *sensus communis*], and does not in the latter case proceed to judge that the imagination is thereby faithfully reporting the objects of the senses [i.e., the bodies acting on the sense-organs] or that the senses take over the true shapes of things [i.e., take on, in the manner of wax when acted on by a die, an *exact* imprint] or, in short, that external things always are as they appear to be. For in all such judgments we are liable to error, and are guilty of it when, for instance, someone relates a fable to us, and we believe it to have actually happened, or when on suffering from jaundice (when the eye is therefore tinged with yellow color) we judge all things to be yellow, or when the [corporeal] imagination being damaged, as happens in those suffering from melancholia, we judge its disordered phantasmata to represent real things. But the understanding of the wise man will not be thereby deceived. Whatever may come to him from the imagination [i.e., from the bodily seat of the *sensus communis*] he will judge to be indeed truly imprinted there, and yet will never assert that it has passed complete and without alteration from external things to the senses, and from the senses to the phantasy, unless he has been previously assured of this on some other ground. For it is we ourselves who are compounding the things that engage our thoughts, in all of those cases in which we [allow ourselves to] believe that in them there is something of which our mind has no immediate experience—as when the sufferer from jaundice persuades himself that the things at which he is look-

---

[113] *rem sibi objectam, prout illam habet vel in se ipso vel in phantasmate.*

ing are yellow. Any such thought will be composite, made up partly of what his phantasy represents to him, and partly of what he is of himself assuming, namely, that the color appears yellow, not owing to a defect in his eye, but because the things at which he is looking really are yellow. The conclusion follows, that we can fall into error only when the things we believe are in some way products of our own compounding.

Seventhly, we declare that this compounding can come about in three ways, namely (*a*) by impulse,[114] (*b*) by conjecture, or (*c*) by deduction. (*a*) All those who in the forming of their judgments on things are led to such beliefs by their native make-up[115] are to be counted as acting through impulse. They are not persuaded by reason or evidence,[116] but are determined merely, either by some superior power [that which has determined their native make-up] or by their own free-will or by the play[117] of their phantasy. The first-named power is never a source of error, the second rarely, the third almost always. Impulse [when determined in the first-named manner] does not indeed concern us, since it is not subject to our human control.[118] (*b*) As to conjecture, nothing that we conjecturally compound really deceives us, so long as we judge it to be no more than probable, and never affirm it to be true. Such conjectures, indeed, aid in our self-instruction; for instance, when from the fact that water, which is more remote than earth from the center of the globe, is also less dense than earth, and that the air which is above the water is less dense than water, we proceed to hazard the guess that above the air there is nothing but a very pure ether, much rarer than the air itself.

There remains, therefore, only (*c*), deduction; through it alone can we be certain that in compounding things we do so comformably with truth. Yet in it also there can be many de-

114 *per impulsum.*
115 *suo ingenio.*
116 *nulla ratione persuasi.*
117 *dispositione.*
118 *sub artem non cadit.*

fects.[119] Thus if, from the fact that in a space full of air we perceive nothing either by sight, touch or any other sense, we conclude that this space is empty, we are in error, wrongly conjoining the nature of this space with that of a vacuum. And this is what happens as often as we judge that we can deduce from what is particular or contingent something general and necessary. But it is within our power to avoid this error, namely, by never conjoining objects save only those which we intuit as being necessarily conjoined, as, for instance, when, from our intuiting shape and extension as being necessarily conjoined, we deduce that nothing can have shape save that which is extended, etc.

In view of all the above considerations we conclude, first, that we have expounded distinctly, and as I think by an adequate enumeration, what at the start could be stated only confusedly, *rudi Minerva;* namely, that no paths leading to certainty in the knowledge of truth are open to men save self-evidencing intuition and necessary deduction. We have also shown what those [simple] natures are to which reference is made in the eighth rule. And it is evident that the mind's intuitive power extends to all those simple natures and to the knowing of the necessary connections between them,[120] and, in short, to everything which the mind accurately[121] experiences as existing either in itself or in the phantasy. Regarding deduction, however, more will be said in what follows.[122]

Secondly, we have concluded that no special labor is required in knowing those simple natures, because they are in

[119] On pp. 12, 14, Descartes has stated that deduction can never be wrongly performed by us. Evidently he is here using the term in a looser popular sense, i.e., as covering not only what in the next paragraph he entitles "necessary deduction" but also reasoning which, falling short of this, yet claims to have a cogency quite other than that of the conjectures, the guesses, dealt with in the preceding paragraph.

[120] Here, as in the preceding paragraph, Descartes is, by implication, taking *relations* as a class of ideas, distinguishable from simple natures.

[121] *praecise,* i.e., when not added to or altered by any mental operation into which the will enters.

[122] Cf. below, p. 68: "Fifthly . . ."

and by themselves sufficiently known. Effort is called for only in separating them off from each other and in intuiting each separately with steadfast mental penetration. No one is of such feeble *ingenium* as not to be able to perceive that when he is seated he in some way differs from himself when upright on his feet; but not everyone separates equally distinctly the nature of posture from the other features in this thought, or can assert that nothing has altered save only the posture. We have good reason for insisting upon this. For often the learned have a way of being so clever that they have contrived to blind themselves even to those things which are in themselves evident and of which the rustic is never ignorant. This is what happens when they set themselves to explain things which are in themselves evident by something yet more evident. For what they in fact then do is to explain something else or nothing at all. Who, for instance, does not apprehend all that there is to apprehend, in respect of his change when he changes location; yet who, on being told that "locus is the surface of the surrounding body," will thereby be enabled to conceive what change of location is? For that surface can be changed, although I have not moved and thus have not changed location; or, on the other hand, it can so move along with me that, though it still surrounds me, I am nevertheless no longer located in the same place. Or again, they would seem to be using magic words, which have an occult power that exceeds the grasp of the human mind. Thus they declare *motion,* a thing completely familiar to everyone, to be *actum entis in potentia, prout est in potentia.* Is there anyone who understands these words? And is there anyone who is ignorant what motion is? Must not everyone recognize that these learned men have been seeking to find a knot in a bulrush?[123] We have there-

---

[123] Gilson (*L'Esprit de la philosophie médiévale* [1932], p. 70) makes the not unjust comment: "C'est une définition dont, depuis Descartes, il est admis que l'on a le droit de se moquer, et celle de Descartes semble assurément beaucoup plus claire, mais c'est peut-être, comme l'a bien vu Leibniz, parce qu'elle ne définit aucunement le mouvement. Ce n'est pas la définition d'Aristote qui est obscure, c'est le mouvement même qu'elle définit; ce qui est acte, puisqu'il est, mais

fore to maintain that no definitions are to be used in explaining things of this kind. To do so is mistakenly to substitute composites for simples. What alone is required is that we each of us intuit the simples apart from all else, attentively turning upon them the light native to his *ingenium*.

Thirdly, we have concluded that the whole of human science [science as distinguished from immediate experience] consists in this, that we have [clear and distinct] understanding of the manner in which those simple natures combine to compose other things. That this be noted is of first importance. For how often, when some difficult matter is proposed for investigation, almost all halt at the very threshold, uncertain as to which of their thoughts they ought to give heed, and obstinately inclined to believe that what they have to be doing is to search for some new kind of entity previously unknown to them! Thus if the question be as to the nature of the magnet, these people, foreseeing nothing but difficulties ahead, turn their minds away from whatever is [simple and] evident, and straightway occupy them instead with whatever is most difficult, in the vague hope that perchance, by roving over the unfruitful field of manifold causes, the novelty they are looking for will be found. On the other hand, he who reflects that in the magnet there can be nothing to know which does not consist of certain simple natures, known in and by themselves, has no doubts as to how he should proceed. First of all, he diligently collects all the experiences to be had in regard to this stone, and from these he then endeavors to infer[124] what the character of that mixture of the simple natures must be if it is to be effective in producing all of the effects thus experienced in the magnet. On determining this mixture, we can at once boldly assert that we have learned the true nature

qui n'est pas actualité pure, puisqu'il devient, et dont cependant la potentialité tend à s'actualiser progressivement, puisqu'il change. Lorsqu'on dépasse ainsi les mots pour attendre les choses, on ne peut pas ne pas voir que la présence du mouvement dans un être, est révélatrice d'un certain manque d'actualité."

[124] *deducere conatur*—a tentative process, calling for "sagacity" and for "suppositions," not "deduction" in any stricter sense.

of the magnet, in so far as it can be discovered by man from his given experiences.

Fourthly, it follows as a final consequence, from what has been said, that we must not fancy that some portions of our knowledge are more obscure [or difficult] than other portions, since all of them are of the same nature throughout, consisting entirely in the combining of things known in and of themselves. This is a truth which very few have hitherto recognized. Prejudiced in favor of the contrary opinion, the more confident among them have not hesitated to uphold, as though they were sound demonstrations, what are merely conjectures of their own, attaching to their concepts certain words by means of which they are in the habit of proclaiming and elaborately discussing many doctrines of which neither they nor their hearers have any real understanding. On the other hand, the more modest often refrain from many an investigation which is yet quite easy and of high practical importance, merely because of their considering themselves unequal to it; and believing, as they do, that such issues allow of being mastered by others better endowed, they adopt the opinions of those in whose authority they have most confidence.

Fifthly,[125] we say that no deduction can be made save of things by way of words, or of causes by way of effects, or of effects by way of causes, or of like by way of like, or parts or the whole by way of parts. . . .[126]

In conclusion [and in anticipation of our argument in Part II], lest perchance the chain-like sequence of our rules be overlooked, we divide all that can be known into simple data and questions. In respect of simple data,[127] the only requirements on which we insist are those which prepare our power of knowing for the more distinct [i.e., perspicuous] intuiting

---

[125] Following the Leibniz MS., the Amsterdam edition has "octavo," i.e., as following on "seventhly"; above, p. 65.

[126] There is here a gap in the text. Descartes at time of writing would seem to have been in doubt as to what he should or should not include within the scope of this rule. Cf. below, p. 74.

[127] *propositiones simplices.* Descartes still continues to distinguish between intuition and judgment. Cf. also below, p. 73.

of objects whatever the objects be, and for the more sagacious examination of them. For these simple data must come before the mind of themselves; they cannot be reached by way of inquiry. This part of our task we have covered in these first twelve rules; in them we have, we believe, taken account of everything that, in our view, can in any way prove helpful in the employment of our reason [in the knowing of the simple data]. As to questions,[128] some of them are perfectly understood, even while we are still in ignorance of their solutions; and these we shall deal with in the next twelve rules. There are others not perfectly understood; and these, in turn, we reserve for treatment in twelve further rules. In making this division between perfectly and imperfectly understood questions, we have had two considerations in view: that we may be able [in the next following twelve rules] to avoid having to speak of anything that presupposes a knowledge of what comes later: and that there may be opportunity of inculcating what, in the disciplining of the mental powers, ought, we hold, to be our first concern. For, be it noted, no questions are to be taken as being perfectly understood, save those in which we apprehend distinctly the three prerequisites: (1) what the marks are that enable us to recognize what we are seeking when we come upon it; (2) from what precisely we ought to deduce this; and (3) the manner in which these two [the data and the conclusion to which they lead] are proved so to depend each on the other that it is impossible for either to be changed in any respect while the other remains unchanged. Thereby we are assured of having all the required premises; nothing remains to be determined save the manner in which the conclusions may be discovered. This will not be a matter of deducing something from one simple thing (that, as we already said can be done without the aid of rules)[129] but of disengaging some one thing which depends on many others mingled together, and of doing this in so artful a manner that at no point [in the course of the inquiry] is any greater mental

[128] Elsewhere Descartes entitles them "difficulties."
[129] Cf. above, pp. 10, 14.

capacity required than in making the simplest illation. Questions of this perfectly understood kind, because of their being highly abstract[130] and being for the most part[131] met with only in the fields of arithmetic and geometry, may seem to the inexperienced to be of mediocre utility. But I here give warning that should they desire to gain full mastery of the concluding part of this method, in which we shall be dealing with all the other [imperfectly understood] questions, they must continue to busy and exercise themselves in the prolonged study of this first kind of question.

---

[130] I.e., as calling for abstraction "from all that is superfluous." Cf. Rule XIII.

[131] *fere tantum.*

RULE XIII

For the perfect understanding of a question we must abstract it from all that is superfluous, rendering it as simple as possible, and, resorting to enumeration, divide it into its minimal parts.

THIS is the one respect in which we imitate the dialecticians. Just as, in the treatment of the forms of the syllogisms, they assume that the terms or matter of the syllogisms are known, so too we here lay it down as a prerequisite that the question at issue be perfectly understood [i.e., that we are from the start in possession of all the data required for its solution]. We do not, however, like them, distinguish two extremes and a middle term. This noted, let us now consider the whole matter afresh. Firstly, there must in every question be something not yet known; otherwise inquiry would be to no purpose. Secondly, the not yet known must be in some way marked out; otherwise we should not in our investigation be determined to it instead of to something else. Thirdly, it can be so marked out only by way of something that is already known. All these prerequisites are found even in imperfectly understood questions. Thus if the question be what is the nature of the magnet, we already know what is meant by those two words, "magnet" and "nature," and thereby are determined to this instead of to some other inquiry; and so in other cases. But over and above this, if the question is to be perfectly understood, we require that it be made so completely

[132] Cf. above, p. 1 n.

determinate that we have no need to seek for anything beyond what can be deduced from the [already known] data.[133] For instance, (a), should someone question me as to what is to be inferred regarding the nature of the magnet when we argue exclusively from those observations[134] which Gilbert claims to have made, be those observations true or be they false; or (b), if I be asked what precisely I should infer as to the nature of sound,[135] basing the inference exclusively on the following data: that three strings A, B and C emit exactly similar sounds; that the strings are being supposed to be so related that B is twice as thick as A but no longer, and kept in tension by a weight twice as heavy; that C in turn, while twice as long is yet no thicker, and is kept in tension by a weight four times as heavy; or (c), if I be asked some other such determinate question—in all such cases we are enabled to see how all imperfect questions can be reduced to questions that are perfectly understood, as will be explained more at length in due course.[136] We see also how this rule can be observed in such wise that our difficulty, rightly understood, is held apart from everything superfluous, and how in that way it can be so reduced that we no longer regard ourselves as dealing with this or that [concrete particularized] subject but solely *in genere* with certain magnitudes in respect of their interrelations. Thus, for instance, once we have decided that only such and such observations regarding the magnet are to be considered, there is no longer any need for us to hesitate in abstracting in thought from all the others.

In addition we prescribe that the difficulty ought to be made as simple as possible in accordance with Rules V and VI, and divided in accordance with Rule VII. Thus if, in studying the magnet, I rely on certain observations, I shall run them over

---

[133] *ex datis.*

[134] *experimentis.*

[135] Cf. *A.T.* x, pp. 337, 431, 488, in Beeckman's Journal.

[136] Cf. below, Rule XIV, pp. 80 ff., leading up to the conclusion, p. 83, "Let us then take it as agreed and certain that questions which are perfectly understood raise scarcely any difficulty save that which consists in so treating proportions as to arrive at equations."

separately, one after another. Or if it is sound I am studying, as in the above instance, I shall separately compare the strings A and B, then A and C, in such wise that I thereby embrace them one and all in a sufficient enumeration. These three rules are the only rules which the pure understanding is called upon to use in respect of the terms of any question before advancing to its ultimate solution—an advance which calls for the employment of the next following eleven rules. The third part of this treatise will further explain how this should be done.[137] By questions, be it understood, we intend to signify all those matters in which the true or the false is found; and in listing the different kinds of questions our purpose is to determine what we can be in a position to accomplish in each kind.

We have already said[138] that there can be no falsity in the bare intuition of things, whether the things be simple or conjoined. As thus apprehended, we do not entitle them "questions"; they do, however, acquire that title, as soon as we are called upon to pass some determinate judgment regarding them. We do not, however, limit the title to questions asked us by other people. Socrates' own ignorance, or rather his own doubting, itself set him a question, when, on first taking note of it, he began to inquire whether it was true that he was in doubt regarding all things, and claimed that he was.

Now in our questions we are seeking either things by way of words, or causes by way of effects, or effects by way of causes, or the whole or other parts by way of parts,[139] or have several such questions simultaneously in view.

We say that we are seeking things by way of words, when the difficulty consists in obscurity of language. To this kind of question are referred not only all riddles, like that of the Sphinx about the animal which to begin with is a quadruped, then a biped and, finally, three-footed; or the riddle regarding the fishermen, who, standing on the shore, provided with

[137] I.e., XIV-XXIV. Cf. below, p. 89 n.
[138] Cf. above, pp. 25, 68.
[139] Cf. above, p. 68.

rods and hooks for the catching of fish, declared that they no longer had those which they had caught, but on the other hand had those which they had not yet been able to catch, etc.[140] But quite apart from such deliberate ambiguity of language, in the great majority of matters about which the learned dispute, the question is almost always one of names. There is, however, no need to judge so ill of the mental powers of the learned as to think that when they thus explain things in unsuitable terms they are wrongly conceiving the things themselves. When, for instance, they call "place"[141] the "surface of the surrounding body," they are not thinking any false thing but only misusing the term "place," which in common use signifies that simple and self-evidencing nature in respect of which a thing is said to be here or there. This consists wholly in a certain relation of the thing that is said to be *in loco* to the parts of the space external to it. Some people, on noting that what is thus named the place of anything is the space occupied by the surface surrounding it, have improperly entitled the latter the thing's absolute place:[142] and similarly in other cases. Indeed, these verbal questions are of such frequent occurrence that if philosophers agreed among themselves in their use of words, almost all their controversies would thereupon cease.

We seek causes by way of effects, when we inquire concerning anything whether it exists or what it is. . . .[143]

[Now all questions are either of words or of things. By questions of words I here mean, not those in which we inquire into words, but those in which by way of words we inquire into things—such questions as those in which we set

[140] The answers to these riddles are given below, p. 77.

[141] *locum.*

[142] *ubi intrinsecum.*

[143] Here again there is a lacuna in the text. Happily it can be filled out, in part at least, from the paragraphs in Arnauld's *Logic* (Paris, 1662), which, as he tells us, he has taken over from the MS. copy of the *Regulae* lent him by Clerselier. Cf. *A.T.* x, pp. 470-75; and Baynes' translation of the "Port-Royal Logic," given here within brackets.

ourselves to find the answer to a riddle or to explain from obscure and ambiguous words what an author has been intending to say.

Questions of things may be reduced to four chief kinds.

(1) The first is, when we seek causes by way of effects. We know, for example, the various effects of the magnet, and inquire into their causes. We know the various effects which we are wont to ascribe to *horror vacui,* and inquire if this is the true cause [and have found that it is not].[144] We know the ebb and flow of the sea, and ask what can be the cause of a movement so great and so regular.

(2) The second is, when we seek effects by way of causes. We have always, for instance, known that wind and water have a great power of moving bodies; but the ancients, not having sufficiently examined what the effects may be of these causes, did not apply them as they have since been applied, by means of mills, to a great number of purposes very useful to our human societies and which so notably lighten the labor of men, the harvest appropriate to a true physics. Thus we may say that the first kind of question, in which we seek causes by way of effects, constitutes the speculative part of physics, and this second kind, in which we seek effect by way of causes, is the whole of applied physics.[145]

(3) In the third kind of question we seek the whole by way of the parts, as when, having several numbers, we seek their sum by adding one to another; or when, having two numbers, we seek their product by multiplying the one by the other.

(4) The fourth kind is when, having the whole and some part, we seek another part; as when having one number and another which is to be subtracted from it, we seek what thereupon remains, or when, having a number, we seek what such and such a part of it will be.

144 Added by Arnauld in the 1664 edition of his *Logic.* The reference is presumably to Pascal's treatise which appeared in 1663.

145 This reads like a paraphrase, in which Arnauld is using his own preferred modes of expression, not a literal transcript of Descartes' text. As to this, however, we can only conjecture.

But we must note that, in order to afford due extension to those two last kinds of questions, and in order that they may include what cannot properly be brought under the two first kinds, we have to take the word "part" in a more general sense, as comprising its modes, its extremities, its accidents, its properties, and in general all its attributes,[146] so that, for example, we shall be seeking a whole by way of parts when we seek to find the area of a triangle by way of its height and base, and on the other hand, a part by way of the whole and of another part when we seek to find the side of a rectangle by way of our knowledge of its area and one of its sides.[147]]

But, as often happens, when a question is propounded to us for a solution, we do not at once recognize the kind to which it belongs, nor consequently whether things are to be sought by way of words, or causes by way of effects, etc. It is useless, therefore, as it seems to me, to treat here of the different kinds in more detail. It will tend to greater brevity and be more useful, if instead we go over all that has to be attended to in the solution of any and every difficulty, considering all of their requirements in order and together. Now in doing so, what we must first, and above all else, strive to obtain—no matter what the question may be—is a distinct understanding as to what it is that we are seeking.

Frequently people are in such a hurry in their investigations, that they bring only a vagrant mind to their solution, not having first considered by what marks they are to recognize what they are seeking, should they chance upon it. They are proceeding as foolishly as a servant sent on some errand by his master, should he be so eager to obey that he hurries off without having received his instructions, and without knowing where he is ordered to go.

[146] Attributes (like substance) is a term which nowhere occurs in the *Regulae,* in Descartes' own text.

[147] This is the end of the missing part of Descartes' text. In his next following paragraphs Arnauld, as we find, is paraphrasing somewhat freely (and with the teaching of the *Discourse* and the *Meditations* also in view) the remainder of Rule XIII and the beginning of Rule XIV.

In every question there has indeed to be something un-known; otherwise there would be no reason for asking it. None the less this unknown something must be marked out by conditions sufficiently definite to determine us to seek one thing rather than another. And, as we are maintaining, our attention must be concentrated on these conditions from the very start. We have to direct the mind's attention to the in-tuition of each of these conditions, diligently asking how far the unknown something for which we are seeking is limited by this and that condition. For our human minds are here liable to error in one or other of two ways; either by our assuming something more than is given in the statement of the question, or on the other hand by our omitting something.

In other words, we have to guard against reading into the question more than is given, and also at the same time against taking the given in too restricted a sense. This is especially so in the case of riddles and other such questions artificially invented for the very purpose of misleading the mind, but sometimes too in other questions—those in which something is being assumed as being certain, and when this is an assump-tion to which we are committed merely by opinion of long standing, and not by any well-grounded reason [i.e., when this something is indeed not to be found among our data]. For example, in the riddle set by the Sphinx,[148] we ought not to believe that the word "foot" refers only to animals' feet: we have to note that it may be otherwise applied, as happens when it is used to describe the hands of an infant or an old man's staff, these being, in each case, employed as feet are in walking. So likewise in the fishermen conundrum, we have to guard against allowing the thought of fish to occupy our minds to the exclusion of those [smaller] animals which the poor often carry about with them all unwillingly, and cast away when caught. Or again, suppose we are inquiring into the construction of a vessel, such as I have seen, in the midst of which stood a column, and lying on the column the figure of a Tantalus in the posture of a man bending down to drink.

148 Cf. above, p. 73.

When water is poured into this vessel, it rises in the vessel, and continues to rise so long as it is not high enough to enter Tantalus' mouth; and immediately it reaches his disappointed lips, at once the whole of the water flows away. At first sight, the whole device seems to connect with the figure of Tantalus, which yet in actual fact is merely accessory and in no wise conditions the question. For the whole difficulty consists exclusively in this: how the vessel can be so constructed that the whole of the water flows away immediately it reaches a certain height, while yet maintaining it up to this level. Or to take a last example [of the other, more serious type above mentioned]: if from all the observations we have regarding the stars, we seek to discover what can be asserted regarding their motions, we may not gratuitously assume that the earth is immobile and is located at the center of things, as the ancients declared—on no better ground than that from infancy it has seemed to us to be so. This we ought to treat as dubious, that we may thereupon proceed to examine what certainty we can have in the matter. And so in other cases.

On the other hand, we sin by omission when we fail to bear in mind some condition which is prerequisite for the determination of the question, and which is either expressly stated in it or is in some way implied in it. Should we, for instance, inquire into the question of perpetual motion, not as we have it in nature, in the motion of stars and of fountains, but as contrived by human skill. Some inquirers have believed that this can be done. Viewing the earth as being in perpetual motion around its axis, and holding that the lodestone retains all the properties of the earth, they have accordingly believed that for the invention of perpetual motion all we have to do is to contrive that the lodestone revolve circularly, communicating to a piece of iron not only its other powers but also its own motion. But even if this could be done, they would not then be producing perpetual motion *artificially;* they would only be utilizing a natural motion, a motion no less natural than that of a wheel exposed to the current of a river. They would thus have been neglecting to take account of a condition essential for the determination of the question.

Once the question is sufficiently understood, what we have next to consider is in what precisely its difficulty consists, in order that, as abstracted from all else, it may be the more easily resolved.

For to know in what precisely the difficulty of a question consists, the understanding of the question does not always of itself suffice; in addition, we have to direct our attention to the several features which go to constitute it. Those features which offer no special difficulty of apprehension, we leave aside; and on their removal, only that of which we are still in ignorance remains. Thus in the case of the Tantalus vessel, above described, we can then easily understand how it has to be constructed. The column as standing in its midst,[149] the bird painted [the figure of Tantalus, etc.], all of these are un-essential; and on leaving them aside, as not bearing on the question at issue, the difficulty then appears in all its naked-ness, how the water previously contained in the vessel, on rising to a certain height, flows entirely away? That is what we have been trying to discover.

What we declare to be alone promising of reward for our labors amounts, therefore, to this: the reviewing of all the factors which are given in the question set, the rejecting of those which we clearly see to be irrelevant, the retaining of those which are necessary, and the reserving of all those which are dubious for a more careful examination.

[149] The column, as we find on solving the problem, conceals a siphon.

RULE XIV

The preceding Rule bears on, and should be applied in the study of, the real extension of bodies. That extension has to be brought before the mind exclusively by means of bare shapes depicted in the [corporeal] imagination. For this is the way in which it is most distinctly apprehended by the understanding.

BUT if we are to make use of the imagination as an aid to understanding, it is essential to note that, in resorting to it, we are not looking to it for the invention of new entities. When something hitherto unknown is deduced from something previously known, we are not thereby discovering some new kind of entity: all we are doing is to extend our total knowledge in such a way that we are enabled to see that the thing sought participates in this or that way in the nature of the data provided in the question which is being asked. For example, if a man has been blind from birth, it is not to be expected that we shall be able by any train of reasoning to make him have true ideas of the colors which we have obtained from our senses. Once, however, a man has seen the primary colors, though he has never seen the intermediate and mixed colors, it is possible for him to construct the images of those which he has not seen from their likeness to the others, by a sort of deduction. Similarly, if in the magnet there be some kind of entity the like of which our understanding has never yet apprehended, it is hopeless to expect that we shall ever be able to know it by way of reasoning; we should have to be furnished either with some new sense or with a divine mind. We shall believe ourselves to have attained whatever in this matter can be accomplished by way of our human equipment,[150] if we discern with all possible distinctness that combination of already known entities or natures which gives rise to those effects which make their appearance in the magnet.

Indeed each of those already known entities, viz., extension, shape, motion and the like, the enumeration of which does not at present concern us, is known by means of an idea which is one and the same in the diverse subjects;[151] the shape of a silver crown we image precisely as we image that of a crown which is golden. This common idea [i.e., this common shape] is carried over from one subject to another by way of a simple comparison that enables us to affirm that the thing which is being inquired into is in this or that respect like, or identical with, or equal to a certain given thing. Consequently in every train of reasoning it is solely by way of comparison that we attain to a precise knowledge of the truth. To take an example: all A is B, all B is C, therefore all A is C. Here we compare with one another a *quaesitum* and a *datum,* viz., A and C [the relation of which to one another we are *seeking* to determine] in the light of what is *given,* viz., that both are B, etc. But because, as we have already often declared, the syllogistic forms are of no assistance in discovering the truth of things, it will be to the reader's profit to reject them altogether and to recognize that all knowledge whatsoever, other than that which consists in the simple and naked intuition of one single thing, is to be had by the comparison of two or more things with each other. Indeed almost the whole task set the human reason consists in preparing for this operation. For when the operation is open and simple we need no assistance from art; in the intuiting of the truth which the comparison yields to us the light of nature [i.e., our native power of direct face-to-face awareness] is all-sufficing.

[150] *ab humano ingenio.*

[151] *in diversis subjectis.* "Subject" Descartes is here using in its realist, etymological sense as meaning that which underlies and embodies the shape in question, i.e., as so far synonymous with "substance," a term which nowhere occurs in the *Regulae.*

It should be noted that the comparisons can be said to be simple and open, only when *quaesitum* and *datum* participate equally in a certain nature. The only reason why preparation is required is that in comparisons not of this simple character, the common nature is not found equally in both, but by way of certain other relations[152] or proportions in which it is involved. The chief part of our human labor consists in so simplifying these proportions as to show clearly an equality between the *quaesitum* and the something else already known.[153]

Next we should note that nothing can be reduced to this equality save that which admits of a greater or a less, and that all such matters are covered by the term "magnitude." Consequently, when, as required by the preceding rule, in difficult issues, its terms are abstracted from every subject [i.e., from all the particular instances in which they are found], all that is left for us to do consists exclusively in the treatment of magnitudes *in genere* [i.e., in universal terms].

Even so, we shall still be making use of the imagination, employing not the pure understanding but the understanding as aided by the species [i.e., the figures, the shapes or patterns, the images] depicted in the phantasy; and thus finally we have to note that nothing can be asserted of magnitudes *in genere* save what can be found to hold true of some magnitude *in specie*[154] [i.e., through our apprehension of particular instances of them, as imaged by us].

From this we easily conclude that there will be no small profit in relating[155] whatsoever can be intelligibly said of magnitudes *in genere* to that species which, of all others, is most easily and distinctly depicted in the imagination. Now it follows from what has been said in Rule XII that the magnitude

[152] *habitudines.*

[153] Cf. below, p. 89.

[154] The Latin term "species" in its active use signifies seeing, and in its more usual passive use signifies that which is seen, i.e., the outward appearance, figure, shape or pattern. In this latter sense it was employed to translate the Greek εἶδος and ἰδέα. We therefore find Aquinas speaking both of *species sensibiles* (what he elsewhere entitles *phantasmata*) and of *species intelligibiles.*

[155] *transferamus.*

which can be most easily and distinctly depicted is the real extension of a body [i.e., of some given body particularized in shape] abstracted from everything else save only from its shape. For in that twelfth rule we have shown the phantasy, together with the ideas[156] existing in it, to be itself no other than a truly real body, extended and shaped.[157] It is likewise evident that in no other subject[158] [i.e., in no other type of subject] do proportions of any and every kind exhibit their differences more distinctly. Though one thing can be said to be more or less white than another, a sound more or less sharp, and so on, it is yet impossible to determine exactly whether the greater exceeds the less in the proportion of two to one, or three to one, etc., unless by way of a certain analogy to the extension of a body that has shape. Let us then take it as agreed and certain that questions, when perfectly determined, raise scarcely any difficulty save that which consists in so treating proportions as to arrive at equations. We may argue that everything in which this precise difficulty is met with can easily be, or ought to be, separated off from every other [type of] subject and stated [exclusively] in terms of extension and shapes. For this reason we shall, up to the twenty-fifth rule, treat of extension and shapes alone, omitting consideration of everything else.

At this juncture I would rejoice to find the reader disposed to the study of arithmetic and geometry, though I should indeed prefer him never to have occupied himself with them rather than that he should have learned them in the usual manner. The practice of the rules which I am engaged in propounding is indeed much the easiest method of learning these sciences, and is amply sufficient for doing so, the rules being easier of application in them than in any of the other disciplines; and yet so great is their utility for the acquiring of a yet wider range of knowledge, that I have no hesitation

---

[156] Here, it may be noted, Descartes does not hesitate to speak of the corporeal phantasmata as ideas. Cf. *New Studies,* pp. 52, 147-48.

[157] *verum corpus reale extensum et figuratum.*

[158] Cf. above, p. 81 n.

in saying that this part of our method has not been invented for the purpose of solving mathematical problems, and that on the contrary these problems should be studied almost exclusively for the sake of training in this method. I shall therefore suppose no knowledge of these disciplines save what is evident in itself and within the reach of everyone. Such knowledge of arithmetic and geometry as is ordinarily met with in those who have mastered them, while it may not be vitiated by any manifest errors, is yet obscured by many equivocal and ill-conceived principles; and these, in the course of our discussion, as occasion offers, we shall endeavor to correct.

By extension we understand whatever has length, breadth and depth, not inquiring whether it be truly body or merely space. It does not, indeed, appear to require further explanation, since there is nothing that our imagination frames for us more easily. But since the learned often employ distinctions so subtle that they extinguish the natural light, and find obscurities in matters of which even the rustic is never ignorant, we give warning that by extension we do not here mean anything distinct and separate from that which is extended,[159] and that we refuse to recognize, in this field, philosophical entities which cannot be imaginatively envisaged. For though some may, for instance, persuade themselves that even supposing every extended object in the universe were annihilated this would not prevent extension existing by itself alone, in so thinking they would not be making use of any corporeal idea,[160] but of a misjudgment of the understanding relying on itself alone. They will themselves admit this, if they direct their attention to that very image of extension which, as will then happen, they will be striving to fashion in their phantasy. For they will then notice that they do not apprehend it in isolation from any and every subject, and that their imaging of it is thus quite other than they have believed it to be. Consequently, whatever the understanding [acting by itself] may think to be true in this regard, these abstract entities can

[159] *ab ipso subjecto.*
[160] *idea corporea.*

never be formed in the phantasy separately from their subjects.

Since, then, we are henceforth [in dealing with questions treating of real extension] to attempt nothing without the aid of the imagination, it will repay us to distinguish with care the ideas [i.e., the *figuras,* the patterns] which, in each case, are to convey to the understanding the meaning of the words we employ. To this end we submit for consideration these three ways of speaking: "extension occupies place," "body possesses extension," and "extension is not body."

The first shows how extension may be taken as being that which is extended. Clearly, if I say "extension occupies place" I am in effect saying "the extended occupies place." Yet this is no reason why, in order to avoid ambiguity, it should be better to use in place of "extension" the expression "that which is extended." For the latter does not indicate sufficiently distinctly what we are conceiving, namely that a subject occupies place because of its being extended. When so expressed, the assertion made is liable to be interpreted as meaning only that "that which is extended is the subject occupying place," just as if I were to say "that which is animate occupies space." This explains why we have said that here we would treat of extension rather than of that which is extended, although we hold that extension does not allow of being conceived otherwise than as that which is extended.

Let us now pass to these words: "body has extension." Here we do indeed understand by the term "extension" something other than body; none the less we are not forming in our phantasy two distinct ideas, one of body and another of extension, but only one single idea of a body that is extended; and from the point of view of the thing[161] it is precisely as if I had said: "body is that which is extended," or rather, "that which is extended is that which is extended." This is a peculiarity of those entities which have their being only in something else, and which can never be conceived

161 *a parte rei.*

without a subject. How different is it with those entities which allow of being really distinct from their subjects! Should I, for example, say "Peter has wealth," my idea of Peter is diverse from that of wealth. Accordingly, should I proceed to say "Paul is wealthy" I am imaging something quite different than if I said "the wealthy is wealthy." Many thinkers, failing to recognize the diversity of the two assertions, are falsely of opinion that extension contains something distinct from that which is extended, in the same way as Paul's wealth is indeed something over and above Paul.

Finally, the statement: "extension is not body." The term extension is here taken quite otherwise than as above; and when it is so used, there is no proper[162] idea [i.e., image] corresponding to it in the phantasy. In fact this entire enunciation is the work of the pure understanding, which alone has the power of separating off abstract entities of this type. For the majority of men, this is, however, an occasion of error. Not recognizing that extension, viewed in this manner, cannot be grasped by the imagination, they yet represent it to themselves by the true idea [i.e., by the corresponding image]. Now such an idea necessarily carries with it the notion of body; and if they say that extension thus apprehended is not body, they are needlessly involving themselves in the contradiction of saying that "the same thing is at once body and not body." It is therefore very important to distinguish the affirmations in which such words as "extension," "shape," "surface," "line," "point," "unity," etc., are used in a sense so restricted as to exclude something which those affirmations do in fact imply. Thus when we say "extension or shape is not body," "number is not the thing that is counted," "a surface is the limit of a body," "a line the limit of a surface," "a point the limit of a line," "unity is not a quantity," etc., all these and other similar propositions would have to be taken entirely outside the bounds of the imagination, even should they be

---

[162] *peculiaris.*

true. Consequently we shall not be concerned to treat of them.[163]

But we should carefully note that in all the other propositions in which these words (notwithstanding their being used in the above restricted sense, in abstraction from their subjects) do not exclude or deny anything from which they are not really distinct, we can and we ought to make use of the imagination as an aid. For though the understanding is in strictness attending only to what is signified by the word, the imagination ought nevertheless to form a true idea of the thing, in order that the understanding may be able, at need, to direct its attention to such other conditions belonging to it as are not expressed by the word, and that it may never imprudently judge that they have been excluded. Thus, if the question be in regard to number, we imagine some subject that is measurable through a plurality of units. Now although it is allowable for the understanding to confine its attention for the moment solely to the multiplicity displayed by the subject, we must nevertheless be on our guard against being thereby led to a conclusion which supposes that what is numbered has been excluded from our thought. That, however, is what those do who ascribe to numbers mysterious properties, idle fancies to which they certainly would not yield any such credence, were it not that they are thinking numbers to be something distinct from the things numbered. In the same way, if we are dealing with shape, let us bear in mind that we are dealing with an extended subject, though we are indeed restricting ourselves to thinking of it merely as shaped. When we are dealing with body, let us bear in mind that we are dealing with what has to be taken as possessing length, breadth and depth. When we are dealing with a surface, our subject will still be the same, though we are thinking of it as having length and breadth, and omit depth, while not denying it. So, too, in the case of the line, we are

[163] E.g., not concerned to discuss whether angelic, disembodied spirits can apprehend extension.

then still thinking of body though only in respect of its length. And in the case of the point, we are still thinking of body though without taking account of anything save that it is what it is.

Notwithstanding all that I have thus far said, I fear that men's minds are so deeply prejudiced that very few are free from the danger of losing their way here, and of finding my lengthy discourse all too brief. Arithmetic and geometry, though the most certain of all the arts, themselves lead us astray here. Does not every calculator believe not merely that his numbers have been abstracted by the understanding from all subject-matter, but that they are also genuinely distinguishable for the imagination? Do not geometers obscure the evident character of the object with which they deal, employing irreconcilable principles? They tell us that lines have no breadth, surfaces no depth, while yet they subsequently wish to obtain the one out of the other, not recognizing that a line, the fluxion of which is conceived as creating a surface, is really a body. How can the line which has no breadth have being save as a mode of body? But not to delay longer over these considerations, we may briefly explain the manner in which we are supposing that our object should be conceived, our purpose being to show how we may most easily demonstrate whatsoever is true in arithmetic and geometry.

Here, therefore, we are dealing with an object that is extended, considering in it nothing save only the extension itself, and purposely refraining from using the word quantity, since there are certain philosophers who are so subtle-minded as to distinguish it even from extension. We suppose all our questions to have been so simplified that there is nothing else to be inquired into save only the knowing of a certain extension by the comparison of it with a certain other already known extension. For we are not here looking to obtain knowledge of any new entity;[164] what we are endeavoring to do is only to simplify the ratios, be they never so in-

[164] Cf. above, p. 80.

volved, so that we may thereby discover an equality between the *quaesitum* and something already known. What is certain is that whatever differences in ratio exist in other subjects can be found to hold also between two or more extensions. Accordingly, our endeavor is sufficiently met if in extension itself we consider all the things that can aid us in the comprehension of differences in the ratios; and these things, as we find, reduce to three: dimension, unity and shape. . . .[165]

[165] Descartes managed to complete Rules XIV to XVII, partially to complete Rule XVIII, and to settle the titles of Rules XIX to XXI, at which point the treatise abruptly ends. The projected Part III is entirely lacking.

DISCOURS
DE LA METHODE

Pour bien conduire ſa raiſon,& chercher
la verité dans les ſciences.

PLUS

LA DIOPTRIQVE.

LES METEORES.

ET

LA GEOMETRIE.

Qui ſont des eſſais de cete METHODE.

A LEYDE
De l'Imprimerie de IAN MAIRE.
CIƆIƆCXXXVII.
Auec Priuilege.

DISCOURSE ON METHOD

OF RIGHTLY CONDUCTING THE REASON AND OF SEEKING FOR TRUTH IN THE SCIENCES[1]

If this discourse appears too lengthy to be read all at once, the reader may take note of its six parts. In the first he will find various considerations bearing on the sciences; in the second the chief rules of the method which the Author has devised; in the third some moral rules which he has derived

[1] Published in Leyden, 1637; and, as Descartes had long intended (cf. *A.T.* i, pp. 23, 85, 340), anonymously, that "caché derrière le tableau" he might overhear what was said of it. (The Latin translation, published under his name in Amsterdam seven years later, has on its title-page: *Ex Gallico translata, et ab Auctore perlecta, variisque in locis emendata.*) The title as given on the title-page takes the place of the more elaborate title which in March 1636 (cf. *A.T.* i, p. 339) he still thought of using: *Le projet d'une Science universelle qui puisse élever nostre nature à son plus haut degré de perfection. Plus la Dioptrique, les Météores et la Géométrie; où les plus curieuses Matières que l'Auteur ait pu choisir pour rendre preuve de la Science universelle qu'il propose, sont expliquées en telle sorte, que ceux mêmes qui n'ont point étudié les peuvent entendre.* Descartes' reason for adopting the term *Discours* he has explained to Mersenne (March 1637, *A.T.* i, p. 349): "I do not entitle it *Traité de la Méthode* but *Discours de la Méthode,* which amounts to saying *Préface ou Advis touchant la Méthode,* in order to signify that my design is not to teach the method but only to converse about it. For as can be seen from what I have said of it, it consists much more in practice than in theory [cf. below, p. 94 ff.]. I name the treatises which follow upon it, *Essais de cette Méthode,* because I claim that the things they contain could not have been discovered without it, and it is by way of them we come to know its value. This, too, is why I have included in the introductory *Discours* some little metaphysics, physics and medicine, namely, in order to show that the method applies to every kind of topic." As Descartes himself revised the Latin translation of 1644, I have drawn freely on it. The textual variations and additions are, however, too numerous for special mention. I have separately noted only those changes and additions which seem to me to raise questions of interpretation.

from this method; in the fourth the reasoning[2] by which he proves the existence of God and of the human soul, the foundations of his metaphysics; in the fifth the order of the questions bearing on his physical investigations, and, in particular, the explanation of the heart's motion and of certain other difficulties pertaining to medicine, as also the difference between our soul and that of the brutes; and then, in the last part, the things which the Author believes to be required for further advance in the study of nature than has yet been achieved, with the reasons which have led him to write.

[2] *Les raisons.*

PART I

GOOD sense is of all things in the world the most equitably distributed; for everyone thinks himself so amply provided with it, that even those most difficult to please in everything else do not commonly desire more of it than they already have. It is not likely that in this respect we are all of us deceived; it is rather to be taken as testifying that the power of judging well and of distinguishing between the true and the false, which, properly speaking, is what is called good sense, or reason, is by nature equal in all men; and that the diversity of our opinions is not due to some men being endowed with a larger share of reason than others, but solely to this, that our thoughts proceed along different paths, and that we are, therefore, not attending to the same things. For to be possessed of good mental powers is not of itself enough; what is all-important is that we employ them rightly. The greatest minds, capable as they are of the greatest virtues, are also capable of the greatest vices; and those who proceed very slowly may make much greater progress, provided they keep to the straight road, than those who, while they run, digress from it.

For myself, I have never supposed my mind to be in any way more perfect than that of the average man; on the contrary, I have often wished I could think as quickly, image as accurately and distinctly, or remember as fully and readily as some others. Beyond these I know of no other qualities making for the perfection of the mind; for as to reason, or sense, inasmuch as it is that alone which renders us men, and distinguishes us from the brutes, I am disposed to believe that it is complete in each one of us; and in this I am following the common opinion of those philosophers who say that differences of more and less hold in respect only of *accidents,* and not in respect of the *forms,* or natures, of the *individuals* of the same *species.*

I have, however, no hesitation in declaring that I have had the great good fortune of finding myself, already in early years, traveling by paths that have led to the reflections and maxims from which I have formed a method.[3] By this method, as it seems to me, I can by degrees increase my knowledge, raising it little by little to the highest point which my quite ordinary mental abilities and the shortness of my life may permit me to attain. Although in the judgment I form of myself I strive always rather to be self-questioning than to be over-bold, and although, when I review with a philosophical eye the diverse actions and enterprises of men, I find scarcely any which do not seem to me vain and useless, yet I am not thereby discouraged. For so abundant are the fruits I have already reaped by way of my method in the search after truth, so complete is my satisfaction in the progress I deem myself to have made, that I cannot but continue to entertain corresponding hopes for the future, thus venturing to believe that if there be any one of all the occupations proper to men, simply as men, which is reliably good and important, it is that which I have chosen.

It may be that in this I am deluding myself, and that what I am taking for gold and diamonds is but a little copper and glass. I know how liable we are to be mistaken in what affects the self, and also how much the judgments of our friends ought to be distrusted when they are in our favor. Nevertheless in this discourse it will be my pleasure to show what the paths are which I have followed, delineating my life as in a picture, in such wise that each of my readers may be able to judge for himself, and also that I, too, on learning from current report the opinions formed in regard to these paths, may thereby have a new means of self-instruction, in supplement to those I have been in the habit of employing.

[3] Cf. *Regulae,* above, p. 42.

Thus my present design is not to teach a method which everyone ought to follow for the right conduct of his reason, but only to show in what manner I have endeavored to conduct my own. Those who undertake to give precepts ought to regard themselves as wiser than those for whom they prescribe; and if they prove to be in the least degree lacking, they have to bear the blame. But in putting forward this piece of writing merely as a history, or, if you prefer so to regard it, as a fable,[4] in which, among some examples worthy of imitation, there will also, perhaps, be found others we should be well advised not to follow, I hope that it will be of use to some without being harmful to anyone, and that all will welcome my plain-speaking.

From my childhood I have been familiar with letters; and as I was given to believe that by their means a clear and assured knowledge can be acquired of all that is useful in life, I was extremely eager for instruction in them. As soon, however, as I had completed the course of study, at the close of which it is customary to be admitted into the order of the learned, I entirely changed my opinion. For I found myself entangled in so many doubts and errors that, as it seemed to me, the endeavor to instruct myself had served only to disclose to me more and more of my ignorance. And yet the School in which I was studying was one of the most celebrated in Europe, where I thought there must be men of learning, if such were anywhere to be found. I was taught all that others learned there, and not content with the sciences taught us, I glanced over all the books which fell into my hands treating of those esteemed most curious and rare. Moreover I knew the judgments that others had formed of me, and although there were among my contemporaries some already quite evidently destined to replace our teachers, I did not feel that I was esteemed inferior to them. And finally, our age appearing to me to be no less flourishing, and no less rich in men of ability

---

[4] I.e., a story with a professedly profitable moral. Cf. Gilson, *Commentary on the Discourse*, p. 68.

than any of the preceding, I felt free to judge of all men whatsoever by myself, and so to conclude that there was no body of knowledge in the world of such worth as I had previously been led to expect.

I continued, however, to hold in esteem the exercises practiced in the Schools. I knew that the languages they teach are required for the understanding of the writings of the ancients; that fables charm and awaken the mind; that the histories of memorable deeds exalt it, and when read with discretion aid in forming the judgment; that such reading of good books is, as it were, to engage in talk with their authors, the finest minds of past ages, artfully contrived talk in which they give us none but the best and most select of their thoughts; that eloquence has incomparable power and beauty; that poetry has its ravishing graces and delights; that in mathematics there are highly subtle inventions which do much to gratify the inquisitive as well as to further the arts and to lessen man's manual labors; that the writings which treat of morals contain numerous precepts and many exhortations to virtue which are very helpful; that theology points out the path to heaven; that philosophy enables us to speak with an appearance of truth on all matters, and secures to us the admiration of the less learned; that jurisprudence, medicine and the other sciences bring honors and riches to those who cultivate them; and, in short, that there is no one of them, even of those most abounding in superstition and falsity, the acquaintance with which is not of some utility, if only as enabling us to estimate it at its true value and to guard ourselves against being deceived by it.

As regards languages, I believed that I had already devoted sufficient time to them, and even also to the writings of the ancients, to their histories and mythical stories. To hold converse with those of other ages is almost, as it were, to travel abroad; and travel, by making us acquainted with the customs of other nations, enables us to judge more justly of our own, and not to regard as ridiculous and irrational whatever is at variance with them, as those ordinarily do who have never seen anything different. When, however, too much time is employed in travel, we become strangers in our own country; and when over-curious regarding what was practiced in the past, we tend to be unduly ignorant of what is done here and now. Then, too, the mythical stories represent, as having happened, many things which are in no wise possible. Even the most trustworthy of the histories, if they do not change or exaggerate the import of things, in order to make them seem more worthy of perusal, at least omit almost all the more commonplace and less striking of the background circumstances, and the account they give of them is to that extent misleading. Those who regulate their conduct by examples drawn from these sources are all too likely to be betrayed into romantic extravagances, forming projects that exceed their powers.

I esteemed eloquence highly, and was enamored of poetry. Both, however, I regarded as being natural gifts rather than fruits of study. Those in whom the gift of reasoning is strongest and who are careful to render their thoughts clear and intelligible, are always the best able to convert others to what they propose, even if they speak Breton and are ignorant of rhetoric. Similarly those who are endowed with the most agreeable powers of fancy and who can express themselves with a wealth of enchantment, are still the best poets, even though they have made no study of the art of poetry.

Above all I delighted in mathematics because of the certainty and evidence of their reasonings. But I had not as yet discovered their true use; and believing that they contributed only to the mechanical arts, I was astonished that foundations so firm and solid should have nothing loftier erected upon them. On the other hand, in contrast to them, I pictured to myself the works of the ancient pagan moralists as being, as it were, palaces arrogantly magnificent, with no better foundations than sand and soft shifting ground. They place the virtues on a lofty pedestal, and exhibit them as being of value above all other things in the world, yet do not succeed in teaching how to know what they are. Often what they honor with that fine title is but insensibility, or pride, or despair, or parricide.[5]

I revered our theology, and would be as desirous as anyone to reach heaven, but being reliably given to understand that the way to it is not less open to the most ignorant than to the most learned, and that the revealed truths which afford us guidance are above our powers of understanding, I did not dare to test them by the feebleness of my reasonings. I recognized that to enter on an examination of them, and to succeed in so doing, I should require to have some special help from above, and to be more than man.

As to philosophy, I shall say only this: that when I noted that it has been cultivated for many centuries by men of the most outstanding ability, and that none the less there is not a single thing of which it treats which is not still in dispute, and nothing, therefore, which is free from doubt, I was not so presuming as to expect that I should succeed where they had failed. When, further, I considered how many diverse opinions regarding one and the same matter are upheld by learned men, and that only one of all these opinions can be true, I accounted as well-nigh false all that is only probable.[6]

As regards the other sciences, inasmuch as they borrow their principles from philosophy, I judged that nothing solid can have been built on foundations so unstable. Neither did the honors and riches they promise incline me to cultivate them. For, thanks be to God, I was not so placed as to be obliged, for the improvement of my fortune, to adopt science as a profession; and though I might not pretend in the manner of the Cynics to despise all honors, I held in no great esteem honors which I could hope to acquire only on false pretenses. And finally, as to the sciences falsely so-

[5] Parricide is here taken in its wider sense as covering Stoic eulogy of L. J. Brutus' execution of his children and M. J. Brutus' assassination of Caesar. Cf. Gilson, *Com.*, p. 132.

[6] *tout ce qui n'était que vraisemblable,* i.e., probable, in the sense of plausible or arguable.

called, my knowledge of them was, I thought, already sufficient to guard me from being any longer liable to be deceived by the professions of an alchemist, the predictions of an astrologer, the impostures of a magician, or by the artifices and boastings of those who profess to know what they do not know.

For these reasons, as soon as my age allowed of my passing from under the control of my teachers, I entirely abandoned the study of letters; and resolving to seek no other science than that which can be found in myself and in the great book of the world, I spent the remainder of my youth in travel, visiting courts and armies, in intercourse with men of diverse dispositions and callings, amassing varied experiences, testing myself in the various situations in which fortune landed me, and at all times making reflections on the things that came my way, and by which I could in any wise profit. For it seemed to me that I might find much more truth in the reasonings each makes regarding the matters in which he is immediately interested, and the outcome of which must very soon punish him if he judges wrongly, than in those made by a man of letters in his study in respect of speculations which are of no practical moment, having for him no further consequence, save perhaps as flattering his vanity, owing to his belief that his skill and artifice in giving them the semblance of truth must have been proportionate to their remoteness from common sense. And throughout I was obsessed by the eager desire to learn to distinguish the true from the false, that I might see clearly what my actions ought to be, and so to have assurance as to the path to be followed in this life.

Yet, here again, so long as I gave thought only to the manners and customs of men, I met with nothing to reassure me, finding almost as much diversity in them as I had previously found in the opinions of the philosophers. The chief profit I derived from study of them was therefore this: observing that many things, however extravagant and ridiculous they may in our view appear to be, were yet very generally received and approved by other great nations, I learned not to be too confident in any belief to which I had been persuaded merely by example or custom; and thus little by little I delivered myself from many errors powerful enough to darken the natural light, i.e., to incapacitate us from listening to reason. When, however, I had occupied myself some years in thus studying in the book of the world and in striving to widen the range of my experience, I one day resolved to take myself too as an object of study, and to employ all the powers of my mind in choosing the paths I should follow; and in this I have succeeded, as it seems to me, far better than I could have done had I never quitted my country or put aside my books.

PART II

I WAS then in Germany, drawn thither by the wars which are not yet ended; and on my return to the army, from the coronation of the Emperor, the setting in of winter detained me in a locality where, finding no congenial associates and being otherwise, as it fortunately happened, untroubled by cares or passions of any kind, I remained all day long secluded in a stove-heated room, undistractedly at leisure, communing with my own thoughts. Among the first that came to me was this, that often there is less perfection in works composed of several parts and the product of several different, hands, than in those due to a single master-workman. Thus we see that buildings planned and executed by a single architect are usually much more beautiful and better proportioned than those which others have attempted to improve, adapting walls to serve purposes other than that for which they were originally designed. So, too, in the case of those ancient villages which have, in course of time, become great cities. How ill-designed they are compared with those which have been devised on a vacant plain by an engineer, free to plan as he pleases! Though some of the buildings, considered each apart from the others, may often, as works of art, surpass those in the newly devised city, yet how ill-arranged they are, large and small haphazardly, and the streets crooked and irregular! Their layout, it would seem, has been due more to chance than to any rationally controlled decisions of men. Even should we take account of the fact that all along there have been certain officials responsible for seeing that private buildings meet the requirements of public amenity, we cannot but recognize how difficult it is, while relying on the labors of others, to achieve what is truly perfect. I had similar thoughts in regard to those nations which, from being at first semi-barbarous, are civilized only gradually. Their laws have been determined for them mainly by embarrassments due to the crimes and quarrels which have forced their adoption; and they cannot, therefore, be as well ordered as those societies which from the very start have held fast to institutions devised by some prudent legislator. So too the province of true religion, the ordinances for which have been made by God alone, is, as is indeed certain, incomparably better regulated than any other. Speaking again of human affairs, I believe that if Sparta did in its time enjoy great prosperity, that was not because of the goodness of each and every one of its laws (for many of them were very strange and even contrary to good morals), but because, having been devised by one single legislator, they one and all had in view the same end.

Thus I came to think that the sciences found in books, at least those whose reasonings are made up merely of plausible arguments and yield no demonstrations, built up, as they are, little by little, from the opinions of many different contributors, do not get so near to the truth as the simple reasonings which a man of good sense, making use of his natural powers, can carry out respecting what happens to come before him. Then further, since we have all passed through the state of infancy before being men, and have therefore of necessity been long governed by our sensuous impulses and by our teachers (teachers who were often at variance with one another, and none of whom, perhaps, counseled us always for the best), I also came to think that it is well-nigh impossible our judgments can be so correct and so reliable as they would have been, had we from the moment of our birth been in entire possession of our reason and been all along guided by it alone.

To be sure, we do not proceed to pull down all the houses of a town, simply for the purpose of rebuilding them differently, to make the streets more beautiful. Often, however, it does happen that this or that house is pulled down with a view to rebuilding; and sometimes this is due to their being

in danger of themselves falling, their foundations being in-
secure. In analogy with this, I persuaded myself that it is
not indeed reasonable for a private individual to think of
reforming a State by changing everything in it, overturning
it in order to re-establish it; and that it is not likely that the
whole body of the sciences, or the manner of teaching them,
as established in the Schools, can be remodeled. In respect,
however, of the opinions which I have hitherto been entertaining, I thought that I could not do better than decide on
emptying my mind of them one and all, with a view to the
replacing of them by others more tenable, or, it may be,
to the re-admitting of them, on their being shown to be in
conformity with reason. I was firmly of the belief that by
this means I should succeed much better in the conduct of
my life than if, building on the old foundations, I relied on
principles of which in my youth I had allowed myself to
be persuaded, and into the truth of which I had never inquired. Of the many difficulties involved I was very well
aware. These are not, however, without remedy, nor are
they comparable to those which face us in reforming, even
in quite minor ways, what is of direct public concern. Great
public institutions, if once overthrown, are excessively difficult to re-establish, or even to maintain erect if once seriously shaken; and their fall cannot but be very violent. As
to their imperfections, if they have any—and their very diversity is sufficient to assure us that they do—usage has
doubtless greatly mitigated them, eliminating, or at least
insensibly correcting, many evils which could never have
been so effectively countered in a deliberately reflective manner. Almost always the imperfections are more tolerable
than the changes required for their removal. Do not high-
ways that wind about among the mountains, by being much
frequented, become gradually so smooth and convenient,
that the following of them is vastly preferable to attempting
the straighter route, scaling high rocks and clambering down
precipices?

   This is why I cannot at all approve of those reckless,

quarrelsome spirits who, though not called by birth or fortune to take part in the management of public affairs, yet never fail to be always on the hunt for some new reform. If I thought that in this essay there were the least ground for supposing me to be guilty of any such folly, I should never willingly consent to its publication. My design has all along been limited to the reform of my own thoughts, and to the basing of them on a foundation entirely my own. Although these labors have given me considerable satisfaction—this is what has led me to give you an account of them—I have no desire to counsel all others to engage in them. Those whom God has more amply endowed will perhaps entertain more exalted designs; but I fear that even what I am here proposing will for many be too hazardous. The resolve to strip oneself of all opinions hitherto believed is not one that everyone is called upon to take. There are among men two types of mind, to neither of which is it at all suited: first, those who, owing to undue confidence in their powers, are precipitate in their judgments and have not the patience required for the orderly arranging of their thoughts. Should men of this type assume themselves free to doubt received opinions and to deviate from the common highway, they will never be able to find, and to hold to, the one straight path that leads aright. Instead they will, throughout all the rest of their lives, find themselves hopelessly astray. Secondly, there are those who have reason or modesty enough to realize that they are less capable of distinguishing between the true and the false than others from whom they can gain instruction. They ought to be well content to follow the opinions of those others, and not to attempt to improve on them by efforts of their own.

As for myself, I should no doubt have belonged to the latter class, had I never had more than one instructor and had I never known how from time immemorial even the most learned of men have continued in disagreement one with another. Already in my college days I had been brought to recognize that there is no opinion, however strange, and however difficult of belief, which has not been upheld by one or other of the philosophers. Afterwards, too, in the course of my travels, I observed that those whose sentiments are very contrary to ours are not on this account barbarous and savage, and that many of them make as good or, it may be, better use of reason than we do ourselves. Bearing also in mind how the selfsame man, with the mental equipment proper to him, if nurtured from infancy among the French or the Germans, would come to be different from what he would have been had he lived always among the Chinese or the cannibals; and how, in respect of fashions in dress, what pleased us ten years ago, and which will again please ten years hence, appears to us at the present moment extravagant and ridiculous. Thus I came to see that custom and example have a much more persuasive power than any certitude obtained by way of inquiry. In respect of truths which are not readily discoverable, plurality of supporting votes is of no value as proof; it is much more likely that the discovery will be made by one man than by all and sundry. I was, however, unable to decide on any one person whose opinion seemed worthy of preference, and so had no option save to look to myself for guidance.

But like those who walk alone and after nightfall, I resolved to proceed so slowly, and with such meticulous circumspection, that if my advance was but small, I should at least guard myself from falling. I had no intention of forthwith discarding any of the opinions which had established themselves in my mind unintroduced by reason. Like the dwellers in an outworn house, who do not start to pull it down until they have planned another in its place, I had first to allow myself time to think out the project on which I was entering, and to seek out and decide on the true method, a method that I could rely upon as guiding me to a knowledge of all the things my mind is capable of knowing.

Along with other philosophical disciplines I had, in my early youth, made some little study of logic, and, in the mathematical field, of geometrical analysis and of algebra—

three arts or sciences, which, it seemed to me, ought to be in some way helpful toward what I had in view. But on looking into them I found that in the case of logic, its syllogisms and the greater part of its other precepts are serviceable more for the explaining to others the things we know (or even, as in the art of Lully,[7] for speaking without judgment of the things of which we are ignorant) than for the discovery of them; and that while it does indeed yield us many precepts which are very good and true, there are so many others, either harmful or superfluous, mingled with them, that to separate out what is good and true is almost as difficult as to extract a Diana or a Minerva from a rough unshaped marble block. As to the analysis of the ancients and the algebra of the moderns, besides extending only to what is highly abstract and seemingly of no real use, the former is so confined to the treatment of shapes that it cannot exercise the understanding without greatly fatiguing the imagination, and the latter is in such subjection to certain rules and other requirements that out of it they have made an obscure and difficult art, which encumbers the mind, not a science helpful in improving it. I was thus led to think that I must search for some other method which will comprise all that is advantageous in these three disciplines, while yet remaining exempt from their defects. A multiplicity of laws often furnishes the vicious with excuses for their evil-doing, and a community is much the better governed if, with only a very few laws, it insists on a quite strict observance of them. So, in like manner, in place of the numerous precepts which have gone to constitute logic, I came to believe that the four following rules would be found sufficient, always provided I took the firm and unswerving resolve never in a single instance to fail in observing them.

The first was to accept nothing as true which I did not evidently know to be such, that is to say, scrupulously to avoid precipitance and prejudice, and in the judgments I

---

[7] Raymond Lully's *Ars brevis*, composed in 1308, was printed for the first time in 1481, and repeatedly thereafter.

passed to include nothing additional to what had presented itself to my mind so clearly and so distinctly that I could have no occasion for doubting it.

The second, to divide each of the difficulties I examined into as many parts as may be required for its adequate solution.

The third, to arrange my thoughts in order, beginning with things the simplest and easiest to know, so that I may then ascend little by little, as it were step by step, to the knowledge of the more complex, and, in doing so, to assign an order of thought even to those objects which are not of themselves in any such order of precedence.

And the last, in all cases to make enumerations so complete, and reviews so general, that I should be assured of omitting nothing.

Those long chains of reasonings, each step simple and easy, which geometers are wont to employ in arriving even at the most difficult of their demonstrations, have led me to surmise that all the things we human beings are competent to know are interconnected in the same manner, and that none are so remote as to be beyond our reach or so hidden that we cannot discover them—that is, provided we abstain from accepting as true what is not thus related, i.e., keep always to the order required for their deduction one from another. And I had no great difficulty in determining what the objects are with which I should begin, for that I already knew, viz., that it was with the simplest and easiest. Bearing in mind, too, that of all those who in time past have sought for truth in the sciences, the mathematicians alone have been able to find any demonstrations, that is to say, any reasons which are certain and evident, I had no doubt that it must have been by a procedure of this kind that they had obtained them. In thus starting from what is simplest and easiest I did not as yet anticipate any other advantage than that of accustoming my mind to pasture itself on truths, and to cease from contenting itself with reasons that are false. Nor while doing so, had I any intention of endeavoring to master all the various sciences which are commonly entitled mathematical. Having observed that however different their objects, all agree in considering only the diverse relations or proportions to be found as holding between them, I thought it best to treat only of these proportions, taking them in a quite general manner, and without ascribing to them any other objects than those which might serve to facilitate the knowing of them (though without in any way restricting them to these objects), so that afterwards I might be the better able to transfer them to all the other things to which they may apply. Then, noting that to obtain knowledge of these proportions I should sometimes have to consider them one by one, and sometimes to retain them in memory, or to embrace several together, I decided that for the better apprehending of each singly, I should view it as holding between lines, there being nothing simpler and nothing that I can represent more distinctly by way of my imagination and senses; and that for the retaining of several in the memory, or for embracing several things simultaneously, I should express them by certain symbols [i.e., numbers or letters] as briefly as possible. In this way, I should be borrowing all that is best in geometry and algebra, and should be correcting all the defects of the one by help of the other.

This, I venture to assert, is what I have in fact achieved. The exact observance of these few precepts has given me such facility in unraveling all the questions dealt with by these two sciences, that in the two or three months I devoted to their examination—commencing with the simplest, the most general, each truth so discovered being a directive that helped me in the discovery of others—not only did I find the answer to many questions I had formerly judged very difficult, I was also in due course able, as it seemed to me, to determine, in respect even of those which I could not thus answer, by what means and to what extent an answer was yet possible. That in making this claim I am not being vainglorious will perhaps become evident to you if you reflect that on each particular issue there is but one true solution, and that whoever finds it knows all that can be known regarding it. The child, for example, who has been taught [the method prescribed in] arithmetic, and has made an addition in accordance with its rules, can rest assured that he has found, in respect of the sum of the numbers about which he was inquiring, all that the human mind can know regarding it. For the method which teaches us to follow the true order, and to enumerate exactly one and all of the items constitutive of what is being inquired into, comprises all that gives certitude to the rules of arithmetic.

But what pleased me most in this method I had discovered was that it afforded me assurance that in all matters I should be employing my reason, if not perfectly, at least as well as it was in my power to do. Besides I felt that in practicing it, I was accustoming my mind little by little to apprehend its objects more precisely and more distinctly; and that as I have not limited it to any particular subject-matter, I might encourage myself in the hope of being able to apply it in coping with the difficulties of the other sciences no less serviceably than I had succeeded in doing in the case of algebra. I had no thought, however, of forthwith tackling all the various questions that might then come up for answer. That would, indeed, have been contrary to the order which the method prescribes. And having come to recognize that the principles of the sciences which deal with these further questions have all to be borrowed from philosophy, and that in philosophy I had hitherto found nothing certain, I considered that before proceeding to treat of them, I must first endeavor to establish what those principles are. And since there can be no task of greater moment than this, and none in which there is greater need to guard against preconceptions and prejudices, I also recognized that I had no right to venture upon it till I had reached a more mature age than that of three and twenty (my age at that time), and that I must spend some considerable time in preparing myself for it, not only by eradicating from my mind all the mistaken opinions I had hitherto been holding, but also by laying up a store of experiences to serve as matter for my reasonings, and by constant practice of my self-prescribed method to strengthen myself ever more in the effective use of it.

PART III

AND finally, it is not enough, before starting to rebuild the house in which we live, that it be pulled down, and materials and builders provided, or that we engage on the work ourselves on a plan we have carefully prepared. We have also to provide ourselves with some other house in which we can be conveniently enough lodged during the rebuilding. Accordingly, lest I should remain irresolute in my actions in the interval during which reason obliges me to be so in my judgments, and that I might not in the meantime be prevented from living as happily as I could, I drew up for myself a provisional code of morals, consisting of some three or four maxims which I propose to enumerate as follows.

The first was to obey the laws and customs of my country, adhering unwaveringly to the religion in which, by God's grace, I had been educated from my childhood, and in all other matters regulating my conduct in conformity with the most moderate opinions, those furthest removed from extremes, as commonly exemplified in the practice of the most judicious of those among whom I might be living. For since I was proposing, from then on, to place no reliance on my own opinions, my intention being to submit them one and all to examination, I was convinced that the best I could do was to adopt in their place those held by the most reliable people; and though there may be, among the Persians and Chinese as among ourselves, persons of this trustworthy kind, it seemed to me more expedient to regulate my conduct on the pattern of those with whom I should have to live. Also it appeared to me that in determining what their opinions really are, I ought to give heed more to what they practiced than to what they said. For owing to the corruption of our minds, not only are few disposed to say all they believe, many are not indeed aware what it is they believe; the act of thought by which we believe a thing is different from that by which we apprehend that we are believing it, and the one is often found without the other. When several opinions were of equally good repute I chose always the most moderate; not only because they are the most auspicious for action, and likely to be the best (all excess tending to be harmful), but also because, in case I have been misled, I shall have been straying less far from the truth path than if, on my choosing one of the extremes, it was the other that I should have followed. I especially reckoned among the excesses all those engagements by which we in any respect limit our freedom. Not that I disapprove the laws which, to provide against the inconstancy of the weak-minded, permit (when it is something good that is intended, or even, it may be, the securing of commercial dealings where the question of good intention does not arise) the taking of vows and the making of contracts, binding the parties to their fulfilment. But finding in the world nothing that is not subject to change, and counting myself as under engagement to perfect my judgments ever more and more, and never to permit of their worsening, I thought that I should be sinning against good sense if, just because I approved something at a given time, I therefore bound myself to reckon it as good at a subsequent time when it may have ceased to be so, or when I have ceased to esteem it such.

My second maxim was to be as unwavering and as resolute in my actions as possible, and having once adopted opinions to adhere to them, however in themselves open to doubt, no less steadfastly than if they had been amply confirmed. In this I am following the example of travelers who, on finding themselves astray in some forest, realize that they ought not to vacillate, turning now in one direction and now in another, and still less to stop moving, but to keep always in as straight a line as possible, never for any minor reason changing direction, even though at the start it may have been chance alone which determined them in their choice of direction. If, in thus proceeding, they do not advance in the direction they expected, they will at least, in the final outcome, find themselves better located than in mid-forest. In the same way, since often, in actual living, the requirements of action allow of no delay, it is very certain that when it is not in our power to determine which opinions are truest, we ought to follow those seemingly most likely; and that in those cases in which we fail to observe any greater likelihood in some than in others, we should nevertheless give our adherence to certain of them, and thereafter (since this was our motive for adhering to them) consider them, in their bearing on action, as no longer doubtful, but very true and certain. This decision was sufficient to deliver me from all the repentings and feelings of remorse which are wont to disturb the consciences of those weak, unstable beings who in a vacillating manner abandon themselves to the acting out, as if it were good, what the next moment they are prepared to recognize as being evil.

My third maxim was to endeavor always to conquer myself rather than fortune, and to change my desires rather than the order of the world, and in general to habituate myself in the belief that save our thoughts there is nothing completely in our power, and so to recognize, in respect of the things which are external to us, that when we have done our best, whatever is still lacking to us is, so far as we are concerned, absolutely impossible of achievement. This, it seemed to me, is sufficient to prevent me from desiring for the future anything which I knew myself incapable of having, and so to render me content. For since our will does not of itself lead us to desire anything save what our understanding exhibits as being in some fashion possible of attainment, it is evident that if we consider external goods as being all alike beyond our power, we shall no more regret the absence of goods that seem due to our station, should we through no fault of our own be deprived of them, than we do in not possessing the kingdom of China or Mexico. Making thus, so to speak, a virtue of necessity, we shall no more desire health when ill, or freedom when in prison, than we now do bodies made of a matter as little corruptible as diamonds, or to have wings to fly like birds. There is, however, I confess, need of a prolonged discipline, and of meditation frequently renewed, if we are to hold firmly to this attitude in all circumstances; and this, I believe, was the main secret of those philosophers who in former times were able to free themselves from subservience to fortune, and in spite of sufferings and poverty to rival in felicity the happiness of their gods. Ceaselessly occupied, as they were, in attending to the limits set them by nature, they were so completely convinced that there was nothing in their power save their thoughts, that this of itself sufficed to preclude them from any attachment to other things; and so absolute was the control they thus exercised over their thoughts, that in this they had indeed some ground for esteeming themselves richer and more powerful, freer and happier than other men. However favored others may be by nature and by fortune, having no such philosophy at their disposal, they can never succeed in bringing events into line with their desires.

Lastly, to complete this moral code, I thought it advisable to review the various occupations of men in this life, in order that I might make choice of the best. Without wishing to pass judgment on other men's occupations, I thought that, for myself, I could not do better than continue in that in which I found myself engaged, that is to say, in devoting my whole life to the cultivation of my reason, and in making such progress as I could in the knowledge of truth, in accordance with the method I had prescribed to myself. I cannot believe that any more delightful or more innocent satisfactions can be enjoyed in this life than those which I have experienced since I began to make use of this method. Discovering by its means, day by day, truths which have seemed to me not unimportant, and with which other men are unacquainted, the contentment it has brought me has so filled my mind that in comparison nothing else has seemed to count. Further, the three preceding maxims have their ground solely in the intention I had of continuing to instruct myself. Since God has given each of us a light[8] for the distinguishing of the true from the false, I could not believe that I ought to remain content for a single moment with the opinions of others, unless indeed I was minded to employ my own judgment in examining them at some more fitting future time. Nor could I have kept myself free of scruple had I supposed that in so accepting them I should be losing the opportunity of finding better opinions, should such exist. In short, I could not have been able to set limits to my desires, and to be content, were it not that I have taken a path by following which I can hope to be assured of acquiring all the knowledge of which I am capable—all the more so that by this same path I should, I expected, acquire all the true goods I could ever hope to secure. For since our will does not incline us to seek or to shun any object save in so far as our understanding represents it as good or harmful, all that is required for right action is right judgment, and for the doing of our best the judging as best we can. This, I say, is sufficient for the acquiring of all the virtues, with all the other goods that are worth acquiring and within our power. When assured of this we cannot fail to be contented.

Having thus assured myself of the trustworthiness of these maxims, and having placed them on one side along with the truths of our Faith, I judged, in respect of all the rest of my opinions, that I might freely set about ridding myself of them. Hoping, as I did, to be in a better position to do so through intercourse with my fellow-men than by remaining any longer shut up in the stove-heated room where I had had these thoughts, I resumed my travels while the winter was still not over; and throughout all the nine following years I did nothing but roam about the world, seeking to be a spectator rather than an actor in all life's dramas. In all circumstances I especially endeavored to reflect on whatever might seem doubtful and might be a source of deception, and

---

[8] *quelque lumière,* i.e., the natural light of reason; in the Latin version, *aliquod rationis lumen.*

thereby I rooted out from my mind all the errors which had previously gained footing in it. Not that in this I imitated the skeptics who doubt only for doubting's sake and profess to be always non-committal; on the contrary, my purpose was solely to find ground of assurance, casting aside the loose earth and sand, that I might get down to rock or clay. In this, as it seems to me, I succeeded fairly well. Endeavoring as I was to discover the falsity or uncertainty of the propositions I examined, doing so not by way of mere conjectures but by clear and reliable reasonings, I met with nothing so doubtful as not to yield some conclusion of sufficient certainty, even though, as might be, merely the conclusion that the proposition in question was lacking in certainty. Just as in pulling down an old house the fragments are usually of service in the building of some new house, so likewise, in the process of overthrowing all those of my opinions that I judged to be ill-founded, I made a variety of observations and experiments which have helped me in establishing conclusions of greater certainty. In this way I continued to exercise myself in my self-prescribed method. For besides taking care, in a general manner, to be all the time conducting my thoughts in conformity with its rules, I reserved certain hours which I expressly devoted to practicing myself in the solution of mathematical difficulties, as also in the solution of difficulties in other sciences, difficulties that I was able to make almost mathematical, detaching them from all such principles as in those sciences I found to be insufficiently secure. And thus without appearing to be living otherwise than those who have no occupation save that of passing their lives quietly and innocently (scrupulously separating pleasure from vice, and that their leisure be not spoilt by boredom, allowing themselves all irreproachable amusements), I was all the time engaged in carrying out my design, gaining an ever better understanding of truth and progressing in the knowledge of it—more effectively, perhaps, than I should have done, had I, instead, spent all my days in the reading of books and in the company of men of letters.

It was not, however, until those nine years had elapsed that I came to any determinate decision regarding the difficulties currently discussed among the learned, or had so much as begun to attempt to establish any philosophy more certain than the vulgar. The example set by so many outstanding men who in former times had made the attempt, with, as it seemed to me, no success, led me to imagine it to be a task so beset with difficulty that I would not, even yet perhaps, have ventured to undertake it, had I not learned of a widespread rumor that I had already carried it through to completion. I am unaware what grounds were given in support of this rumor; and if anything I have myself said has played any part in starting it, that must have been owing to my confessing my ignorance more candidly than those who make claim to learning are wont to do, and perhaps also through my having given voice to the reasons I had for doubting many of the things which others regard as certain; it could not have been through my having boasted of any positive doctrinal teaching.[9] But being honest enough not to wish to appear different from what I really am, I thought that I must by every means in my power strive to render myself worthy of the reputation in which I was being held; and it is now exactly eight years since this resolve led me to settle myself at a distance from all the places where I might be in the way of meeting acquaintances, and to retire to this country.[10] The long duration of the war has here conduced to the establishment of such well-ordered discipline that the sole use of the standing armies would appear to be that of enabling the inhabitants to enjoy the fruits of peace with so much the more security. Here, in the crowded throng of a great nation, ever active and more concerned with their own affairs than curious about those of others, I have been able to be no less solitary and retired than in deserts the most remote.

[9] *d'aucune doctrine.* Here, it may be, Descartes is referring to his public encounter with Chandoux. Cf. *New Studies,* p. 40 ff.

[10] Descartes departed for Holland in September 1628; the eight years bring us to September 1636.

PART IV

I HESITATE to tell you of the first meditations there made by me; they are so metaphysical and so unusual as not, perhaps, to be generally acceptable. None the less, since they are necessary in judging whether the foundations I have laid are sufficiently secure, I have no option save to speak of them. In practical life, as I had long observed, it is sometimes necessary to follow opinions which we know to be highly uncertain; and, as above said, to hold steadfastly to them, as if they were indeed indubitable. But as I was then minded to give myself entirely to the search for truth, I thought that what was required of me was the directly opposite course, and that I ought to reject as downright false all opinions which I could imagine to be in the least degree open to doubt—my purpose being to discover whether, after so doing, there might not remain, as still calling for belief, something entirely indubitable. Thus, on the ground that our senses sometimes deceive us, I was prepared to suppose that no existing thing is such as the senses make us image it to be; and because in respect even of the very simplest geometrical questions some men err in reasoning and commit paralogisms, I therefore rejected as false (recognizing myself to be no less fallible than others) all the reasonings I had previously accepted as demonstrations; and, finally, when I considered that all the thoughts we have when awake can come to us in sleep (none of the latter being then true), I resolved to feign that all the things which had entered my mind were no more true than the illusions of my dreams. But I immediately became aware that while I was thus disposed to think that all was false, it was absolutely necessary that I who thus thought should be somewhat;[11] and noting that

11 *quelque chose.*

118

this truth *I think, therefore I am,* was so steadfast and so assured that the suppositions of the skeptics, to whatever extreme they might all be carried, could not avail to shake it, I concluded that I might without scruple accept it as being the first principle[12] of the philosophy I was seeking.

Next, on attentively examining what I was, while recognizing that I could feign that I had no body, that there was no world, nor any place in which I might be, I likewise noted that, notwithstanding this, I could not on that account feign that I was not. Quite the contrary: from this very circumstance that I thought to doubt the truth of those other things, it very evidently and very certainly followed that I was, whereas I had only to cease to think for an instant of time and I should then (even although all the other things I had imaged still remained true [i.e., real existents]) have no ground for believing that I can have existed in that instant. From this I knew that I was a substance whose whole essence or nature consists entirely in thinking, and which, for its existence, has no need of place,[13] and is not dependent on any material thing; so that this I, that is to say, the soul[14] by which I am what I am, is entirely distinct from the body, and is indeed more easy to know than the body, and would not itself cease to be all that it is, even should the body cease to exist.

I then proceeded to consider, in a general manner, what is requisite to the truth and certainty of a proposition. Having found one—*I think, therefore I am*—which I knew to be true and certain, I thought that I ought also to know in what this certainty consists; and having noted that in this proposition nothing assures me of its truth save only that I

[12] *principe,* in its etymological sense, as equivalent to *initium.* In the Latin version, *primum fundamentum.*

[13] I.e., of spatial location; cf. Gilson, *Com.,* p. 306.

[14] *l'âme.* Descartes' use of the term *l'âme* is here unusual. As a general rule, in his other writings, he employs the terms *l'esprit* and *mens* when viewing mind in its distinction from the body, reserving the terms *l'âme* and *anima* to designate the mind in its union with the body.

see very clearly that in order to think it is necessary to be, I judged that I could take as being a general rule, that the things we apprehend very clearly and distinctly are true— bearing in mind, however, that there is some difficulty in rightly determining which are those we apprehend distinctly.

Reflecting in accordance with this rule on the fact that I doubted, and that consequently my being was not entirely perfect (seeing clearly, as I did, that it is a greater perfection to know than to doubt), I resolved to inquire whence I had learned to think of something more perfect than I myself was; and I saw clearly that it must proceed from some nature that was indeed more perfect. As to the thoughts I had of other things outside me, such as the heavens, the Earth, light, heat and a thousand others, I had not any such difficulty in knowing whence they came. Remarking nothing in them which seemed to render them superior to myself, I could believe that, if they were true, they were dependencies of my nature in so far as my nature had a certain perfection; and that if they were not true, I received them from nothing, that is to say, that they were in me in so far as I was in some respects lacking in perfection. But this latter suggestion could not be made in respect of the idea of a being more perfect than myself, since the receiving the idea from nothing is a thing manifestly impossible. And since it is no less contradictory that the more perfect should result from, and depend on, the less perfect than that something should proceed from nothing, it is equally impossible I should receive it from myself. Thus we are committed to the conclusion that it has been placed in me by a nature which is veritably more perfect than I am, and which has indeed within itself all the perfections of which I have any idea, that is to say, in a single word, that is God. And since some perfections other than those I myself possess were known to me, I further concluded that I was not the only being in existence (here I shall, with your permission, freely use the School terms).[15] There must of necessity exist some other more perfect being upon whom I was dependent, and from whom I had received all that I had. For if I alone had existed, independently of all else, in such wise that I had from myself all the perfection, however small in amount, through which I participated in the perfections of Divine Existence, I should have been able, for the same reason, to have from myself the whole surplus of perfections which I know to be lacking to me, and so could of myself have been infinite, eternal, immutable, omniscient, all-powerful—in short, have been able to possess all the perfections that I could discern as being in God.

Consequently, in order to know the nature of God (in extension of the above reasonings in proof of His existence) so far as my own nature allows of my doing so, I had only to consider in respect of all the things of which I found in myself any idea, whether the possession of them was or was not a perfection; thereby I was at once assured that none of those which showed any imperfection was in Him, and that all the others were—just as I had learned that doubt, inconstancy, sadness and such like, could not be in Him, seeing that I myself should have been very glad to be free from them. In addition to these latter I had ideas of things which are sensible and corporeal. For although I might suppose that I was dreaming, and that all I saw or imaged was false, I yet could not deny that the ideas of them were indeed in my thought. But because I had already very clearly discerned in myself that the intelligent is distinct from the corporeal, and since I had also observed that all composition witnesses to dependence and that dependence is manifestly a defect, I therefore judged that it could not be a perfection in God to be composed of two natures, and that He was not so compounded. At the same time I likewise concluded

15 As Gilson has pointed out (*Com.*, p. 332), such scholastic expressions as *avoir de soi-même, participer,* etc., were not yet in general use: *participer* stands in counter-opposition to *être par essence.*

that if there be in the world any bodies, or even any intelligences or other natures, which are not wholly perfect, their being must depend on His power in such a way that without Him they could not subsist for a single moment.

I then set myself to look for other truths, and having directed my attention to the object dealt with by geometers, which I took to be a continuous body, a space indefinitely extended in length, breadth, height and depth, which allowed of diverse shapes and sizes, and of their being moved or transposed in all sorts of ways (for all this the geometers take as being in the object of their studies), I perused some of their simplest demonstrations; and while noting that the great certitude which by common consent is accorded to them is founded solely upon this that they are apprehended as evident, in conformity with the rule above stated,[16] I likewise noted that there is nothing at all in them which assures me of the existence of their object. Taking, for instance, a triangle, while I saw that its three angles must be equal to two right angles, I did not on this account see anything which could assure me that anywhere in the world a triangle existed. On the other hand, on reverting to the examination of the idea of a Perfect Being, I found that existence is comprised in the idea precisely in the way in which it is comprised in the idea of a triangle that its three angles are equal to two right angles, or in that of a sphere that all its parts are equally distant from its center, and indeed even more evidently; and that in consequence it is at least as certain that God, who is this Perfect Being, is or exists, as any demonstration of geometry can possibly be.

The reason why many are persuaded that there is difficulty in knowing this truth, as also in knowing what their soul is, is that they never raise their minds above the things of sense, and that they are so accustomed to consider nothing except what they can image (a mode of thinking restricted to material things), that whatever is not imageable seems to them not intelligible. Even the philosophers in their schools do

[16] Above, p. 106.

so, as is sufficiently manifest from their holding as a maxim that there is nothing in the understanding which was not previously in the senses, where, however, it is certain, the ideas of God and of the rational soul have never been. Those who employ their power of imagery to comprehend these ideas behave, as it seems to me, exactly as if in order to hear sounds or smell odors they sought to avail themselves of their eyes—unless, indeed, there is this difference, that the sense of sight does not afford any less truth than do hearing and smell. In any case, neither our imagination nor our senses can ever assure us of anything whatsoever save so far as our understanding intervenes.

Finally, if there still be men who are not sufficiently persuaded of the existence of God and of their soul by the reasons which I have cited, I would have them know that all the other things which they think to be more assured, as that they have a body and that there are stars and an Earth, and such like things, are less certain. For though the moral assurance we have of these things is such that there is an appearance of extravagance in professing to doubt of their existence, yet none the less when it is a metaphysical certitude that is in question, no one, unless he is devoid of reason, can deny that we do have sufficient ground for not being entirely assured, namely, in the fact that, as we are aware, we can, when asleep, image ourselves as possessed of a different body and as seeing stars and another Earth, without there being any such things. For how do we know that the thoughts which come in dreams are more likely to be false than those we experience when awake? Are not the former no less vivid and detailed than the latter? The ablest minds may treat of this question at whatever length they please, but I do not believe that they will be able to find any reason sufficient to remove this doubt, unless and until they presuppose the existence of God. For, to begin with, even the maxim which a short time ago I adopted as a rule, viz., that the things we cognize very clearly and very distinctly are all true, is reliable only because God is or exists, because He is a Perfect Being, and because all that is in us comes from Him. Thereupon it follows that our ideas or notions, as being of real things, and as coming from God, must in so far as they are clear and distinct be to that extent true. So that, though quite often we have ideas which contain some falsity, this can only be in the case of those in which there is some confusion or obscurity, i.e., owing to their participation, in this respect, in nothingness; or, in other words, that in us they are thus confused because we are not wholly perfect. And it is evident that it is not less repugnant that the falsity or imperfection, in so far as it is such, should proceed from God, than that truth or perfection should proceed from nothing. If, however, we did not know that whatever in us is real and true comes from a Being perfect and infinite, our ideas, however clear and distinct, would yield us no ground of assurance that they had the perfection of being true.

Now, once the knowledge of God and of the soul has thus rendered us certain of the reliability of this rule, we have no difficulty in recognizing that what we picture to ourselves in sleep ought not to make us in any way doubtful of the truth of the thoughts we have when awake. For if in our dreams there comes to us some quite distinct idea, if, for instance, a geometer should discover some new demonstration, its coming during sleep would not militate against its truth. As for the most usual error in dreams, that which consists in their representing to us various objects in the same fashion as do our external senses, this may indeed lead us to distrust the truth of such ideas. But what of that? They often deceive us even when awake, as when sufferers from jaundice see everything yellow-colored, or when the stars and other distant bodies appear smaller than they are. For whether awake or asleep, we ought never to allow ourselves to be persuaded save on the evidence of our reason. And be it noted, I speak of our reason, and not of our imagination or senses. Although we see the sun very clearly, we ought not on this account to judge that it is of the size we see; and we can quite distinctly image a lion's head on the body of a goat without having to commit ourselves to the conclusion that a chimera exists. For reason does not require us to believe that whatever we see or image is true; it does, however, insist that all our ideas or notions must have some basis of truth. Otherwise it could not be that God, who is altogether perfect and trustworthy, should have placed them in us. And inasmuch as our reasonings are never during sleep so evident nor so complete as when we are awake (although sometimes our dream-images are then as lively and detailed, or indeed more so), reason also tells us that, since we are not beings wholly perfect and since our thoughts cannot therefore all be true, the truth they have should rather be met with in those we have in our waking moments than in those of our dreams.

PART V

I WOULD very gladly have proceeded to expound the complete chain of truths which I have deduced from these primary truths, but as this would have required me to speak of many questions in dispute among the learned and as I have no desire to be thus embroiled with them, I believe it will be better for me to abstain. I shall relate, in outline, merely what these truths are; those best qualified to judge may then decide whether a more detailed account of them would be to the public advantage. I have remained ever constant in my resolution not to assume, in demonstrating the existence of God and of the soul, any other principle than that of which I have been making use, i.e., to accept as true nothing which does not appear to me even clearer and more certain than the demonstrations of the geometers had formerly seemed. None the less I venture to declare that not only have I, in a short time, found means to satisfy myself on all the chief difficulties usually discussed in philosophy, but have also taken account of certain laws which God has so established in nature, and of which He has impressed such notions in our souls, that once we have reflected sufficiently upon them, we can no longer doubt their being accurately observed in all that exists or happens in the world. And on surveying the ordered sequence of these laws, I have, it seems to me, discovered many truths more useful and more important than all I had previously learned or even hoped to be able to learn.

But having set myself to expound the most important of these discoveries in a treatise[17] which certain considerations prevent me from publishing,[18] I can best explain what may

[17] *Le Traité du Monde ou de la Lumière,* published by Clerselier in 1671.

[18] I.e., the condemnation of Galileo in 1633.

126

here be suitably said about them by a statement of the contents of this treatise. I had planned, before I set about the writing of it, to include all that I thought I knew regarding the nature of material things. But just as painters, on finding themselves unable, on a plane surface, to represent equally well all the various aspects of the solid body, select one chief aspect on which alone they make the light fall, with the others thrown into the shade and allowed to appear only as they can be seen while looking at the principal aspect, so fearing lest I should not be able to include in my discourse all I had in mind, I resolved to expound at any length only my views regarding light; and then, in sequel, to add something on the sun and the fixed stars, since light proceeds almost wholly from them; on the heavens, since they transmit it; on the planets, comets and the Earth, since they reflect it; and particularly on all the bodies which are upon the Earth, since they are colored, or transparent, or luminous; and finally on man, since he is the spectator of all these objects.

[As stated in the "Prefatory Note by the Author" (above, p. 91), Descartes proceeds to expound: "the questions bearing on his physical investigations, and, in particular, the explanation of the heart's motion and of certain other difficulties pertaining to medicine, as also the difference between our soul and that of the brutes."]

What is worthy of remark is that though many animals manifest in some of their actions more skill than do we ourselves, those same animals, in some of their other actions, are found to show none at all. Thus their doing certain things better than we do is no proof of their being endowed with mind. For on that assumption they would have to possess more of it than any of us do, and ought to surpass us in all things. On the contrary, what it shows is that they are destitute of mind and that it is nature which

19 For an account of Descartes' "physical and psychological" doctrines in the paragraphs here omitted, cf. *New Studies*, p. 103 ff.

acts in them according to the disposition of their organs, just as a clock, which is composed only of wheels and weights, can number the hours and measure time more exactly than we can with all our knowledge.

Next I had described the rational soul[20] and shown that it can in no wise be derived from the power of matter as can the other things of which I have spoken, and must be due to a special act of creation. I also showed that it is not sufficient that the soul be lodged in the human body like a pilot in his ship, unless perhaps for the moving of its members, but that it needs to be joined and united with it more closely, in order that, in addition to any such motor function, it may have sensations and appetites similar to ours and thus constitute a true man. As the soul is a topic of supreme importance, I have, in concluding, dwelt upon it at some length. For next to the error of those who deny God, an error which I have, I think, already sufficiently refuted, none is more effectual in diverting weak minds from the straight path of virtue than that of imagining the soul of the brutes to be of the same nature as ours, and consequently that after this life there is not for us, more than for the flies or the ants, anything either to hope or to fear. On thus coming to know how different the animals are from us, we comprehend so much better the reasons which prove the soul to be of a nature entirely independent of the body, and therefore not bound to die with it. Then, finally, inasmuch as we observe no other causes capable of destroying it, we are naturally led to judge that it is [in fact] immortal.

20 I.e., as contrasted with *celle des bêtes.*

PART VI

IT is now three years since I finished the treatise which dealt with all these matters;[21] and I was starting to revise it, with a view to placing it in the printer's hands, when I learned that certain persons to whose opinion I deferred, and whose authority over my actions can hardly be less than that of reason over my thoughts, had disapproved a certain physical theory published a short time previously by another person.[22] I will not say that I agreed with the theory in question, but only that prior to this censure I found in it nothing which I could imagine to be prejudicial either to religion or to the state, and nothing therefore which would have prevented me from considering it, if reason had persuaded me of its truth. This made me fear lest some one of my own opinions might be found open to misunderstanding, despite the great care I have always taken not to accept any new belief unless I could demonstrate it in the most certain manner, and not to write anything which could tend to anyone's disadvantage. These considerations sufficed to make me alter my purpose of publishing the treatise. For although the reasons leading to my previous decision were indeed strong, my distaste for the writing of books—an occupation to which I have always been little disposed—immediately enabled me to find many other reasons for shirking the task; and these reasons, on the one side and on the other, are such that not only am I here committed to a statement of them, but the public also may perhaps be interested to know what they are.

[21] I.e., treatise finished in or about July 1633. Cf. Descartes' letter to Mersenne (July 22, 1633), *A.T.* i, p. 268.
[22] Galileo's *Dialogues on the Two Great Systems of the World* was condemned by the Inquisition on June 23, 1633; and this became known to Descartes some five months later.

I have never regarded as of much account what has proceeded from my own native powers,[23] and so long as the harvest I reaped from the method I employed was no other than that of having satisfied myself regarding some difficulties which concern the speculative sciences, or of being helped to regulate my manner of life by the reasons it has taught me, I have not felt obliged to commit any of it to writing. As regards matters of conduct, if others besides those whom God has established as the supreme rulers of His peoples or to whom He has given sufficient grace and zeal to be prophets, are to be permitted to share in choosing for us our ways and customs, reformers will be found to be as numerous as heads, so convinced is everyone of his own abounding good sense. My speculations were indeed truly pleasing to me; but I recognize that other men have theirs, which perhaps please them even more. As soon, however, as I had acquired some general notions regarding physics, and on beginning to make trial of them in various special difficulties had observed how far they can carry us and how much they differ from the principles hitherto employed, I believed that I could not keep them hidden without grievously sinning against the law which lays us under obligation to promote, as far as in us lies, the general good of all mankind. For they led me to see that it is possible to obtain knowledge highly useful in life, and that in place of the speculative philosophy taught in the Schools we can have a practical philosophy, by means of which, knowing the force and the actions of fire, water, air, of the stars, of the heavens, and of all the bodies that surround us—knowing them as distinctly as we know the various crafts of the artisans—we may in the same fashion employ them in all the uses for

[23] In this respect, as also in their distaste for the labors of formal expository writing, Descartes and Newton very closely resemble one another. Like Newton, Descartes was primarily interested in the processes of inquiry and discovery; and as Descartes has stated (to Father Vatier, February 22, 1638, *A.T.* i, p. 559), the "ordre pour chercher les choses . . . est assez différent de celui dont j'ai cru devoir user pour les expliquer."

which they are suited, thus rendering ourselves the masters and possessors of nature. This is to be desired, not only with a view to the invention of an infinity of arts by which we would be enabled to enjoy without heavy labor the fruits of the earth and all its conveniences, but above all for the preservation of health, which is, without doubt, of all blessings in this life, the first of all goods and the foundation on which the others rest. For the mind is so dependent on the temper and disposition of the bodily organs that if any means can ever be found to render men wiser and more capable than they have hitherto been, I believe that it is in the science of medicine that the means must be sought. It is true that medicine, as currently practiced, contains little of any notable utility. With no wish to depreciate it, I am yet sure there is no one, even of those engaged in the profession, who does not admit that all we know is almost nothing in comparison with what remains to be discovered; and that we could be freed from innumerable maladies, both of body and of mind, and even perhaps from the infirmities of age, if we had sufficient knowledge of their causes and of the remedies provided by nature. Intending, therefore, as I do, to devote all my life to the search for this indispensable science,[24] and having discovered a path which, as it seems to me, must, if we follow it out, infallibly guide us to our goal, provided we be not hindered by the shortness of life or through lack of empirical data,[25] I judged that there was no better means of overcoming these two impediments than to communicate to the public all the little I have myself found, and to summon those who are well-disposed and suitably equipped to help, each according to his inclination and ability, in the making of the required observations,[26] and in making public all the things each has thereby learned. In this way those who follow will be enabled to begin where their predecessors have left off. By thus uniting the lives and labors of many,

[24] Cf. below, p. 143.
[25] *des expériences;* Lat. *experimentorum.*
[26] *expériences.*

we should collectively advance much further than each by himself could contrive to do.

With regard to [the making of] observations, I also noted that they become the more necessary the further we advance in knowledge. At the start, however, it is better to make use only of those which spontaneously present themselves to our senses, and of which, no matter how slight be our attention to them, we cannot be ignorant, than of those which are more rare and recondite. What has commended this order of procedure to me is that so long as the causes of the more common are still unknown, those which very rarely occur are all too apt to mislead us, the circumstances on which they depend being nearly always so special[27] and so minute that they are extremely difficult to bring under observation. The order I have adopted is therefore this: first, I have endeavored to find in a general manner the principles, i.e., the first causes, of all that is or can be in the world, and while so doing to direct my mind to God alone who has created that world, and to deduce the causes from no other source than certain seeds of truth with which our souls are naturally endowed. Then, secondly, I have examined the first and most familiarly known effects deducible from these causes; and therewith, as it seemed to me, I have come to know the heavens, the stars, an Earth, and likewise on the Earth water, air, fire, the minerals and several other such things—things which are, of all things, the most common and which are consequently the easiest to know. Then thirdly, when I sought to descend to those which were more special, so many and so diverse were the things that presented themselves to me, that I could not think it possible for the human mind to distinguish the forms or species of bodies which are on the Earth from an infinity of others that might have been had God willed to set them there, nor consequently to make them serviceable to us [in our search for explanation of them] save by discovering from [study of] the effects what are their causes, availing ourselves for this purpose of

[27] *particulières.*

some of the rarer, special experiences. Thanks to this [three-fold] procedure, on reviewing all the objects that have ever presented themselves to my senses, I can indeed venture to say that I have not observed any which I could not appropriately explain by the principles I had discovered. But, as I have also to confess, the power of nature is so ample, so vast, and these principles are so simple and so general, that of the particular effects there is hardly one that I do not recognize as allowing of being accounted for in several different ways; and usually my greatest difficulty is to discover in which of these various ways it has to be viewed. And for this purpose I know of no other expedient than again to descend to the [special, less familiar] experiences, and among them to look for those which can be what they in fact are only as explained in some one, and not in any other, of those various possible ways. As to what remains to be done, I am now, as it seems to me, in the position to decide how we ought to proceed in order to render the majority of these latter [rarer, more recondite] effects helpful to us in our inquiries. But I also see that they are such, and so numerous, that neither my energies nor my income (even were that income a thousand times larger than it is) could suffice for making all the required observations. Accordingly, my progress in the knowledge of nature will be greater or less according as I shall have the means of making more or fewer observations. This is what I hoped to make known by the treatise I had written, showing so convincingly the advantage which would thereupon accrue to the public, that all those who have the good of mankind at heart—all who are virtuous indeed and not in mere outward seeming—would feel under obligation to communicate to me the observations they have made, and to assist me in obtaining those that remain to be made.

But I have since bethought myself of other reasons which have caused me to change my opinion. My duty, as I now see it, is to continue to write of all the things I judge to be of importance (provided I find them to be indeed true), bestowing the same care upon them as I should have done, had it been my intention to have them published. Thereby I secure for myself further opportunity of examining them more closely. Do we not always give closer attention to what we believe will be read by others than to what is written only for ourselves? How often what has seemed true to me when first thought of, has seemed false on my attempting to commit it to writing. In this way I also make sure of not missing the chance of benefiting the public to the full limits of my capacities. For should my writings contain anything of value, those into whose hands they may come after my death will then be in position to make such use of them as may seem proper. I was still, however, definitely resolved that I should by no means permit their being published during my lifetime. The oppositions and controversies to which they might well give rise, even the reputation, such as it might be, which they would bring me, would be bound to deprive me of the leisure that I hoped to employ in self-instruction. Everyone is indeed under obligation, in proportion to his abilities, to promote the good of others; to be of service to no one is indeed to be worthless. But it is no less true that our cares ought to extend beyond the present, and that it is well to omit what is of possible profit to the living when what we have in view will be of much greater benefit to posterity. I am more than willing it should be known that the little I have as yet learned is almost nothing in comparison with that of which I am ignorant; but this does not mean that I despair of being able to attain the wider knowledge. Those who little by little discover truths in the sciences are very much like those who begin to become rich; they have then less trouble in obtaining great acquisitions than they previously had, when poorer, in making much smaller acquisitions. Or we may compare them to the commanders of armies, whose forces usually increase in proportion to their victories. After the loss of a battle, they have need of greater powers of command in holding together what remains of their troops than, after a victory, in the taking of towns and provinces. For to conquer all the difficulties and combat all the errors which prevent us from arriving at knowledge of the truth is, indeed, to engage in battles; and to yield credence to false opinion concerning a matter of any far-reaching importance is to lose one of these battles, so much greater is the skill required to recover the previously held position than to make notable progress after well-assured beginnings. For myself, if I have succeeded in discovering several truths in the sciences (and I trust that the matters contained in this volume will show that I have found some) they have, I can certify, depended on, and followed upon, my surmounting of some five or six principal difficulties, which I reckon as battles in each of which fortune has favored me. Indeed I will not hesitate to declare my conviction that for the completion of my designs I have need of no more than two or three other such victories, and that my age[28] is not so advanced but that I may still, in the ordinary course of nature, have sufficient time for this task. But the more assured I am of being thus able to employ my time to advantage, the more I believe myself bound to make the most of the time remaining to me; and were I to make public the fundamentals of my physics, I should undoubtedly be creating the situations that would rob me of it. For although the fundamentals of my physics are almost all so evident that they have only to be understood to be believed, and although there is, I claim, not one of them which I am not in position to demonstrate, none the less, since it is impossible that they should accord with all the diverse opinions of other men, I foresee that I should often be drawn into the controversies to which they would give rise.

These controversial discussions, it may be urged, would be useful in making me aware of my errors, and, if my writings contain something of value, in bringing others to a fuller understanding of it; also I should already be beginning to enlist the services of those who might assist me —a multiplicity of observers being able to see more than

[28] Descartes was then, in 1637, forty-one years of age.

can a single observer—with their discoveries. But though I recognize that I am extremely liable to error, and though I almost never trust thoughts on their first occurring to me, my experience of the kind of objections likely to be made to my views prevents me from looking for any profit from them. Already I have had frequent experience of the judgments passed by those I esteem my friends, and by some others whom I thought to be neutrally disposed toward me, and even too by some whose malignity and envy would, I knew, make them endeavor to discover what affection concealed from the eyes of my friends. Yet rarely has it happened that anything has been objected to me which I had not myself foreseen, except when it was something remote from what I was discussing. Hardly ever, therefore, have I met with any critic of my opinions who has not seemed to me less rigorous or less impartial than myself. Nor have I ever observed that previously unknown truth has been discovered by way of the disputations practiced in the Schools. Each participant, striving for victory, is more concerned to dwell on whatever has the appearance of truth than to weigh the reasons for and against: those who have for long been good advocates are not afterwards on that account the better judges.

As to the advantage which others might receive from the communication of my thoughts, it could not be very great. For I have not yet carried them sufficiently far. Much still remains to be added before use can be made of them; and I can say, I think, without vanity, that if there is anyone capable of completing them, that person should be no other than myself: not that there may not be in the world many incomparably superior to me in ability, but because no one can understand what he has learned from another, and make it his own, so well as he who has discovered it for himself. This is especially true in the matters which are here engaging us. I have often explained some of my opinions to men of very good intelligence; and while I talked with them, they seemed to be understanding them quite adequately. When, however, they repeated them, I noted that almost always they were so changed that I could no longer acknowledge them as mine. Apropos of this, I welcome the opportunity of begging posterity never to believe —unless I have myself declared it—what on common report they may find ascribed to me. I am not in the least surprised at the extravagances ascribed to those of the ancient philosophers whose writings we do not possess, and refuse to believe their thoughts to have been of that absurd kind. Were they not among the ablest minds of their times? Is it not rather that they have been misrepresented? As we find, scarcely ever have they been surpassed by any one of their disciples. I am indeed confident that those who, in these present days, are most insistent in adhering to the teaching of Aristotle would consider themselves fortunate if they had as much knowledge of nature as he possessed, even if this were on the condition that they should never obtain more. They are like the ivy which never strives to rise above the tree that sustains it, and often indeed falls backwards after reaching its top. For, as it seems to me, they too lose their balance, that is to say, render themselves in some manner less intelligent than they would have been if they had abstained from study. Not content with knowing all that is intelligibly explained in their author, they insist on also finding in him the solution of various difficulties in regard to which he has nothing to say, and of which he has perhaps never even thought. This manner of philosophizing is well suited to those whose mental powers are of a decidedly mediocre quality. The very obscurity of the distinctions and principles on which they rely is precisely what enables them to speak with as much confidence as if they had understanding of them, enabling them to hold to them even in face of the most subtle and skilful opponents—there being no possibility of their being [enlightened and thereby] refuted. In this they seem to me to resemble a blind man who, in order to fight without disadvantage with an opponent who sees, would have him descend to the bottom of a very dark cave. Such adversaries, I may add, have an interest in my refraining from publishing the principles of the philosophy I employ. So simple and so evident are they, that in publishing them I should, as it were, be opening windows and admitting daylight into the cave where they have retreated for the conduct of the fight. Even those of superior ability have no good reason for wishing to know them. If their ambition is to be able to speak on any and every topic and to acquire a reputation for learning, they will do so more easily by remaining satisfied with what has the appearance of truth—and in all sorts of matters that is easily found—than by seeking truth itself. Truth we discover only little by little, on some few issues; and it obliges us, when called upon to speak of other matters, frankly to confess our ignorance of them. Should they, on the other hand, prefer some little knowledge of truth to the vanity of appearing ignorant of none, and so be desirous of following a course of action similar to mine, there is no need that I should, for their assistance, add anything to what I have already said in this *Discourse*. If they are capable of advancing further than I have thus far done, they should likewise be the better able to discover for themselves all that I believe myself to have found. For proceeding as I have done, that is to say, examining nothing save in due order [from the simple to the more and more complex], we can be certain that what remains to be discovered is in itself more difficult, more deeply hidden, than anything I have thus far studied, and that they would have much less satisfaction in hearing of it from me than from themselves. Moreover, through always engaging first in what is easy, and then passing slowly, step by step, to what is more difficult, they will acquire habits of mind which will benefit them much more than any instructions of mine could do. To take my own case, I am convinced that if I had been taught from my youth all the truth of which I have since sought out the demonstrations, and so had learned them without labor, I should never, perhaps, have come to know any others; at least, I should never have acquired the habit and facility, which I consider myself now to have, of always discovering new truths in proportion to my efforts in searching for them. In short, if there is any work in the world which cannot be so well carried through by another as by him who initiated it, it is that at which I labor.

As regards the observations which can be helpful in this work, it is true that one man is not equal to making all of them. But the only hands he could usefully employ besides his own are those of artisans or people of that kind, whom he can pay, and who may be induced by hope of gain (a very effective incentive) to carry out accurately all the directions he might give them. For as to those who, whether from curiosity or desire to learn, may perchance of their own accord come forward to assist him, not only are they wont to make many promises which they do not fulfill, planning ambitious projects not one of which is ever practicable; invariably they require to be repaid by help in several of their difficulties, or at least by compliments, and by interviews so useless that all time spent in them is time lost. As for the observations which others have already independently made, even should they be willing to communicate them (which those who entitle them secrets would never do),[29] they are for the most part accompanied by so many superfluous circumstances and details as to make it extremely difficult to discover in them what is veritably relevant. Besides, they are likely to be found almost all of them so illdescribed, or so false (those who report them having been anxious to make them appear to be in conformity with the principles they themselves hold) that even if some of them might be serviceable, this would not compensate for the time which would have to be spent in making the selection. Accordingly, if there were anywhere in the world someone whom we knew to be assuredly capable of making discoveries

[29] A reference to those chemists who know "quantité de ces petits secrets de chimie qui se débitent entre gens de ce métier." Cf. Descartes to Mersenne (December 7, 1642), *A.T.* iii, p. 598. Cf. Gilson, *Com.*, p. 465.

of supreme importance and of the greatest possible utility
to the public, and if all other men were therefore eager to
assist him to complete his labors by every means in their
power, I yet do not see how they could do anything for him
beyond contributing to the expenses of the observations he
would require to have made, and for the rest seeing to it that
he was not deprived of his leisure by any personal impor-
tunities. But, besides not esteeming myself so highly as to
be willing to make promises of anything extraordinary, nor
being so vain as to imagine the public ought to interest itself
greatly in my projects, my soul is not so base as to be
willing to accept from anyone a favor that I might be thought
not to have merited.

The joint force of those various considerations was what,
three years ago, decided me against publishing the treatise
I had completed. This too was why I even went so far as
to resolve never to publish during my life any other of that
wide general kind, or any by which the foundations of my
physics might be understood. Since then, however, two further reasons have determined me to append here some
sample specimens, and to render the public some account of
my action and projects. The first of these reasons is that if I
failed to do so, those who have been cognizant of my previous intention to publish certain writings might imagine my
reasons for not doing so were less to my credit than they
really are. For although I am not immoderately enamored
of fame, and even, if I may presume to say so, am averse to
it, in so far as I judge it to be inimical to the repose that I
value above all other things, none the less I have never sought
to conceal my actions as if they were crimes. Nor have I
taken elaborate precautions to ensure my remaining unknown, partly because I should have regarded that as likely
to disquiet me, disturbing the perfect repose of mind that I
sought, and partly because, while always myself indifferent
as to whether I was or was not known, I have yet been unable
to prevent myself acquiring some sort of reputation, and so
have thought that I ought to do my best to save myself at

least from having an evil reputation. The other reason which
has obliged me to write this *Discourse* and these *Essays* is
that daily I am becoming more and more consciously aware
of being delayed in my project of self-instruction because of
the innumerable observations of which I stand in need, and
which it is impossible for me to make without the aid of
others. While not flattering myself with any expectation that
the public will be seriously interested in my projects, I am
yet unwilling to be so far wanting in the duty I owe to
myself as to give those who shall survive me occasion for
their some day reproaching me that I might have left them
something much better than anything I have in fact left, had
I not been all too neglectful in not showing them how they
could have come to my help.

I therefore bethought myself that it would be easy for
me to select certain matters which would not be likely to
give rise to controversies, and also not oblige me to declare
more of my principles than I wish, while yet exhibiting sufficiently clearly what I can or cannot do in the sciences.
Whether or not I have succeeded, it is not for me to say.
In speaking, as I have done, of my writings, I have had no
intention of anticipating the judgments of others regarding
them. I shall, however, be grateful if they will examine
them; and that they may feel the more free to do so, I beg
all of those who have any objections to make, to be so good
as to report them to my publisher, who will notify me of
them so that I may at once set about appending to them
my reply. My readers, seeing both the objections and my
replies, will then the more easily judge what they should
take the truth to be. I make no promise of lengthy replies,
but only that I shall quite frankly acknowledge my errors,
should I recognize them to be such. Or if I am unable to
regard them as errors, I shall state no more than what I consider to be required in defense of what I have written, being
careful not to enter on the discussion of any new matters, and
so to avoid becoming engaged in further controversies.

If some of the statements I have made in the beginning

of the *Dioptric* and *Meteors* be found startling, because of my calling them suppositions, and my seeming not to be concerned with proof of them, I beg my readers to have the patience to read attentively the essays in their entirety. They will then, I trust, find themselves satisfied. The reasonings in these essays are, it appears to me, so closely interconnected, that as the last in order are demonstrated by the first which are their causes, so the first are in their turn proved by the last which are their effects. It must not be imagined that in this I am committing the fallacy which logicians entitle circular reasoning. For since experience renders the greater part of these effects most certain [i.e., *quâ immediately* apprehended], the causes from which I deduce them serve not so much to prove as to explain them, whereas on the contrary, it is the effects which [by the certainty of their occurrence] prove the [actuality of the] causes. I have called them suppositions in order that it may be known that I believe myself able to deduce them from those primary truths which I have explained above; and in thus deliberately deciding not to deduce them, my aim has been to prevent certain persons from making use of them in the erection of an extravagant philosophy upon what they take to be my principles, and for which I should have to bear the blame. The persons I have here in mind imagine that in a day, and after hearing no more than two or three words on the subject, they can master all that another has taken twenty years to discover. They are the more liable to error, and the less capable of discerning the truth, in proportion as they are subtler and more lively. As to the opinions which are wholly and truly mine, I do not plead for them on the ground of their being new. On the contrary, if the reasons for them be duly considered, I am convinced that they will be found to be so simple and so conformable to common sense as to appear less extraordinary and less paradoxical than any others which can be entertained in respect of the issues involved. And I make no boast of being the first discoverer of any of them; I have adopted them not because they have been held by others, nor because they have not been so held, but solely because reason has commended them to me.

Though artisans may not be at once able to execute the invention explained in the *Dioptric*,[30] I do not think that it can on that account be declared defective. Since skill and practice are required in the making and adjusting of the machine, and though no essential detail is lacking in my description of it, I would be just as astonished if they were successful in their first attempt, as I should be if someone were in a single day to learn to play the lute, merely through having been given a good sheet of suitable music. And if I write in French, which is the language of my country, in preference to Latin, which is that of my teachers, this is because I hope that those who rely entirely on their unspoiled natural reason will be better judges of my opinions than those who give credence only to the writings of the ancients. As for those who combine good sense with study, whom alone I should choose to have as judges, they will not, I feel sure, be so partial to Latin as to refuse to listen to the reasons I expound in the vulgar tongue.

To conclude, I have no wish to dwell on the progress I hope to make in the sciences in the coming years, nor to make any promises to the public which I am not certain of fulfilling. This only will I say, that I have resolved to devote the years remaining to me exclusively in the endeavor to acquire such knowledge of nature as will enable me, in the field of medicine, to draw up rules of greater certainty than any hitherto practiced; and that my inclination is so strongly opposed to all other pursuits, and especially to those which can be useful to some only by being harmful to others,[31] that if circumstances had been such as to constrain me to engage in them, I do not believe that I should have been able to succeed. I am well aware that in saying this I am doing what cannot tend to my worldly advancement, but

[30] *Tenth Discourse, A.T.* vi, p. 211.

[31] The profession which Descartes seems here to have specially in mind is that of military engineer.

with that I am in no wise concerned; and I shall always hold myself more obliged to those by whose favor I am left to enjoy my leisure without interruption, than to any who might offer me the most honored preferments.

DESCARTES' THEORY OF VISION AS EXPOUNDED IN HIS *DIOPTRIC*[1]

[*La Dioptrique,* the first of the three "Essays" prefaced by the *Discourse on Method,* consists of ten Discourses, (1) on light, (2) on refraction ("Dioptric" can be described as being that part of optics which treats of the transmission of light from one medium to another), (3) on the eyes, (4) on the senses in general, (5) on the images which form on the back-part of the eye, (6) on vision, (7) on our means of improving vision, (8) on the shapes transparent bodies should have for the refracting of light in all the ways which aid vision, (9) on the telescope, (10) on the shaping of glass or crystal lenses. The sections here translated are from the fourth,[2] fifth and sixth of these Discourses.]

WE must be careful not to suppose that in order to sense,[3] the mind has to contemplate images which are [emitted by objects and] despatched by them to the brain, as our philosophers commonly assert; or, at least, we have to conceive the nature of those images in an entirely different manner. For in so far as these philosophers take no account of anything in the images beyond the resemblance they should have to the objects they represent, they are unable to show how they can have been formed by these objects, received by the organs of the external senses, and transmitted by the nerves to the brain. Their only reason in supposing them is that they have observed how our thought can easily be

[1] *A.T.* vi, pp. 112-14.
[2] The *Dioptric,* it may be noted, is twice as long, and the three "Essays" together four times as long, as the *Discourse on Method.*
[3] *pour sentir.*

excited by a picture to conceive the object pictured, and that
it has therefore seemed to them that in the same way the
objects affecting our senses ought to be apprehended by

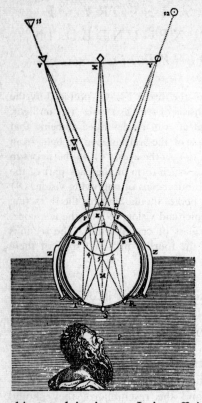

means of certain small
pictures which shape
themselves in the head.
We ought, however, to
bear in mind that there
are several things besides
images which can excite
our thought, as for in-
stance, signs and words,
which have no manner of
resemblance to the things
they signify. And if—
making the least possible
departure from received
opinions—we agree to
recognize that the ob-
jects which we sense do
in fact send these images
into the brain, we must
at least recognize that
none of them can re-
semble in all respects the
object it represents; for
there would then be no
distinction between the

object and its image. It is sufficient that images resemble
their objects in some few respects [i.e., in respect of extension, shape and size]; and often, indeed, their perfection
depends on their not resembling them as much as they might
have done. Thus, in the case of engravings, made up of a
little ink disposed here and there on the paper, we see how
they represent forests, towns, men and even battles and tem-
pests, while yet of the infinity of diverse qualities which they
make us conceive in these objects, the only one of these

qualities to which they bear any proper resemblance is the quality of shape; and even this is a very imperfect resemblance, since it is on a completely flat surface that they represent bodies diverse in height and distance, and further that in accordance with the rules of perspective they often represent circles better by ovals than by other circles, and squares by four-sided figures which are not squares, and similarly in the case of all other shapes. And thus it comes about that often, precisely in order to be more perfect in their quality as images, i.e., the better to represent an object, they ought not to resemble it. Now it is in this way that we must think of the images which take form in the brain, and must recognize that the only question we need raise is that of knowing how the images can supply to the mind the means of sensing all the diverse qualities [including color, sound, heat, etc.] of the objects to which they stand related, and not how in themselves they bear resemblance to them. For just as when the blind man, of whom we have spoken above, touches this and that body with his staff, it is certain that these bodies do not transmit anything to him save only this, that in making his staff move diversely according to the diverse qualities that are in them, they thereby move the nerves of his hand, and in sequence thereupon the points in his brain from which those nerves come. This gives occasion to his soul to sense as many different qualities in these bodies as there are varieties in the movements which are caused by them in his brain.

Fifth Discourse: On the images which form on the back-part of the eye[4]

We thus see that in sensing the soul has no need to contemplate images which present to us precisely the things sensed. This in no way conflicts with what is yet the case, that the objects which we are looking at impress sufficiently perfect images of themselves on the back-parts of our eyes. . . .

[4] *A.T.* vi, p. 114.

But I must explain more at length how this picture is formed; for thereby I shall be able to explain several things pertaining to vision.

Consider, then, first of all, that from each part of the objects V, X, Y, there enter the eye and penetrate to RST all those rays which the opening of the pupil FF can compass, and that, in accordance with what has been said above, owing as much to the nature of the refraction as to that of the three humors KLM, all those rays which come from the same point are bent in traversing the three surfaces BCD, 123 and 456, in such fashion as is required for their reassembling again at an approximately identical point. . . . The rays which come from the point X assemble at the point S, those from V at R, and those from Y at T. And reciprocally, that no ray comes toward S save from the point X; and almost none toward R save from the point V, and similarly with those from T and all the other points intermediate between T and R. . . . If the rays from X are the motions that constitute yellow light, those from Y the motions that constitute blue light, and those from R red light, the three points RST will be moved correspondingly in these three different ways. . . .

But, having spoken of the perfection of this picture, we must also consider its defects. The first and chief of these is that whatever shapes the parts of the eye may be able to assume, it is impossible for them to make the rays coming from diverse points all assemble at as many other diverse points. The best they can do is to secure that only those coming from some point, such as X, assemble at another point, e.g., S, in the center of the back-part of the eye, in which case, some only of those from the point V can then assemble precisely at the point R or from the point Y precisely at the point T; the other rays have to scatter a little around the points T and R. . . . This is what prevents the picture from ever being as distinct toward its extremities as it is in the center. . . . We also note that the rays which come from the point V would be scattered yet more widely around the point R than they now are, should the point V, from which they come, be much nearer to the eye, e.g., at 10, or further removed, as toward 11, than is X, to the distance of which I am supposing the shape of the eye to have been proportioned, with the result that they would render the part R of this picture less distinct than they now do. . . . The other defects of this picture consist in this, that its parts are reversed, i.e., are in positions quite contrary to that of the objects; and in this, that the parts are diminished and abridged, some more, some less, owing to the

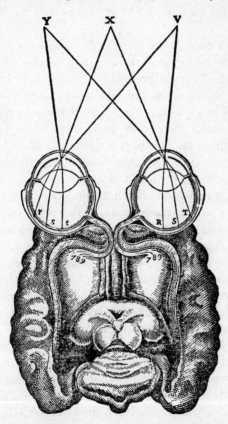

diverse distances and locations of the things they represent, much in the same manner as in a picture executed in perspective. Thus [in the diagram on p. 146] T which is to the left represents what is toward the right, and R which is toward the right represents V which is toward the left. And further, the shape of the object V should not occupy more of the space toward R than that of the object 10 which is smaller but closer, nor less than that of object 11, which is larger but proportionately more distant. . . . And, finally, that the straight line VXY is represented by the curve RST. . . .

Further, not only do the images of objects thus form themselves on the back-part of the eye, they likewise pass beyond to the brain. This will be readily understood if we bear in mind that, for instance, the rays which come into the eye from the object V touch at the point R the extremity of that one of the small fibers of the optic nerve which has its beginning in the point 7 of the interior surface of the brain 789. The rays from X touch at the point S the extremity of another of those fibers, that which has its beginning at the point 8. The rays of the object Y similarly touch another at the point T which corresponds to the point of the brain marked 9, and so with all the others [intermediate between V and Y]. Now since light is nothing else than a movement, or an action which tends to cause some movement, those of its rays which come from V toward R have the power of moving the whole fiber R7, and thereby the point in the brain marked 7; those which come from X toward S, the power of moving the whole fiber S8, and even of moving it differently from the way it moves R7, inasmuch as the objects X and V are of two different colors. Similarly the rays from Y move the point 9. Thus it is evident that again an image 789 is formed this time on the interior surface of the brain . . . sufficiently similar to the objects V, X, Y. From there we can again transport it to a certain small gland which is located toward the center of the brain-concavities and which [alone] strictly [speaking] is the seat of the *sensus communis*. . . .

[The following diagram, used in the *Principles*, Pt. III (cf. at close of *A.T.* xi, Fig. 35), shows the manner in which the double organs of sight and of smell may be conceived as causing single impressions on the pineal gland.]

Sixth Discourse: On vision[5]

Now, while this picture, in thus passing into our head, always retains some degree of resemblance to the objects from which it proceeds, we yet need not hold, as I have already sufficiently shown, that it is by means of this resemblance that it enables us to perceive them, as if there were again in our brain yet other eyes with which we are able to apprehend it,[6] but rather that it is the movements that go to com-

[5] *A.T.* vi, pp. 130-47.
[6] Cf. Newton's remark that the function of the organs of sense is that of carrying the species of things into the sensorium, not that of enabling the soul to be aware of them (cited in *New Studies*, p. 147); cf. also below, p. 157.

pose the picture, which, acting immediately on our mind, inasmuch as it is united to our body, are so instituted by nature as to make it to have such and such sensations. This is what I propose to explain more in detail.

All the qualities which we apprehend in the objects of vision can be reduced to six principal qualities: light, color, situation, distance, magnitude and shape. First, as to light and color, which alone are peculiar to the sense of sight, we have to think of our soul as being of such a nature that the force of the movements which take place at the points in the brain at which the small fibers of the optic nerve terminate, determine it to have the sensation of light, and the particular character of these movements to determine the sensation of color. Thus it is that the movements of the nerves which respond to the ears determine us to hear sounds, those of the tongue to savor tastes, and, in general, movements of the nerves from all parts of the body to sense a certain tickling when they are moderate, and pain when they are too violent. Yet in all this there need be no resemblance between the ideas apprehended and the movements which cause these ideas. . . .

But we must here consider more particularly in what the quantity of the light which is seen consists, i.e., the quantity of the force with which it moves each one of the small fibers of the optic nerve. For it is not always equal to the light which is in the objects, but varies in proportion to their distance and to the size of the pupil and also in proportion to the space which the rays coming from each part of the object can occupy in the back-part of the eye. Since for instance, it is manifest that the point X would send more rays into the eye than it does, if the opening of the pupil were wider, and that it sends as many into the eye which is near it and in which the pupil is narrowed, as it does into the eye in which the pupil is larger but proportionately farther removed. Again . . . if the object is nearer, and the rays enter through a smaller pupil, the rays from the object will be acting on a smaller area in the back of the eye and will there act with

greater force on each of the nerve-fibers which they touch.
This is very easily calculated. For if, e.g., the area of the
retina affected is four times smaller in the one case than in
the other, and if in the larger area the number of the fibers
is four thousand, in the smaller area it will be only one
thousand. Consequently each of the small fibers in the smaller
area will be moved by the thousandth part of the total forces,
and in the larger area only by a quarter part of the thousandth part of the total.

We have also to consider that we can discriminate the
parts of the bodies we are looking at, only in so far as they
differ in their coloring, and that the distinct seeing of colors
does not depend only on this, that all the rays which come
from each point of the object assemble themselves on approximately as many other diverse points in the back of the
eye, and on this that no others come from elsewhere toward
these same points . . . but also on the number of the small
optic nerve-fibers in the area which the image occupies in
the back of the eye. For though, e.g., the object VXY is
composed of ten thousand parts which are in a position to
send rays toward the back of the eye RST in ten thousand
different modes and consequently to make us see at one and
the same time ten thousand colors, they cannot enable the
mind to distinguish more than a thousand at most, if we
suppose that there are only a thousand optic nerve-fibers in
the space RST. For ten of the parts of the object, acting
together upon each of these fibers, can move it only in one
single mode, composed of all those that are acting upon it,
with the result that the area occupied by each one of these
fibers has to be considered as if it were a point. This is why
a meadow, which is painted over with an infinity of quite
diverse colors, often appears, as seen from far-off, to be all
white or all blue; and in general that all bodies are seen less
distinctly from a distance than from close at hand; and
finally that the larger the space the image of an object can
be made to occupy at the base of the eye, the more distinctly
it can be seen. Of this we shall have much more to say later.

As regards situation, i.e., the side toward which each part of the object is located relatively to our body, we do not perceive it otherwise by our eyes than by our hands. Our knowledge of it does not depend on any image or action which comes to us from the object, but solely on the situation of the small parts of the brain whence the nerves take their origin. For this situation—a situation which changes with every change however small in the points at which these nerve-fibers are located—is instituted by nature in order to secure, not only that the mind be aware of the location of each part of the body which it animates, relatively to all the others, but also that it be able to transfer its attention to all the positions contained in the straight line that can be imaged as drawn from the extremity of each of these parts, and as prolonged to infinity. Just as when the blind man, of whom we have already spoken, turns his hand A toward E, or his hand C toward E, the nerves inserted in this hand cause a certain change in his brain which supplies his mind

with the means of knowing not merely the location A or C but also all the others which are in the straight line AE or CE, in such wise that it can direct its attention to the objects B and D, and determine the locations where they are, and this without knowing or thinking of the locations proper to the two hands. Similarly, when our eye or head turns in some particular direction, our mind is notified of it by changes which the nerves inserted in the muscles that serve in these movements cause in our brain. . . . We should not, therefore, find it strange that the [distant] objects can be seen in their true situation notwithstanding that the picture which they imprint in the eye is of so contrary a character; just as our blind man can sense at one and the same moment the object B, which is to the right, by means of his left hand, and D, which is to the left, by means of his right hand. Again, like the blind man, we do not judge that a body is double when we touch it with our two hands. So, too, our two eyes, directed in the manner required for carrying our attention to one and the same location, need make us see only one single object, notwithstanding that a picture forms itself in each of them.

The seeing of distance does not depend, any more than that of location, on images despatched by the objects, but, primarily, on the shape of the body of the eye. For, as we have noted, this shape has to be a little different in enabling us to see what is farther away; and in the measure that we change it in proportioning it to the distance of the objects, we likewise change a certain part of our brain, in a manner so instituted by nature that the mind is able to apprehend this distance. Usually this comes about without our reflecting upon it, just as, when we clasp a body with our hand, we conform the hand to the size and shape of the body, and thereby sense the body, without having need to think of those movements of the hand. Secondly, we know the distance by the relations in which the two eyes stand to one another. For, just as the blind man, holding the two sticks, AE, CE, of which I am supposing that he ignores the length, knowing only the interval between his two hands, A and C, and the magnitude of the angles, ACE, CAE, can thereby, as by a natural geometry, know where the point E is; so when our two eyes RST and rst, are turned toward X, the magnitude of the line Ss, and that of the two angles XSs and XsS, enable us to know where the point X is. We can do this also by the use of a single eye, through change of its position. If, holding it turned toward X, we place it first at the point S, and immediately thereafter at the point s, this will suffice to bring it about that the size of the line Ss and of the two angles XSs and XsS find themselves together in our phantasy, and make us apprehend the distance of the point X; and this by an action of the thought which, quite simple though it be as an imagination, none the less in itself covers a reasoning quite similar to that which surveyors make when, by means of two different stations, they measure inaccessible points.

We have still another way of apprehending distance, viz., by the distinctness or confusion of the shape, and in general by the force or weakness of the light. When we look fixedly toward X, the rays which come from objects at 10 and 12 do not assemble so exactly toward R and toward T, at the back of the eye, as they would if they were at the points V and Y. Thereby we see that they are farther removed or closer to us than is X. Then from the fact that the light, which comes toward the eye from an object at 10, is stronger than if this object were toward V, we judge it to be nearer; and from the fact that the light which comes from an object at 12 is weaker than if it were at Y, we judge it to be more distant. Finally, when we already, on whatever grounds, know the magnitude of an object, or its situation, or the distinctness of its shape and colors, or merely the force of the light which comes from it, this may serve, not strictly in seeing, but in determining the distance. Thus in observing from far off a body which we have been accustomed to see close at hand, we judge of its distance much better than we should if its magnitude had been less known to us. In viewing a mountain, lit up by the sun, beyond a forest covered with shadow, it is solely the situation of this forest [i.e., its being below and in front of the mountains] that makes us judge it to be the nearer of the two. And in viewing on the sea two vessels, one of which is much smaller than the other, but proportionately nearer to us, in such fashion that they appear equal, we can by the difference in their shapes, in their colors, and in the light that they transmit to us, judge which is the more distant.

On the manner in which we see the magnitude and shape of objects, I need not particularly dwell, since it is all comprised in our manner of seeing the distance and situation of their parts. Their magnitude is estimated by the knowledge or opinion we have regarding their distance, compared with the magnitude of the images they impress on the back of the eye, and not absolutely by the magnitude of those images, as is sufficiently manifest from this, that while these may be, for instance, a hundred times larger when the objects are very near us than when they are ten times farther away, they do not on this account make us see them a hundred times larger, but [as] almost equal [in size], at least if we are not deceived in respect of their distance. And it is also manifest that the shape is judged by the knowledge or opinion we have of the situation of the diverse parts of the objects and not by resemblance to the pictures which are in the eye. For those pictures ordinarily contain only ovals and lozenge-shapes, and yet what they make us see are circles and squares.

But in order that there may be no continuing doubts that vision operates in the manner I have been explaining, let us here consider the reasons why it sometimes comes about that it deceives us. First, because it is the soul that sees, and not the eye, and because the soul sees immediately only by the intervention of the brain, whence it happens that madmen, and sleepers, often see, or think that they see, diverse objects which are yet not before their eyes. . . . Secondly, because the impressions, which come from without, pass to the *sensus communis* by way of the nerves, and if the situation of these nerves is affected by any unusual cause, it can lead us to see objects in other than their proper locations, as happens when we press one eyeball. On using both eyes the objects then appear to be doubled. In the same way [and for the same reason] if we cross two fingers and place a small ball between them, we think that we are touching two balls. . . .

We have also to recognize that all our means of knowing distance are very uncertain. For, as regards the shape of the eye, it hardly varies at all in any manner at all sensible to us when the object is at more than four or five feet from us, and even when the object is nearer varies so little that we can thence obtain no knowledge at all precise. And as regards the angles contained between the lines drawn from the two eyes and thence to the object, or from two positions of one and the same object, they almost cease to vary at all when the object seen is even a very little farther distant from us. In consequence of this, our *sensus communis* seems to be incapable of receiving in itself the idea of a distance greater than about a hundred or two hundred feet, as can be verified in the case of the moon and the sun, which have to be classed among the most distant bodies that we can see, and of which at their distance the diameters are approximately as one to a hundred. They usually appear to us as of only one or two feet in diameter at most, notwithstanding that, as we are sufficiently assured by our reason, they are extremely large and extremely far distant. This is not due to any fault in our power to conceive them larger than we do; we can very well conceive towers and mountains very much larger; but because, not being able to conceive them as farther removed from us than a hundred or two hundred feet, it follows that their diameter should not appear more than that of one or two feet. Their situation also contributes to deceive us in this regard; for ordinarily heavenly bodies seem smaller when they are very high toward midday than when, on rising and setting, diverse objects intervene between them and our eyes and so cause us to take better notice of their distance. Astronomers, in measuring them with their instruments, definitely prove that their appearing larger in the one situation than in the other is not due to their being seen under a larger angle, but because they are judged to be more distant. And thus it follows that the axiom of the ancient optics, which declares that the apparent magnitude of objects is proportioned to that of the angle of vision, is not always true.

We are also deceived owing to the way in which white or luminous bodies, and in general all those which operate forcibly upon the sense of sight, always appear to be a little nearer or larger than they would appear if they acted less forcibly. . . . In short, pictures in perspective show us how easy it is to be deceived, in judging of distance by magnitude, by shape, by color, or by light. For, inasmuch as the things which are there depicted are much smaller than we imagine they ought to be, with lineaments more confused and their colors duskier and feebler than belongs to them, they often appear to us to be more distant than otherwise they would.

RENATI
DES-CARTES,
MEDITATIONES
DE PRIMA
PHILOSOPHIA,
IN QVA DEI EXISTENTIA
ET ANIMÆ IMMORTALITAS
DEMONSTRATVR.

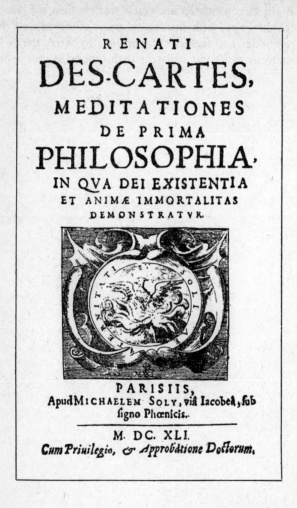

PARISIIS,
Apud MICHAELEM SOLY, viâ Iacobeâ, fub
figno Phœnicis.

M. DC. XLI.
Cum Priuilegio, & Approbatione Doctorum.

MEDITATIONS
ON FIRST PHILOSOPHY

IN WHICH THE EXISTENCE OF GOD AND THE
DISTINCTION IN MAN OF SOUL AND BODY
ARE DEMONSTRATED[1]

[DEDICATION]

To the Most Wise and Illustrious, the Dean and Doctors of
the Sacred Faculty of Theology

MY motive in presenting this work to you is so right and
proper that on learning what I have in view you will, I am
confident, regard it as calling for your support and protec-
tion. Accordingly I can best commend it to you by stating
in a few words what I have set myself to do.

I have always regarded the two questions that bear on
God and the soul, to be the chief of those which ought to be
demonstrated by help of philosophy rather than of theology.
For although to us, the faithful, it may suffice to believe, as

---

[1] Published in 1641. The above is the title as modified in the second
edition, 1642, *Animae immortalitas* being displaced by *Animae
humanae a corpore distinctio*. This change was required by the admission which Descartes has found himself constrained to make,
that the immortality of the soul cannot be philosophically demonstrated, and that belief in it must rest or fall, so far as it is or is not
supported by revelation. Descartes himself carefully revised the 1647
French translation, and in doing so sought by alterations and additions to clarify the Latin text. I have therefore drawn freely on both
versions. The variations in wording and paragraphing are too numerous for special mention; only those changes and additions which
raise questions of interpretation are separately noted. All explanatory additions not in either text I have indicated by inclusion in square
brackets.

being matters of faith, that the human soul does not perish with the body and that God exists, yet assuredly it does not seem possible that infidels should be persuaded of any religion, or almost even of any moral virtue, unless we have antecedently, by way of natural reason, proved to them those two truths. Seeing that, in this life, vices are frequently more highly rewarded than the virtues, few would prefer the right to the useful, had they no fear of God and no expectation of another life. It is indeed true that the existence of God is to be believed on the testimony of the Sacred Scriptures, and likewise that the Sacred Scriptures are to be believed because they come from God. Faith is a gift from God, and in giving us the grace which enables us to believe those other things He can also be enabling us to believe that He exists. This argument, however, can have no force with infidels; they might well reply that we are reasoning in a circle. And, in truth, as I have observed, not only do you with other theologians affirm the sufficiency of natural reason for the proof of God's existence, you likewise recognize Holy Scripture as teaching the knowledge of God to be much easier to us than that of many created things, and indeed as being so easy to acquire that those who have it not are blameworthy. To this effect we have these words in *Wisdom of Solomon,* chap. xiii: *Neither are they to be pardoned. For if they were able to know so much that they could aim at the world, how did they not sooner find out the Lord thereof?* And in Romans, chap. i, it is said that they are *without excuse.* And then also by these words, *That which may be known of God is manifest in them,* we would seem to be admonished that what we may know of God cannot be established save by reasons obtained through inspection of our own minds. This is why I have thought it would not be improper for me to inquire by what means and in what way God can be thus known, that is to say, more easily and certainly than the things of the world.

As regards the soul, while many have judged that its nature cannot easily be determined and some have even gone so far as to say that human reasonings lead them to conclude that it perishes with the body, and that only by faith can the contrary be believed, none the less inasmuch as the Lateran Council held under Leo X (in its eighth session) condemns these opinions, and expressly summons the Christian philosophers to refute such arguments and to employ their powers in establishing the truth, I have ventured to do so in this treatise.

Moreover I am aware that many of the ungodly refuse to believe in the existence of God or to distinguish between soul and body, and this for no other reason than that those two tenets have, they allege, never yet been demonstrated. Though I am far from being of their opinion, and on the contrary hold that almost all the proofs which have been adduced by so many great men have, when rightly understood, demonstrative force, and that it is well-nigh impossible to discover new ones, I yet hold that in philosophy nothing can be of more service than the earnest setting of ourselves to seek out, once for all, the best of these proofs, and the expounding of them with such accuracy and evidence that henceforth it will be universally agreed that they are veritable demonstrations. And lastly, having been importuned to undertake this task by friends who knew of my having practiced a certain method of resolving all kinds of difficulties in the sciences, a method not indeed new (there being nothing older than truth), but which, as they were aware, I have repeatedly used not unsuccessfully in these other fields, I have thought it to be my duty to make trial of its applicability in this field also.

The sum of what I have been able to accomplish is contained in this treatise. Not that I have here attempted to assemble all the reasonings which may be adduced as proofs of the tenets under question. That does not seem worthwhile save where no one proof is sufficiently certain. The first and chief proofs I have expounded in a manner that justifies my presenting them as being demonstrations of the highest certainty and evidence. And I will further declare

that they are such as to have led me to think that there is
no possibility, by way of our human powers, of our ever
discovering other and better proofs. (In making these claims,
the importance of the issues, and the glory of God to which
all this relates, constrain me to speak here of myself somewhat more freely than I am wont to do.) But however certain and evident I consider them to be, I cannot persuade
myself that they are level to the comprehension of all. In
geometry, many of the demonstrations bequeathed us by
Archimedes, Apollonius, Pappus and others, though regarded by everyone as evident and certain, containing, as
they manifestly do, nothing which, considered by itself, is
not quite easy to understand, and no consequences which
fail of accurate coherence with their antecedents, yet, being
somewhat lengthy and calling for the reader's whole attention,
they are understandable only by the few. Similarly, though
I consider the proofs which I have employed to be equal, or
even superior, in certainty and evidence to those of geometry, I fear there will not be many who can adequately
understand them, and this not merely because of their being
lengthy and involved, but more especially because of their
requiring the mind to be entirely free from all prejudices,
and prepared to dissociate itself from its sensuous preoccu-
pations. In truth, aptitude for the metaphysical disciplines is
less general than for those of geometry. And there is also
this further difference between them: since everyone comes
to geometry already convinced that ordinarily in this field
nothing is advanced which is not assuredly demonstrated,
those who are insufficiently versed in it err more frequently
by assenting to what is false than by denying what is true,
this being due to their desire to give the impression that they
understand; in philosophy, on the other hand, where there
is supposed to be nothing which is not open to question, few
give themselves to the search after truth, and the great majority, bent on acquiring the reputation of being bold
thinkers, venture arrogantly to challenge even the most evident truths.

This is why my reasonings, bearing as they do on philosophy, no matter how forceful they may be, cannot be expected to have any great effect on my readers, unless and until you assist them by your patronage. So high is the estimation in which your Faculty is universally held, and so authoritative is the title, THE SORBONNE, not only in matters of faith but also of human philosophy, that no other Body, with the sole exception of the Sacred Council, is held in such respectful deference, everyone recognizing that it is impossible to find elsewhere greater perspicacity and weight, greater wisdom and integrity of judgment. I have no doubt, therefore, that should you deign to give sympathetic attention to this treatise, first of all by your revising of it (for, mindful as I am, not only of my humanity, but more especially of my ignorance, I do not venture to claim that it is free from error); secondly, by your supplementing of it, adding to it whatever is lacking, perfecting what is incomplete, and yourselves giving such fuller explanation as may be required, or at least so advising me in those regards that I may then set myself to remedy them; and finally, should you—once the reasonings contained in it, proving the existence of God and the distinction between mind and body, have been thus brought to that perspicuity which, I am convinced, allows of their being ranked as completely accurate demonstrations—be willing to testify to this being so, and to do so in a public manner, then, as I say, I have no doubt that all the errors and false opinions hitherto entertained on these questions will soon be effaced from the minds of men. The truth will itself serve to bring all other able and learned men into agreement with your verdict; and your authority will cause the atheists, who in general are only pretenders to learning, to lay aside their spirit of contradiction, and may indeed even lead them to come out in support of the reasonings which they find to be thus ranked as demonstrations by all able men, doing so in the fear that otherwise they may seem not to have understanding of them. In short, to so many testimonies, all other men will readily yield credence; no longer will anyone dare to doubt either the existence of God or the real and veritable distinction in man between soul and body. But it is for you, in your singular wisdom, to judge how serviceable my proposals may prove to be, being, as you are, in a position to observe the disorders to which continuing doubt gives rise. It would not here become me to say more in commendation of the cause of God and religion to you who have always been the steadiest supporters of the Catholic Church.

PREFACE TO THE READER

IN the *Discourse on the Method of rightly conducting Reason and of Seeking for Truth in the Sciences,* published in French in the year 1637, I have already touched briefly on the two questions, that respecting God and that respecting the human mind. Not that I had the design of treating them with any thoroughness, but only so to speak in passing, that I might learn from the judgment of my readers as to how subsequently I should deal with them. For these questions appeared to me to be of such moment that I judged it best to deal with them more than once; and since the path I follow in discussing them is so little trodden, and so remote from that usually taken, I thought it inexpedient to dwell upon them at full length in a French discourse that might be read by all and sundry, lest those disqualified through insufficient mental powers should come to believe that they too might travel by this road.

Having, in the *Discourse on Method,* requested all those who might find anything censurable in my writings to do me the favor of acquainting me with it, I have now to report that nothing worthy of remark has been objected, save only on two points, and to these I will here briefly reply, deferring till later my more detailed discussion of them.

The first objection is that though the human mind, when reflecting upon itself, may not apprehend itself to be other than a thinking thing, it does not therefore follow that its nature, i.e., its *essence,* consists only in its being a thing which thinks, at least not in such wise that the word *only* may be taken as excluding all the other things which might perhaps also be said to pertain to the nature of the soul. To this objection I reply that I was not there intending to exclude them in accordance with the order required by the truth in this matter (an issue with which I was not then concerned), but only in accordance with the order of my thinking. All I meant to say was that, in so far as I had awareness of myself, what I alone clearly apprehended as pertaining to my essence was that I was a thinking thing, i.e., a thing having in itself the faculty of thinking. What I shall later show is that, since there is nothing else which I am aware of as belonging to my nature, it follows that nothing else does in truth belong to it.

The second objection is that it does not follow from my having an idea of a thing more perfect than I am that the idea is itself more perfect than I am, and still less that what is represented by the idea exists. I reply that the term idea is here equivocally used; for it may be taken either materially [i.e., actually, in itself] as being an act of the understanding, a sense in which it cannot be said to be more perfect than the self, or it may be taken objectively [i.e., representatively] as being the thing [immediately] apprehended by [way of] this act—a thing which, even though not taken as existing independently of my understanding, may nevertheless be more perfect than myself by reason of its essence. This I propose to show at due length in the present treatise, viz., that simply from there being in me the idea of a thing more perfect than myself, it follows that the thing [so represented] does indeed exist.

In addition to these two objections I have received two lengthy works on these issues. In them, however, it is not so much my reasonings as my conclusions which are called in question; and this by arguments borrowed from the usual atheistic sources. But as arguments of this sort can make no impression on those who understand my reasonings, there is no call for me to refute them. Also there are many men of such irrational and feeble judgment that they are more influenced by the opinions which happen to be first suggested to them, however false and contrary to reason, than by a true and adequate but subsequently obtained refutation of these opinions; and I am therefore the more disinclined to reply to these criticisms, in that, before replying to them, I should be obliged to state what they are. I shall say, in general, only this, that the arguments alleged by the atheists in disproof of the existence of God derive such force as they may have either from our having ascribed to God human affections or from our having arrogated to our minds so much power and wisdom that we have presumed to determine and to comprehend all that God can and ought to do. Nothing that they thus allege need cause us any difficulty, provided we recognize that our minds must be viewed as being finite, and God as being incomprehensible and infinite.

Having thus, by way of the *Discourse,* made trial of the judgments passed by readers on that work, I again, in the present work, take up the two questions, regarding God and regarding the human mind, and in so doing I shall treat of the primary data[2] of all first philosophy, without, however, expecting any popular response, or the securing of more than a small body of readers. I would not, indeed, invite anyone to read it who is not able and willing to meditate earnestly with me, detaching his mind from the senses, and likewise from all prejudices; and I know well that those so disposed are few in number. As to those who, without caring to comprehend the order and connections of my reasonings, are concerned only to query single isolated conclusions, as so many are wont to do, such readers, I say, will not greatly profit by their perusal of this treatise. They may perchance, here and there, find occasion for captious criticisms, but are hardly likely to be in a position to urge any serious objection or anything that genuinely calls for reply.

But as I do not promise that even these few upon whom I am counting will on a first reading be at once satisfied, and as I do not go so far as to claim to have been able to foresee all that may be a source of difficulty to each one of them, I shall, first of all, in these *Meditations,* set forth those considerations by which I believe myself to have been brought to an assured and evident knowledge of the truth,

2 *initia,* here used by Descartes as synonymous with *principia.*

that I may perchance in due course learn whether the reasonings by which I have thus myself been persuaded will also suffice for the convincing of others. Having done so, I shall then proceed to reply to the objections made by some men of outstanding ability and learning to whom these meditations were sent for criticism, before being committed to the press. Those objections are so numerous and varied that I venture to hope that no further criticism, at least none of any consequence, is likely to have been overlooked. This is why I entreat my readers not to pass judgment on these meditations until they have taken care to read all[3] of the objections, with the relative replies.

[3] Passage of time has made the reading of Descartes' very lengthy appendix of objections and his replies less rewarding and less necessary: one chief section is given below, pp. 258-61, and others in *New Studies*.

SYNOPSIS OF THE SIX FOLLOWING MEDITATIONS

In the first meditation I set forth the grounds[4] on which all things, and especially material things, can be doubted—so long, that is to say, as we have no other foundations for the sciences than those on which we have hitherto relied. Although the utility of a doubt so general may not, on first suggestion, be apparent, it is none the less very great. It frees us from all prejudices; it opens to us the easiest way of detaching the mind from the senses; and lastly, it secures us against further doubting of what we shall conclude to be true.

In the second meditation the mind, on making use of the freedom proper to it, finds that it can suppose to be non-existent all those things the existence of which can in any wise be doubted, but while so doing it has perforce to recognize that it must itself exist. This is a point of the greatest importance; it is in this way that the mind is enabled to distinguish easily between the things which pertain to itself, that is, to its intellectual nature, and the things which pertain to the body. Some may, perhaps, be led to expect to find at this stage in my argument a statement of grounds in proof of the immortality of the soul, and I therefore think it proper to give warning that, since it has been my endeavor to write in this treatise nothing of which I cannot give exact demonstration, I have found myself obliged to adopt an order similar to that used by geometers, viz., to state all the premises on which the proposition in question depends, before coming to any conclusion regarding it. Now the first and chief prerequisite for knowledge of the immortality of the soul is our being able to form as

4 *causae.*

perspicuous an apprehension of it as possible, an apprehension completely distinct from all apprehension of body; and this is what has been done in this second meditation. In addition we have to be assured (1) that all the things we judge clearly and distinctly are true in that very mode in which we are judging them, and this could not be proved at any point prior to the fourth meditation; (2) that we have a distinct apprehension of the corporeal, and this I give partly in the second and partly in the fifth and sixth meditations; and (3) that on these grounds we have to conclude that whatever things are clearly and distinctly apprehended as being diverse substances, as are mind and body, are indeed distinct each from the other, a conclusion drawn in the sixth meditation. This is further confirmed in that same meditation, where it is pointed out that we cannot apprehend body save as divisible, nor, on the other hand, the mind save as indivisible. For we cannot think of the half of a mind as we can of the half of any body, however small; so that, as we thus see, not only are their natures diverse but also in some measure contraries. I have not, however, pursued the matter further in this present treatise, not only for the reason that these considerations suffice to show that the extinction of the mind does not follow from the corruption of the body, thus affording men the hope of a life after death, but also because the premises which enable us to infer the immortality of the mind call for an exposition of the whole science of physics. We should have to establish (1) that all substances whatsoever, all things that is to say, which owe their existence to God's creation of them, are by their very nature incorruptible, and that they can never cease to be, unless through God's withdrawing from them His concurrence they are thereby reduced to nothing; (2) that whereas body, taken generally [i.e., taking body collectively, as meaning matter], is a substance, and therefore can never perish, the human body, in so far as it differs from other bodies [i.e., taking "bodies" in the plural, thereby meaning material things], is composed en-

tirely of a certain configuration of members, and other similar accidents, while the human mind is not constituted of
accidents of any kind whatever, but is a pure substance.
For though all the accidents of the mind suffer change,
though, for instance, it thinks of other things, wills others,
and senses others, it is yet always the same mind. The human body, on the contrary, is no longer the same, if a change
takes place in the structure of some of its parts. Thus it follows, that while the body may, indeed, easily enough perish,
the mind is in its own nature immortal.

In the third meditation I have, as it seems to me, de-
veloped at sufficient length my chief argument in proof of
the existence of God. None the less, being anxious to withdraw the minds of my readers from the senses, I was unwilling to make use in that section of any comparisons
drawn from corporeal things, and there may perhaps have
remained many obscurities which, as I hope, may later be
entirely removed by my replies to objections. Thus, to take
one instance [and to employ one such comparison], the
reader may wonder how it can be that the idea of a being
supremely perfect (an idea that is in fact in us) contains so
much objective reality, that is to say participates by representation in so many degrees of being and of perfection,[5]
that it cannot but proceed from a cause supremely perfect.
In replying to objections, I have illustrated my argument by
use of a comparison, that of an ingeniously perfect machine,
the idea of which exists in the mind of some workman. The
objective [i.e., representative] perfection of this idea must
have some cause, viz., either the science of the workman,
or that of some other person from whom he has received
the idea: so likewise, the idea of God, which is in us, must
have God as its cause.

In the fourth meditation it is shown that whatever we
judge clearly and distinctly is true; and also at the same
time it is explained in what the nature of error consists.

[5] This explanatory clause, in explanation of the scholastic term
"objective," added in French version.

Knowledge of these conclusions is required not only for the confirming of the preceding truths but also for the understanding of those that follow. (In passing, I may remark that I do not here treat of sin, that is, of error committed in the pursuit of good and evil, but solely of that which arises in deciding between the true and the false. Nor do I dwell on matters bearing on faith or on the conduct of life, but only on those speculative truths which can be known by way of the natural light.[6])

In the fifth meditation, in addition to a general account of corporeal nature, a new proof is given of the existence of God, a proof not perhaps free any more than the former from certain difficulties. The countering of these difficulties has again to await my reply to objections. I further show in what sense it is true that the certainty even of geometrical demonstrations is dependent on our knowledge of there being a God.

Finally, in the sixth meditation I distinguish the action of the understanding from that of the imagination; their distinguishing characters are described; the mind is proved to be really distinct from the body, and yet to be so closely conjoined with it as to form with it one single thing. All the errors which are wont to originate in the senses are then brought under review, and the manner of avoiding them indicated. Then in conclusion I give an account of all the grounds enabling us to be assured of the existence of material things; not that I consider them to be of great utility in establishing what they prove, viz., that a world does indeed exist, that men have bodies and the like, things which no one of sound mind has ever doubted; but because, on viewing them closely, we come to discern that they are neither so strong nor so evident as those through which we gain knowledge of our mind and of God, so that these latter are, of all the things which can be known through our human powers, the most certain and the most evident. The

[6] Cf. *A.T.* iii, pp. 334-35.

establishing of this conclusion has been my prime aim in these meditations; and that is why, in this synopsis, I have omitted mention of the many other issues on which I have dwelt only incidentally.

MEDITATION I

Concerning the Things of which we may doubt

IT is now several years since I first became aware how many
false opinions I had from my childhood been admitting as
true, and how doubtful was everything I have subsequently
based on them. Accordingly I have ever since been convinced that if I am to establish anything firm and lasting in
the sciences, I must once for all, and by a deliberate effort,
rid myself of all those opinions to which I have hitherto
given credence, starting entirely anew, and building from
the foundations up. But as this enterprise was evidently one
of great magnitude, I waited until I had attained an age so
mature that I could no longer expect that I should at any
later date be better able to execute my design. This is what
has made me delay so long; and I should now be failing in
my duty, were I to continue consuming in deliberation such
time for action as still remains to me.

Today, then, as I have suitably freed my mind from all
cares, and have secured for myself an assured leisure in
peaceful solitude, I shall at last apply myself earnestly and
freely to the general overthrow of all my former opinions.
In doing so, it will not be necessary for me to show that they
are one and all false; that is perhaps more than can be
done. But since reason has already persuaded me that I
ought to withhold belief no less carefully from things not
entirely certain and indubitable than from those which appear to me manifestly false, I shall be justified in setting
all of them aside, if in each case I can find any ground
whatsoever for regarding them as dubitable. Nor in so doing shall I be investigating each belief separately—that, like
inquiry into their falsity, would be an endless labor. The

withdrawal of foundations involves the downfall of whatever rests on these foundations, and what I shall therefore
begin by examining are the principles[7] on which my former
beliefs rested.

Whatever, up to the present, I have accepted as possessed
of the highest truth and certainty I have learned either from
the senses or through[8] the senses. Now these senses I have
sometimes found to be deceptive; and it is only prudent never
to place complete confidence in that by which we have even
once been deceived.

But, it may be said, although the senses sometimes deceive us regarding minute objects, or such as are at a great
distance from us, there are yet many other things which,
though known by way of sense, are too evident to be
doubted; as, for instance, that I am in this place, seated by
the fire, attired in a dressing-gown, having this paper in my
hands, and other similar seeming certainties. Can I deny
that these hands and this body are mine, save perhaps by
comparing myself to those who are insane, and whose brains
are so disturbed and clouded by dark bilious vapors that
they persist in assuring us that they are kings, when in fact
they are in extreme poverty; or that they are clothed in gold
and purple when they are in fact destitute of any covering;
or that their head is made of clay and their body of glass,
or that they are pumpkins. They are mad; and I should be
no less insane were I to follow examples so extravagant.

None the less I must bear in mind that I am a man, and
am therefore in the habit of sleeping, and that what the insane represent to themselves in their waking moments I
represent to myself, with other things even less probable,
in my dreams. How often, indeed, have I dreamt of myself
being in this place, dressed and seated by the fire, whilst all
the time I was lying undressed in bed! At the present moment it certainly seems that in looking at this paper I do

[7] *principia*, i.e., the initial data.
[8] E.g., through hearsay or reading. Cf. *Entretien avec Burman*,
A.T. v, p. 146, Adam's edition, pp. 3-4.

so with open eyes, that the head which I move is not asleep, that it is deliberately and of set purpose that I extend this hand, and that I am sensing the hand. The things which happen to the sleeper are not so clear nor so distinct as all of these are. I cannot, however, but remind myself that on many occasions I have in sleep been deceived by similar illusions; and on more careful study of them I see that there are no certain marks distinguishing waking from sleep; and I see this so manifestly that, lost in amazement, I am almost persuaded that I am now dreaming.

Let us, then, suppose ourselves to be asleep, and that all these particulars—namely, that we open our eyes, move the head, extend the hands—are false and illusory; and let us reflect that our hands perhaps, and the whole body, are not what we see them as being. Nevertheless we must at least agree that the things seen by us in sleep are as it were like painted images, and cannot have been formed save in the likeness of what is real and true. The types of things depicted, eyes, head, hands, etc.—these at least are not imaginary, but true and existent. For in truth when painters endeavor with all possible artifice to represent sirens and satyrs by forms the most fantastic and unusual, they cannot assign them natures which are entirely new, but only make a certain selection of limbs from different animals. Even should they excogitate something so novel that nothing similar has ever before been seen, and that their work represents to us a thing entirely fictitious and false, the colors used in depicting them cannot be similarly fictitious; they at least must truly exist. And by this same reasoning, even should those general things, viz., a body, eyes, a head, hands and such like, be imaginary, we are yet bound to admit that there are things simpler and more universal which are real existents and by the intermixture of which, as in the case of the colors, all the images of things of which we have any awareness be they true and real or false and fantastic, are formed. To this class of things belong corporeal nature in general and its extension, the shape of extended things, their quantity or magnitude, and their number, as also the location in which they are, the time through which they endure, and other similar things.

This, perhaps, is why we not unreasonably conclude that physics, astronomy, medicine, and all other disciplines treating of composite things are of doubtful character, and that arithmetic, geometry, etc., treating only of the simplest and most general things and but little concerned as to whether or not they are actual existents, have a content that is certain and indubitable. For whether I am awake or dreaming, 2 and 3 are 5, a square has no more than four sides; and it does not seem possible that truths so evident can ever be suspected of falsity.

Yet even these truths can be questioned. That God exists, that He is all-powerful and has created me such as I am, has long been my settled opinion. How, then, do I know that He has not arranged that there be no Earth, no heavens, no extended thing, no shape, no magnitude, no location, while at the same time securing that all these things appear to me to exist precisely as they now do? Others, as I sometimes think, deceive themselves in the things which they believe they know best. How do I know that I am not myself deceived every time I add 2 and 3, or count the sides of a square, or judge of things yet simpler, if anything simpler can be suggested? But perhaps God has not been willing that I should be thus deceived, for He is said to be supremely good. If, however, it be repugnant to the goodness of God to have created me such that I am constantly subject to deception, it would also appear to be contrary to His goodness to permit me to be sometimes deceived, and that He does permit this is not in doubt.

There may be those who might prefer to deny the existence of a God so powerful, rather than to believe that all other things are uncertain. Let us, for the present, not oppose them; let us allow, in the manner of their view, that all which has been said regarding God is a fable. Even so we shall not have met and answered the doubts suggested above regarding the reliability of our mental faculties; instead we shall have given added force to them. For in whatever way it be supposed that I have come to be what I am, whether by fate or by chance, or by a continual succession and connection of things, or by some other means, since to be deceived and to err is an imperfection, the likelihood of my being so imperfect as to be the constant victim of deception will be increased in proportion as the power to which they assign my origin is lessened. To such argument I have assuredly nothing to reply; and thus at last I am constrained to confess that there is no one of all my former opinions which is not open to doubt, and this not merely owing to want of thought on my part, or through levity, but from cogent and maturely considered reasons. Henceforth, therefore, should I desire to discover something certain, I ought to refrain from assenting to these opinions no less scrupulously than in respect of what is manifestly false.

But it is not sufficient to have taken note of these conclusions; we must also be careful to keep them in mind. For long-established customary opinions perpetually recur in thought, long and familiar usage having given them the right to occupy my mind, even almost against my will, and to be masters of my belief. Nor shall I ever lose this habit of assenting to and of confiding in them, not at least so long as I consider them as in truth they are, namely, as opinions which, though in some fashion doubtful (as I have just shown), are still, none the less, highly probable and such as it is much more reasonable to believe than to deny. This is why I shall, as I think, be acting prudently if, taking a directly contrary line, I of set purpose employ every available device for the deceiving of myself, feigning that all these opinions are entirely false and imaginary. Then, in due course, having so balanced my old-time prejudices by this new prejudice that I cease to incline to one side more than to another, my judgment, no longer dominated by misleading usages, will not be hindered by them in the apprehension of things. In this course there can, I am convinced, be neither danger nor error. What I have under consideration is a question solely of knowledge, not of action, so that I cannot for the present be at fault as being over-ready to adopt a questioning attitude.

Accordingly I shall now suppose, not that a true God, who as such must be supremely good and the fountain of truth, but that some malignant genius exceedingly powerful and cunning has devoted all his powers in the deceiving of me; I shall suppose that the sky, the earth, colors, shapes, sounds and all external things are illusions and impostures of which this evil genius has availed himself for the abuse of my credulity; I shall consider myself as having no hands, no eyes, no flesh, no blood, nor any senses, but as falsely opining myself to possess all these things. Further, I shall obstinately persist in this way of thinking; and even if, while so doing, it may not be within my power to arrive at the knowledge of any truth, there is one thing I have it in me to do, viz., to suspend judgment, refusing assent to what is false. Thereby, thanks to this resolved firmness of mind, I shall be effectively guarding myself against being imposed upon by this deceiver, no matter how powerful or how craftily deceptive he may be.

This undertaking is, however, irksome and laborious, and a certain indolence drags me back into the course of my customary life. Just as a captive who has been enjoying in sleep an imaginary liberty, should he begin to suspect that his liberty is a dream, dreads awakening, and conspires with the agreeable illusions for the prolonging of the deception, so in similar fashion I gladly lapse back into my accustomed opinions. I dread to be wakened, in fear lest the wakefulness may have to be laboriously spent, not in the tranquilizing light of truth, but in the extreme darkness of the above-suggested questionings.

MEDITATION II

Concerning the Nature of the Human Mind, and how it is more easily known than the Body[9]

So disquieting are the doubts in which yesterday's meditation has involved me that it is no longer in my power to forget them. Nor do I yet see how they are to be resolved. It is as if I had all of a sudden fallen into very deep water, and am so disconcerted that I can neither plant my feet securely on the bottom nor maintain myself by swimming on the surface. I shall, however, brace myself for a great effort, entering anew on the path which I was yesterday exploring; that is, I shall proceed by setting aside all that admits even of the very slightest doubt, just as if I had convicted it of being absolutely false; and I shall persist in following this path, until I have come upon something certain, or, failing in that, until at least I know, and know with certainty, that in the world there is nothing certain.

Archimedes, that he might displace the whole earth, required only that there might be some one point, fixed and immovable, to serve in leverage; so likewise I shall be entitled to entertain high hopes if I am fortunate enough to find some one thing that is certain and indubitable.

I am supposing, then, that all the things I see are false;[10] that of all the happenings my memory has ever suggested to me, none has ever so existed; that I have no senses; that body, shape, extension, movement and location are but mental fictions. What is there, then, which can be esteemed true? Perhaps this only, that nothing whatsoever is certain.

But how do I know that there is not something different from all the things I have thus far enumerated and in regard

[9] Cf. *A.T.* vii, p. 297, l. 22.
[10] I.e., are not independent existents.

to which there is not the least occasion for doubt? Is there not some God, or other being by whatever name we call Him, who puts these thoughts into my mind? Yet why suppose such a being? May it not be that I am myself capable of being their author? Am I not myself at least a something? But already I have denied that I have a body and senses. This indeed raises awkward questions. But what is it that thereupon follows? Am I so dependent on the body and senses that without them I cannot exist? Having persuaded myself that outside me there is nothing, that there is no heaven, no Earth, that there are no minds, no bodies, am I thereby committed to the view that I also do not exist? By no means. If I am persuading myself of something, in so doing I assuredly do exist. But what if, unknown to me, there be some deceiver, very powerful and very cunning, who is constantly employing his ingenuity in deceiving me? Again, as before, without doubt, if he is deceiving me, I exist. Let him deceive me as much as he will, he can never cause me to be nothing so long as I shall be thinking that I am something. And thus, having reflected well, and carefully examined all things, we have finally to conclude that this declaration, *Ego sum, ego existo,* is necessarily true every time I propound it or mentally apprehend it.

But I do not yet know in any adequate manner what I am, I who am certain that I am; and I must be careful not to substitute some other thing in place of myself, and so go astray in this knowledge which I am holding to be the most certain and evident of all that is knowable by me. This is why I shall now meditate anew on what, prior to my venturing on these questionings, I believed myself to be. I shall withdraw those beliefs which can, even in the least degree, be invalidated by the reasons cited, in order that at length, of all my previous beliefs, there may remain only what is certain and indubitable.

What then did I formerly believe myself to be? Undoubtedly I thought myself to be a man. But what is a man? Shall I say a rational animal? No, for then I should have to inquire what is "animal," what "rational"; and thus from the one question I should be drawn on into several others yet more difficult. I have not, at present, the leisure for any such subtle inquiries. Instead, I prefer to meditate on the thoughts which of themselves sprang up in my mind on my applying myself to the consideration of what I am, considerations suggested by my own proper nature. I thought that I possessed a face, hands, arms, and that whole structure to which I was giving the title "body," composed as it is of the limbs discernible in a corpse. In addition, I took notice that I was nourished, that I walked, that I sensed, that I thought, all of which actions I ascribed to the soul. But what the soul might be I did not stop to consider; or if I did, I imaged it as being something extremely rare and subtle, like a wind, a flame or an ether, and as diffused throughout my grosser parts. As to the nature of "body," no doubts whatsoever disturbed me. I had, as I thought, quite distinct knowledge of it; and had I been called upon to explain the manner in which I then conceived it, I should have explained myself somewhat thus: by body I understand whatever can be determined by a certain shape, and comprised in a certain location, whatever so fills a certain space as to exclude from it every other body, whatever can be apprehended by touch, sight, hearing, taste or smell, and whatever can be moved in various ways, not indeed of itself but something foreign to it by which it is touched and impressed. For I nowise conceived the power of self-movement, of sensing or knowing, as pertaining to the nature of body: on the contrary I was somewhat astonished on finding in certain bodies faculties such as these.

But what am I now to say that I am, now that I am supposing that there exists a very powerful, and if I may so speak, malignant being, who employs all his powers and skill in deceiving me? Can I affirm that I possess any one of those things which I have been speaking of as pertaining to the nature of body? On stopping to consider them with closer attention, and on reviewing all of them, I find none of which I can say that it belongs to me; to enumerate them again would be idle and tedious. What then, of those things which I have been attributing not to body, but to the soul? What of nutrition or of walking? If it be that I have no body, it cannot be that I take nourishment or that I walk. Sensing? There can be no sensing in the absence of body; and besides I have seemed during sleep to apprehend things which, as I afterwards noted, had not been sensed. Thinking? Here I find what does belong to me: it alone cannot be separated from me. *I am, I exist.*[11] This is certain. How often? As often as I think. For it might indeed be that if I entirely ceased to think, I should thereupon altogether cease to exist. I am not at present admitting anything which is not necessarily true; and, accurately speaking, I am therefore [taking myself to be] only a thinking thing, that is to say, a mind, an understanding or reason—terms the significance of which has hitherto been unknown to me. I am, then, a real thing, and really existent. What thing? I have said it, a thinking thing.

And what more am I? I look for aid to the imagination. [But how mistakenly!] I am not that assemblage of limbs we call the human body; I am not a subtle penetrating air distributed throughout all these members; I am not a wind, a fire, a vapor, a breath or anything at all that I can image. I am supposing all these things to be nothing. Yet I find, while so doing, that I am still assured that I am a something.

But may it not be that those very things which, not being known to me, I have been supposing non-existent, are not really different from the self that I know? As to that I cannot say, and am not now discussing it. I can judge only of things that are known to me. Having come to know that I exist, I am inquiring as to what I am, this I that I thus know to exist. Now quite certainly this knowledge, taken in the precise manner as above, is not dependent on things the existence of which is not yet known to me; consequently and still more evidently it does not depend on any of the things

11 *Ego sum, ego existo.*

which are feigned by the imagination. Indeed this word *feigning*[12] warns me of my error; for I should in truth be feigning were I to *image*[13] myself to be a something; since imaging is in no respect distinguishable from the contemplating of the shape or image of a *corporeal*[13] thing. Already I know with certainty that I exist, and that all these imaged things, and in general whatever relates to the nature of body, may possibly be dreams merely or deceptions. Accordingly, I see clearly that it is no more reasonable to say, "I will resort to my imagination in order to learn more distinctly what I am," than if I were to say, "I am awake and apprehend something that is real, true; but as I do not yet apprehend it sufficiently well, I will of express purpose go to sleep, that my dreams may represent it to me with greater truth and evidence." I know therefore that nothing of all I can comprehend by way of the imagination pertains to this knowledge I [already] have of myself, and that if the mind is to determine the nature of the self with perfect distinctness, I must be careful to restrain it, diverting it from all such imaginative modes of apprehension.

What then is it that I am? A thinking thing.[14] What is a thinking thing? It is a thing that doubts, understands, affirms, denies, wills, abstains from willing, that also can be aware of images and sensations.

Assuredly if all these things pertain to me, I am indeed a something. And how could it be they should not pertain to me? Am I not that very being who doubts of almost everything, who none the less also apprehends certain things, who affirms that one thing only is true, while denying all the rest, who yet desires to know more, who is averse to being deceived, who images many things, sometimes even despite his will, and who likewise apprehends many things which seem to come by way of the senses? Even though I should be always dreaming, and though he who has cre-

---

[12] *effingo,* italicized as in text.
[13] Italics not in text.
[14] *Res cogitans;* Fr. *une chose qui pense.*

ated[15] me employs all his ingenuity in deceiving me, is there any one of the above assertions which is not as true as that I am and that I exist? Any one of them which can be distinguished from my thinking? Any one of them which can be said to be separate from the self? So manifest is it that it is I who doubt, I who apprehend, I who desire, that there is here no need to add anything by way of rendering it more evident. It is no less certain that I can apprehend images. For although it may happen (as I have been supposing) that none of the things imaged are true, the imaging, *quâ* active power, is none the less really in me, as forming part of my thinking. Again, I am the being who senses, that is to say, who apprehends corporeal things, as if by the organs of sense, since I do in truth see light, hear noise, feel heat. These things, it will be said, are false, and I am only dreaming. Even so, it is none the less certain that it seems to me that I see, that I hear, and that I am warmed. This is what in me is rightly called sensing, and as used in this precise manner is nowise other than thinking.

From all this I begin to know what I am somewhat better than heretofore. But it still seems to me—for I am unable to prevent myself continuing in this way of thinking—that corporeal things, which are reconnoitered by the senses, and whose images inform thought, are known with much greater distinctness than that part of myself (whatever it be) which is not imageable—strange though it may be to be thus saying that I know and comprehend more distinctly those things which I am supposing to be doubtful and unknown, and as not belonging to me, than others which are known to me, which appertain to my proper nature and of the truth of which I am convinced—in short are known more distinctly than I know myself. But I can see how this comes about:

15 Replying to Burman (*A.T.* v, p. 157; Adam's edition, p. 18), Descartes adds: "Whether this being is indeed God, I cannot yet say. Is the genius who is deluding me the Being who also created me? That I do not yet know, and am here speaking only in a confused manner."

my mind delights to wander and will not yet suffer itself to be restrained within the limits of truth.

Let us, therefore, once again allow the mind the freest reign, so that when afterwards we bring it, more opportunely, under due constraint, it may be the more easily controlled. Let us begin by considering the things which are commonly thought to be the most distinctly known, viz., the bodies which we touch and see; not, indeed, bodies in general, for such general notions are usually somewhat confused, but one particular body. Take, for example, this piece of wax; it has been but recently taken from the hive; it has not yet lost the sweetness of the honey it contained; it still retains something of the odor of the flowers from which it has been gathered; its color, its shape, its size, are manifest to us; it is hard, cold, easily handled, and when struck upon with the finger emits a sound. In short, all that is required to make a body known with the greatest possible distinctness is present in the one now before us. But behold! While I am speaking let it be moved toward the fire. What remains of the taste exhales, the odor evaporates, the color changes, the shape is destroyed, its size increases, it becomes liquid, it becomes hot and can no longer be handled, and when struck upon emits no sound. Does the wax, notwithstanding these changes, still remain the same wax? We must admit that it does; no one doubts that it does, no one judges otherwise. What, then, was it I comprehended so distinctly in knowing the piece of wax? Certainly, it could be nothing of all that I was aware of by way of the senses, since all the things that came by way of taste, smell, sight, touch and hearing, are changed, and the wax none the less remains.

Perhaps it has all along been as I am now thinking, viz., that the wax was not that sweetness of honey, nor that pleasing scent of flowers, nor that whiteness, that shape, that sound, but a body which a little while ago appeared to me decked out with those modes, and now appears decked out with others. But what precisely is it that I am here imaging? Let us attentively consider the wax, withdrawing from it all that does not belong to it, that we may see what remains. As we find, what then alone remains is a something extended, flexible and movable. But what is this "flexible," this "movable"? What am I then imaging? That the piece of wax from being round in shape can become square, or from being square can become triangular? Assuredly not. For I am apprehending that it admits of an infinity of similar shapes, and am not able to compass this infinity by way of images. Consequently this comprehension of it cannot be the product of the faculty of imagination.

What, we may next ask, is its extension? Is it also not known [by way of the imagination]? It becomes greater when the wax is melted, greater when the wax is made to boil, and ever greater as the heat increases; and I should not be apprehending what the wax truly is, if I did not think that this piece of wax we are considering allows of a greater variety of extensions than I have ever imaged. I must, therefore, admit that I cannot by way of images comprehend what this wax is, and that it is by the mind alone that I [adequately] apprehend it. I say this particular wax, for as to wax in general that is yet more evident. Now what is this wax which cannot be [adequately] apprehended save by the mind? Certainly the same that I see, touch, image, and in short, the very body that from the start I have been supposing it to be. And what has especially to be noted is that our [adequate] apprehension of it is not a seeing, nor a touching, nor an imaging, and has never been such, although it may formerly have seemed so, but is solely an inspection of the mind which may be imperfect and confused, as it formerly was, or clear and distinct, as it now is, according as my attention is directed less or more to the constituents composing the body.

I am indeed amazed when I consider how weak my mind is and how prone to error. For although I can, dispensing with words, [directly] apprehend all this in myself, none the less words have a hampering hold upon me, and the accepted usages of ordinary speech tend to mislead me. Thus when the wax is before us we say that we see it to be the same wax as that previously seen, and not that we judge it to be the same from its retaining the same color and shape. From this I should straightway conclude that the wax is known by ocular vision, independently of a strictly mental inspection, were it not that perchance I recall how when looking from a window at beings passing by on the street below, I similarly say that it is men I am seeing, just as I say that I am seeing the wax. What do I see from the window beyond hats and cloaks, which might cover automatic machines? Yet I judge those to be men. In analogous fashion, what I have been supposing myself to see with the eyes I am comprehending solely with the faculty of judgment, a faculty proper not to my eyes but to my mind.

But aiming as I do at knowledge superior to the common, I should be ashamed to draw grounds for doubt from the forms and terms of ordinary speech. I prefer therefore to pass on, and to ask whether I apprehended the wax on my first seeing it, and while I was still believing that I knew it by way of the external senses, or at least by the *sensus communis,* as they call it, that is to say by the imaginative faculty, more perfectly and more evidently than I now apprehend it after having examined with greater care what it is and in what way it can be known. It would indeed be foolish to have doubts as to the answer to this question. Was there anything in that first apprehension which was distinct? What did I apprehend that any animal might not have seen? When, however, I distinguish the wax from its external forms; when stripped as it were of its vestments I consider it in complete nakedness, it is certain that though there may still be error in my judgment, I could not be thus apprehending it without a mind that is human.

What now shall I say of the mind itself, i.e., of myself? For as yet[16] I do not admit in myself anything but mind. What am I to say in regard to this I which seems to apprehend this piece of wax so distinctly? Do I not know myself much

[16] Cf. *Meditation* VI, below, p. 230 ff.

more truly and much more certainly, and also much more
distinctly and evidently, than I do the wax? For if I judge
that the wax is or exists because I see it, evidently it follows,
with yet greater evidence that I myself am or exist, inasmuch as I am thus seeing it. For though it may be that
what I see is not in truth wax, and that I do not even possess
eyes with which to see anything, yet assuredly when I see,
or (for I no longer allow the distinction) when I think I
see, it cannot be that I myself who think am not a something. So likewise, if I judge that the wax exists because I
touch it, it will follow that I am; and if I judge that the
imagination, or some other cause whatever it be, persuades
me that the wax exists, the same conclusion follows [viz.,
that I am *thinking* by way of an image and *thinking* what
I thus image to be independently existing]. And what I have
here said regarding the piece of wax may be said in respect
of all other things which are external to me.

And yet a further point: if the apprehension of the wax
has seemed to me more determinate and distinct when sight
and touch, and many causes[17] besides, have rendered it
manifest to me, how much more evidently and distinctly
must I now know myself, since all the reasons which can
aid in the apprehension of wax, or of any body whatsoever,
afford yet better evidence of the nature of my mind. Besides,
in the mind itself there are so many more things which can
contribute to the more distinct knowledge of it, that those
which come to it by way of the body scarcely merit being
taken into account.

Thus, then, I have been brought step by step to the conclusion I set out to establish. For I now know that, properly
speaking, bodies are cognized not by the senses or by the
imagination, but by the understanding alone. They are not
thus cognized because seen or touched, but only in so far as
they are apprehended understandingly.[18] Thus, as I now

17 *causis.*
18 *sed tantum ex eo quod intelligantur;* Fr. *mais seulement de ce
que nous les concevons par la pensée.*

recognize, nothing is more easily or more evidently apprehended by me than my mind. Difficult, however, as it is to
rid oneself of a way of thinking to which the mind has been
so long accustomed, it is well that I should halt for some
time at this point, that by prolonged meditation I may more
deeply impress upon myself[19] this new knowledge.[20]

[19] *memoriae meae;* Fr. *en ma mémoire,* a strangely misleading
term for Descartes to use.
[20] Cf. Descartes' Reply to Objection II (*A.T.* vii, p. 130; *H.R.* ii,
p. 31): "Nothing conduces more to the acquiring of a firm and assured knowledge of things than a preliminary accustoming of ourselves in the doubting of all things and especially of the things that
are corporeal; and though I have, in years long past, seen several
books written by Skeptics and Academics treating of these questions
(and though it is not without distaste that I have again served up
this stale dish), not only have I had no option save to reserve for
them this entire second Meditation, but I have also to request my
readers, before they proceed any further, to expend not merely the
little time required for the reading of it, but several months, or at
least weeks, in thinking over the things of which it treats; only so, I
am convinced, can they hope to profit to the full in their reading of
what follows."

MEDITATION III

Concerning God: that He exists

I SHALL now close my eyes, stop my ears, withdraw all my senses, I shall even efface from my thinking all images of corporeal things; or since that can hardly be done, I shall at least view them as empty and false. In this manner, holding converse only with myself and closely examining my nature, I shall endeavor to obtain, little by little, better and more familiar knowledge of myself. I am a thinking thing, i.e., a thing that doubts, affirms, denies, knows some few things, is ignorant of many, that loves, that hates, that wills, that refuses, that images also and senses. For as I before remarked, although the things which I sense or image are perhaps, apart from me, nothing at all, I am nevertheless certain that those ways of thinking, which I call sensings and imagings, in so far as they are no more than ways of thinking, pertain to me. In those few words I have summed up all that I truly know, or at least all that I have thus far been aware of knowing.

I shall now endeavor to discover whether, on closer attention, there may not perhaps pertain to me other things which I have not yet considered. I am certain that I am a thinking thing. But do I thereby know also what is required to render me thus certain of anything? In this first knowledge there is indeed nothing save the clear and distinct apprehension of what I am affirming; yet this would not suffice to render me certain of its truth, if it could ever happen that anything which I apprehend thus clearly and distinctly should yet prove false; and accordingly I would now seem to be able to adopt as a general rule[21] that everything I apprehend in a genuinely clear and distinct manner is true.

I have, however, been receiving and admitting as altogether certain and manifest[22] several other things which yet I have afterwards found to be altogether doubtful. What were those things? They were the Earth, the sky, the stars, and all the other things I was apprehending by way of the senses. But what was there that I clearly[23] apprehended in them? Nothing save that the ideas or thoughts of such things presented themselves to my mind. And even now I do not deny that those ideas are to be met with in me. There was, however, another thing which I was affirming, and which, being habituated to belief in it, I supposed myself to be apprehending clearly,[24] although in truth I was not so apprehending it, namely that there were things outside me, from which these proceed and to which they are altogether similar. It was in this that I was mistaken; or if I was perhaps judging correctly, assuredly this was not due to any knowledge conveyed to me by way of direct apprehension.

But when I considered something very simple and easy, bearing on arithmetic or geometry, for instance that 2 and 3 together make 5, and other things of this sort, was I not, then at least, intuiting them sufficiently perspicuously[25] to justify me in affirming their truth? If afterwards I entertained doubts regarding them, this was indeed for no other reason than that it occurred to me that a God[26] might perhaps have endowed me with a nature such that I may be

[21] Cf. below, p. 195 ff., where Descartes adds, as being essential, two further prerequisites, that the human *ingenium* can be shown to be divinely conditioned, and that God who thus determines it is no deceiver.

[22] Descartes, it may be noted, is careful to avoid speaking of them as having ever been apprehended either clearly or distinctly.

[23] The French version misleadingly adds—"et distinctement."

[24] *clare;* Fr. *très clairement.* Here again the French version is misleading. For Descartes there can, strictly, be no degrees of immediacy and therefore no degrees of clearness. Cf. *New Studies*, p. 264.

[25] *satis perspicue intuebar;* Fr. *concevais-je assez clairement.*

[26] *aliquem Deum;* Fr. *quelque Dieu.*

deceived even in respect of the things which seem to me
the most manifest of all. For whenever this supposition of
God's omnipotence comes up in my mind, I cannot but
confess that it is easy for Him, if He so wishes, to cause me
to err, even in those matters which I regard myself as intuiting[27] with the eyes of the mind in the most evident manner. None the less, when I direct my attention to the things
which I believe myself to be apprehending quite clearly, I
am so persuaded of their truth that I cannot but break into
protestations such as these: Let who will deceive me, he
will never be able to bring it about that in the very time
during which I shall be thinking that I am a something, I
shall yet be nothing; or that, at some future time, it will be
true that I have never been, it now being true to say that
I am; or that 2 and 3 could make more or less than 5; or that
any other such things which I clearly see, cannot be other
than I apprehend them as being. And certainly since I have
no reason to believe that there is a God who is a deceiver
(and indeed have not yet even considered the grounds for
supposing that a God of any kind exists), the ground of my
doubts, entirely dependent as it is on this supposition, is but
slight, and so to speak metaphysical. But to be able to
eliminate it, I must at the earliest possible opportunity inquire whether there is indeed a God; and should I find there
is a God, I must also inquire whether He can be a deceiver.
For without the knowledge of these two truths I do not see
how I can be certain of anything.

Now in order that I may be enabled to conduct this inquiry without interrupting the order of meditation I have
proposed to myself—namely to pass step by step from the
first notions I discover in my mind to those which I can
afterwards find to be there—I must here divide all my
thoughts into certain kinds, and consider in which of these
kinds truth and error, in the strict sense, are to be found.
Some of my thoughts are, as it were, images of things; and

[27] *intueri;* Fr. *connaître.*

to them alone strictly belongs the title "idea," e.g., when I represent to myself a man, or a chimera, or the sky, or an angel, or even God. Other thoughts have in addition other forms; for instance when I will, fear, affirm, deny, while in so doing I am always indeed apprehending something as the subject of my thought, I am also embracing in thought something more[28] than the similitude of this thing; and of the thoughts of this kind some are called volitions or affections,[29] whereas others are called judgments. If ideas are considered only in themselves, and not as referred to some other thing, they cannot, strictly speaking, be false. For whether I image a goat or a chimera, that I am imaging the latter is no less true than that I am imaging the former. Nor need I fear there may be falsity in the will or in the affections. For though I am able to desire things that are evil, or even what has never existed, it is yet none the less true that I so desire them. There thus remain only our judgments; and it is in respect of them that I must take diligent heed lest I be deceived. And assuredly the chief and most usual error to be met with in them consists in judging that the ideas which are in me are similar to, conformed to, the things which are outside me; if I considered them as being only certain modes or ways in which I think, without referring them to anything beyond, they would hardly afford any material for error.

To consider now the ideas [that are strictly so called], some appear to me to be innate, others to be adventitious, that is to say foreign to me and coming from without, and

[28] *aliquid amplius.*

[29] Descartes has nowhere specified, in any precise manner, the relations in which will, understanding and the affections stand to one another. Fear is the only affection here cited. Both understanding and will enter into willing, affirming and denying, his other three instances. In the sequel it is with judgment alone that he has anything further to say. The natural beliefs which he speaks of as being impulses are not dealt with until *Meditation* VI. Belief as a factor common both to natural and to intellectually grounded belief, he has nowhere been concerned to examine.

others to be made or invented by me.[30] When I apprehend
what a thing is, what a truth is, or what a thought is, I
would seem to be holding the power of so doing from no
other source than my own nature. On the other hand, when
I hear a sound, see the Sun, or sense fire, I have hitherto
judged these to proceed from certain things situated outside
me. Lastly it appears to me that sirens, hippogriffs and other
similar chimeras are my own mental inventions. But perhaps
I may yet come to hold that all of these ideas are of the
kind I call adventitious, coming to me from without, or that
they are all innate, or are all made by me; for I have not
yet clearly discerned their true origin.

Here my chief task must be to inquire, in respect of those
ideas which seem to me to come from things existing outside
me, what grounds there are obliging me to believe they are
similar to the outside things. The first of those grounds is
that I seem to be so taught by nature; and the second, that
I experience in myself that these ideas are not in any wise
dependent on my will, nor therefore on myself. Often they
present themselves to me in spite of myself, as, for instance,
at the present moment, whether I will or not, I feel heat;
and because of this I am persuaded that this sensation or
idea is produced in me by a thing that is different from me,
viz., by the heat of the fire near which I am sitting. And as
it has seemed to me, nothing is more obvious than that I
may therefore judge that what this external thing is impress-
ing on me is not anything different from itself, but its
similitude.

Next, I must consider whether these grounds are sufficiently strong and convincing. When I here say that I am
so taught by nature I understand by the word nature only

[30] *factae;* Fr. *faites et inventées.* In a letter to Mersenne (June 14,
1641) Descartes interprets the term *factae* as follows: "I have distinguished three kinds of ideas; some are adventitious, such as the
idea we commonly have of the sun; others are *factae vel factitiae,*
among which we can class that which the astronomers by their reasonings make of the sun; others are innate, such as the idea of God,
of the mind. . . ." Cf. below, pp. 198-99.

a certain spontaneous impulse which constrains me to this belief, and not a natural light enabling me to know that the belief is true. These two things are widely different; for what the natural light shows me to be true (e.g., that inasmuch as I doubt, it follows that I am, and the like), I cannot anywise call in doubt, since I have in me no other faculty or power whereby to distinguish the true from the false, none as trustworthy as the natural light, and none that can teach me the falsity of what the natural light shows me to be true. As I have often observed, when this question relates to the choice between right and wrong in action, the natural impulses have frequently misled me; and I do not see that I have any better ground for following them in questions of truth and error.[31]

As to the other ground, that these ideas, as not being dependent on my will, must necessarily proceed from things situated outside me, I do not find it any more convincing than that of which I have been speaking. For just as the natural impulses, notwithstanding the fact that they are not always in accordance with my will, are none the less in me, so likewise it may be that I have in me, though indeed unknown to me, some faculty or power capable of producing the ideas, and of doing so without the aid of any external things. That, as I have hitherto thought, is precisely what I am doing when I dream.

And lastly, even should the ideas proceed from things other than myself, it does not therefore follow that they must be similar to those things. On the contrary, I have observed in a number of instances how greatly a thing can differ from our ideas of it. For example, I find present to me two completely diverse ideas of the Sun; the one in which the Sun appears to me as extremely small is, it would seem, derived from the senses, and to be counted as belonging to the class of adventitious ideas; the other, in which the Sun is taken by me to be many times larger than the whole Earth, has

[31] For Descartes' later modification of this provisional conclusion, cf. *Meditation* VI, p. 238 ff.

been arrived at by way of astronomical reasonings, that is to say, elicited from certain notions innate in me, or formed by me in some other manner. Certainly, these two ideas of the Sun cannot both resemble the same Sun; and reason constrains me to believe that the one which seems to have emanated from it in a direct manner is the more unlike.

These various considerations convince me that hitherto it has not been by any assured judgment, but only from a sort of blind impulse, that I have believed in the existence of things outside me and different from me, things which by way of the sense-organs or by whatever means they employ, have conveyed to me their ideas or images, and have thus impressed on me their similitudes.[32]

But there is yet another way of inquiring whether any of those things, the ideas of which are in me, exist outside me. If ideas are taken in so far only as they are certain ways of thinking, I recognize among them no differences or inequality; they all appear to me to proceed from me in the same manner. When, however, they are viewed as images, of which one represents one thing and another some other thing, it is evident that they differ greatly one from another. Those which represent substances are without doubt something more, and contain in themselves, so to speak, more objective reality (that is to say participate by representation in a higher degree of being or of perfection)[33] than those which represent only modes or accidents; and again, the idea by which I apprehend a supreme God, eternal, infinite, immutable, omniscient, omnipotent, and the creator of all things which are in addition to Himself, has certainly in it more objective reality than those ideas by which finite substances are represented.

Now it is manifest by the natural light that there must be at least as much reality in the efficient and total cause as in its effect. For whence can the effect draw its reality if not from its cause? How could this cause communicate to it this

---

[32] *et y imprimaient leurs ressemblances,* added in French version.
[33] Parenthesis added in French version.

reality if it did not itself have it? And hence it follows, not only that something cannot proceed from nothing; but also that what is more perfect, i.e., contains more reality, cannot proceed from what is less perfect. And this is not only evidently true of those effects the reality of which philosophers term actual or formal, but also of the ideas the reality of which is viewed only as being what they term objective[34] [i.e., representational]. Thus, for example, a stone which has not yet existed cannot now begin to be unless it be produced by some thing which possesses in itself, either formally or eminently, all that enters into the composition of the stone (i.e., which contains in itself the same things or others more excellent than those which are in the stone).[35] Thus heat cannot be produced in a subject previously devoid of it save by a cause of an order or degree or kind at least as perfect as the heat, and so in all other cases. But neither can the idea of the heat or of the stone exist in me unless it too has been placed in me by a cause which contains in itself at least as much reality as I am ascribing to the heat or the stone. For although this cause may not communicate to the idea anything of its formal, i.e., of its actual reality, we ought not on that account to view this cause as less real. As we have to recognize, it is the very nature of an idea to require for itself no other formal [i.e., actual] reality save that which it receives and borrows from the thought or mind of which it is a mode, i.e., a manner or way of thinking.[36] But nevertheless, if an idea is to contain one [particular] objective reality rather than some other, it must undoubtedly derive it from some cause in which there is to be found at least as much formal [i.e., actual] reality as in the idea there is ob-

[34] In composing the *Meditations* in Latin, and in addressing them to the learned, Descartes had perforce to make use of the language spoken by the learned. Hence these scholastic terms, which are, as he says, "rude and barbaric even in the Latin, and much more so in the French." Cf. preface to the 1647 French translation. *A.T.* ix, pp. 1-3.

[35] Parenthesis added in the French version.

[36] *c'est-à-dire, une manière ou façon de penser,* added in French version.

jective [i.e., representational] reality. For if anything [of that kind] be allowed as being met with in the idea and yet not in the cause of the idea, it must have derived its origin from nothing. But however imperfect that mode of being—the mode of being objectively in the understanding by way of representation through its idea—we certainly cannot, for all that, declare it to be in itself nothing, nor consequently that the idea owes its origin to nothing.

Nor may I, on the ground that the reality which I ascribe to my ideas is only objective [i.e., representational], suspect it of not being also formally [i.e., actually] present in their causes, and so hold it to be sufficient if in them also it exists only objectively. Just as the objective mode of existence belongs to ideas by their very nature, so the formal mode of existence appertains to the causes of these ideas, at least to the first and chief of their causes, by the very nature of those causes. For although, it may be, one idea gives birth to another, the series of the ideas cannot be carried back *in infinitum;* we must in the end reach a first idea, the cause of which is, as it were, the archetype in which all the reality or perfection that is in the idea only objectively, by way of representation, is contained formally [i.e., actually]. In this way the natural light makes it evident to me that the ideas are in me in the manner of images, which may indeed fall short of the perfection of the things from which they have been derived, but can never contain anything greater or more perfect.

The longer and more carefully I examine all these things, the more clearly and distinctly do I recognize their truth. What then am I to conclude from it all? This, namely, that if the objective reality of any one of my ideas be so great that I am certain it cannot be in me either formally or eminently, and that consequently I cannot myself be the cause of it, it necessarily follows that I am not alone in the world and that there is likewise existing some other thing, which is the cause of this idea. Were no idea of this kind to be met with in me, I should have no argument sufficient to render me certain of the existence of anything different from me. For after careful inquiry in every possible quarter, I have up to the present[37] failed to discover any other.

Now among my ideas in addition to the idea which exhibits me to myself—an idea as to which there can here be no difficulty—there is another which represents God, others representing corporeal and inanimate things, others representing angels, others representing animals, and again others representing to me men similar to myself. As regards the ideas which represent other men, or animals, or angels, I can easily understand that they may have been compounded from those which I have of myself, of corporeal things, and of God, even although there may be, outside myself, neither men, animals nor angels. As regards the ideas of corporeal things, there is nothing in them so great or so excellent that it might not possibly have proceeded from myself, and on considering them closely and examining each separately in the way in which I yesterday examined the idea of wax, I find that there is but little in them which is clearly and distinctly apprehended, viz., magnitude or extension in length, breadth and depth, shape which results from the limitation of extension, the location which bodies have in relation to one another, and motion or change of location, to which may be added substance, duration and number. As to other things such as light and the colors, sounds, odors, tastes, heat and cold and the other tactual qualities, they present themselves to me so confusedly and obscurely that I cannot tell whether they are true or false, i.e., whether the ideas I have of them are ideas of real things or whether they present only chimerical beings which are incapable of [independent] existence. For though, as I have before remarked, it is only in judgments that formal falsity, falsity properly so called, can be met with, there can yet in ideas be a certain material falsity, namely when the ideas represent what is nothing as if it were

---

[37] Later in *Meditation* VI, having meantime confirmed the argument to and from the existence of God, Descartes takes account of the role played by the natural beliefs.

something. For example, so far are the ideas I have of heat and cold from being clear and distinct, that I cannot learn from them whether cold is only a privation of heat or heat a privation of cold, or indeed whether either or neither is a real quality. And inasmuch as ideas are taken as being images [i.e., as standing for something], there cannot be any that do not seem to us to represent something; and accordingly, if it be indeed true that cold is nothing but a privation of heat, the idea which represents it to me as something real and positive may quite properly be termed false; and so in other cases.[38] Ideas of this kind I need not indeed assign to any author other than myself. For, if they are false, i.e., if they represent what is not a thing, then by the light of reason it is known to me that they proceed from nothing, i.e., that they are in me only because of some lack of perfection in my nature. On the other hand, even supposing them to be true, if what they exhibit to me has such little reality—so little that I cannot even distinguish the thing thus represented from not-being—I do not see why they may not have been produced by myself.

As to the clear and distinct ideas I have of corporeal things, there are some which, as it seems to me, I can have obtained from the idea [i.e., the immediate awareness] I have of myself, e.g., those of substance, duration, number and the like. For when I think a stone to be a substance or to be a thing capable of existing by itself, and in like manner think myself to be a substance, though I am then indeed apprehending myself to be a thinking non-extended thing, and the stone, on the contrary, to be an extended non-thinking thing,

[38] Descartes replies to Burman's objection that in our idea of nothing we have an idea which is yet not the idea of a real thing: "That idea is merely negative and can hardly be said to be an idea. I am here taking the word 'idea' in its strict and proper sense. The ideas we have of common notions are not, properly speaking, ideas of things, and we are then taking idea in a wider sense" (*A.T.* v, p. 153; Adam's edition, p. 29). Here, as so often in Descartes, "idea" allows of ambiguous employment. He never quite definitely made up his mind in which of the two very different senses it should be used. Cf. *New Studies*, p. 223.

and though there is accordingly a notable difference between the two, none the less they appear to agree in this, that they represent substances.[39] In the same way, when I apprehend myself as now existing and recollect that I have existed at other times, and when I have thoughts of which I apprehend the number, I acquire the ideas of duration and number, which I can thereafter freely transfer to other things. As to the other qualities composing the ideas of corporeal things, extension, shape, location and motion, it is true that they are not indeed formally [i.e., actually] in me, since I am nothing other than a thinking thing; but as they are merely certain modes of substance—and as it were the vestments[40] under which corporeal substance appears to us—whereas I am myself a substance, it would seem that they may be contained in me eminently.

The only idea that remains for consideration, therefore, is the idea of God. Is there in that idea anything which cannot be regarded as proceeding from myself? By the name God I mean a substance that is infinite, immutable, independent, all-knowing, all-powerful, and by which I myself and everything else, if any such other things there be, have been created. All those attributes are so great and so eminent, that the more attentively I consider them the less does it seem possible that they can have proceeded from myself alone; and thus, in the light of all that has been said, we have no option save to conclude that God exists. For though the idea of substance may be in me in so far as I am myself a substance, yet, being as I am a finite entity, it would not be the idea of an *infinite* substance; it can be this only as having proceeded from some substance which is in itself infinite.

The argument cannot be met by supposing that I apprehend the infinite not through a true idea but only by negation

---

[39] Descartes is here speaking in a semi-popular manner. Strictly, on his teaching, bodies such as a stone, unlike the self, are not special creations: they are modal existences coming into being and passing away. Matter in its singleness, *quâ* extension, is alone substantial and abiding in the manner of the self. Cf. in *Synopsis* above, p. 172.

[40] *comme les vêtements,* added in French version.

of that which is finite, in the manner in which I apprehend
rest and darkness by the negation of motion and light.
On the contrary there is manifestly more reality in the infinite substance than in the finite substance, and my awareness of the infinite must therefore be in some way prior to
my awareness of the finite, that is to say, my awareness of
God must be prior to that of myself. For how could I know
that I doubt and desire, i.e., know that something is lacking
to me and that I am not wholly perfect, save by having in
me the idea of a being more perfect than myself, by comparison with which I may recognize my deficiencies. Nor can
our argument be evaded by declaring that this idea of God
is perhaps materially false, and that consequently, as in the
already mentioned ideas of heat and cold, it may have nothing as its source, i.e., that its existence may be due to my
imperfection.[41] On the contrary, since this idea is completely
clear and distinct, and contains within itself more objective
reality than any other, there can be none which is of itself
more true or less open to the suspicion of falsity. This idea
of a being supremely perfect and infinite is, I maintain, entirely true, for although we may perhaps entertain the supposition that no such being exists, we yet cannot suppose, as
I have been supposing in the case of cold, that the idea of it
exhibits to me nothing real. The idea is also completely[42]
clear and distinct for the further reason that whatsoever I
apprehend clearly and distinctly of the real and of the true,
and of what purports some perfection, is in its entirety contained in it. This holds true, even though it be that I do not
comprehend the infinite, and that in God there is an infinitude of things which I cannot comprehend, or even reach in
any way by thought. For it is of the nature of the infinite that
I, finite as I am and limited, cannot comprehend it. It suffices that I understand this, and that I judge that whatever
I apprehend clearly, and which I know to purport some perfection, and perchance also an infinitude of yet other perfec-

[41] Parenthesis added in French version.
[42] *maxime.*

tions of which I am ignorant, is in God formally or eminently. Consequently, the idea I have of Him is the most completely true, the most completely clear and distinct, of all the ideas that are in me.

But perhaps I am something more than I am supposing myself to be; perhaps all those perfections which I am attributing to God are in some fashion potentially in me, although they do not yet show themselves or issue in action. Indeed I am already aware that my knowledge increases, perfecting itself little by little; and I see nothing to prevent its thus increasing more and more *in infinitum,* nor any reason why on its being thus increased and perfected I may not in this way be able to acquire all the other perfections of the Divine nature, nor finally, why the power I have of acquiring these perfections, if the power be indeed thus already in me, may not suffice to provide the idea of them.

But on closer examination I recognize that this cannot be allowed. For, in the first place, even should it be true that my knowledge, little by little, daily increases, and that many things potentially mine are not yet actual, none the less these powers do not pertain to, or make the least approach to, the idea I have of God in whom nothing is merely potential, and all is actual and operative. There can indeed be no more convincing evidence of the imperfection of my knowledge than that it gradually increases. Again, although my knowledge can be ever more and more increased, I may not, for this reason, suppose that it can ever be actually infinite; for it can never be so increased as not still to allow of yet further increase. But when I judge God to be actually infinite, I do so as judging that nothing can be added to His sovereign perfection. And lastly, I comprehend that what is objective in an idea cannot be produced by a being that exists potentially only—which properly speaking is nothing—but only by a being that is formal, that is to say, actual.

Assuredly, in all that I have been saying there is nothing which is not, on attentive consideration, manifest by the natural light. When, however, my attention is divided, and my mind is, as it were, blinded by the images of sensible things, I do not so readily recollect why the idea of a being more perfect than I, must necessarily have proceeded from a being which is indeed more perfect; and this is why I am concerned to continue the inquiry as to whether I myself, who have this idea of God, could exist, if no such being exists.

I ask, therefore, from what do I derive my existence? Perhaps from myself, or from my parents or from some other causes less perfect than God: for I can think or conjecture nothing more perfect than God, or even equal to God.

But were I independent of everything else, and myself the author of my being, I should not be anywise in doubt or entertain desires for what is other than myself; in short, nothing would be lacking to me. I should have given myself all those perfections of which I had any idea, and should thus be God. Nor should it be imagined that what is lacking to me is more difficult to acquire than what I already possess. On the contrary, it is manifestly much more difficult to bring it to pass that I, i.e., a thing, a substance that thinks, should emerge out of nothing, than it would be to obtain knowledge of many things of which I am ignorant, such knowledge being only an accident of this thinking substance. If I had this greater perfection, that is to say were capable of being myself the author of my existence, I would not have denied myself what is more easy of acquisition, viz., the knowledge in which I am lacking. Nor would I have deprived myself of any of the things which I apprehend as being contained in the idea of God, none of which seems to me more difficult to acquire. Were any one of them more difficult, it would certainly appear to me as being such (supposing I were myself the author of all the other things I possess), because in it I should thereby be experiencing a limit to my power.

Even if I suppose that I have always existed as I now am, I cannot evade the force of this reasoning, on the plea that there will then be no need to seek for any author of my existence. The course of my life can be divided into innumerable parts, none of which is in any way dependent on the others. Accordingly it does not follow that because I was in existence a short time ago I must be in existence now, unless there be some cause which produces me, creates me as it were anew at this very instant, that is to say, conserves me. To all those who consider with attention the nature of time it is indeed evident that a thing in order to be conserved at each of the moments in which it endures has need of the same power and action as would be required to produce and create it anew, if it did not yet exist. That the difference between creation and conservation is a difference solely in our way of thinking is one of the many things which the natural light manifests to us.

What, therefore, is now required is that I interrogate myself as to whether there be in me some power by which I can secure that I who now am shall still be in the time that follows. Since I am nothing but a thinking thing—this at least is the only part of myself which thus far has been definitely in question—if such a power resided in me, I should undoubtedly be conscious of it. But I experience no such power; and thereby I quite evidently know that I am dependent on some being other than myself.

Perhaps, however, the being on which I am dependent is not the being I call God, and that I am produced either by my parents or by some other causes less perfect than God. But this cannot be. As I before said, manifestly there must be at least as much reality in the cause as in the effect. Accordingly, inasmuch as I am a thinking thing and have in me an idea of God, whatever the cause be to which my nature has finally to be traced, it too must be allowed to be a thinking thing, and to possess the idea of all the perfections I attribute to God. We may then inquire whether this cause derives its origin and its existence from itself or from some other thing. If self-existent, it follows from the reasons above cited that it must itself be God; as having the power of self-existence, it must, beyond doubt, likewise have the power of actually possessing all the perfections of which it has in itself the idea, that is, all those which I apprehend as being in God. Should it, however, hold its existence from some cause other than itself, we shall again ask, in the same manner, respecting this other cause, whether it exists of itself or through some other, until we at length reach an ultimate cause, which will be God.

Here, as is evident, there can be no regression *in infinitum;* for the question we are asking is not only as to the cause which has in past time produced me, but more especially as to what it is that is conserving me at the present moment.

Nor may we suppose that several partial causes have concurred in the producing of me; that from one I have received the idea of some one of the perfections I attribute to God; from another the idea of some other, so that while all these perfections exist somewhere in the universe, they are not to be found conjoined together in one entity which is God. On the contrary, the unity, the simplicity, that is the inseparability of all the things which are in God, is one of the chief perfections I apprehend to be in Him; and assuredly this idea of the unity of all God's perfections could not have been placed in me by any cause from which I did not also have the ideas of His other perfections. For how could it have made me understand them to be at once conjoined and inseparable, without at the same time making me know what they are?

Finally, as regards my parents, even though all that I have ever held concerning them were true, it would not follow that it is they who conserve me, nor that they have brought me into being in so far as I am a thinking thing, since what they did was merely to implant certain dispositions in that matter in which I judge that I (that is to say, my mind, which alone at present I identify with myself) reside. Here, therefore, there can be no further question in their regard, and from this alone, viz., that I exist, and have in me the idea of a Being sovereignly perfect, that is to say, God, I have forthwith to conclude that His existence is demonstrated in the most evident manner.

It only remains to me to examine how I have obtained this idea. I have not acquired it through the senses, and it is never presented to me unexpectedly, as sensible things are wont to be, when these act, or seem to act, on the external sense-organs. Nor is it a product or fiction of my mind; for it is not in my power to take from or add anything to it. Consequently the only alternative is to allow that it is innate in me, just as is the idea of myself.

Certainly I ought not to find it strange that God, in creating me, has placed this in me, to be, as it were, the mark of the workman imprinted on his work. Nor need the mark be something different from the work itself. From this alone, that God has created me, it is highly likely[43] that He has in some fashion made me in His image and similitude, and that I apprehend this similitude by means of the same faculty by which I apprehend myself—that is to say, when my mind is

---

[43] *valde credibile;* Fr. *fort croyable.* Cf. Descartes' Reply to Burman's Objection (*A.T.* v, p. 156; Adam's edition, p. 38): "*Objection.* But why so? Could not God have created you and yet not created you in His image? *Reply.* No. For it is an axiom, accepted and true, that 'the effect is similar to the cause.' God is the cause of my being; I am His effect, therefore I resemble Him. *O.* But a builder is the cause of a house, and yet it does not resemble him. *R.* He is not the cause in the sense we are here giving to it. He does no more than apply active things to things that are passive; and his work need not, therefore, resemble him. The cause of which we are here speaking is the *causa totalis,* the cause to which the very existence of things is due. Now a cause of this kind cannot produce anything not similar to itself. For since it is itself an existent and a substance, and in producing something is calling this something into existence, that is to say, is creating something where before there was nothing whatsoever (a mode of production proper only to God), this something must at least be an existent and a substance, and so thus at least be in the similitude and image of God. *O.* But if so, a stone and all other things will be in the image of God. *R.* They too will have His image and similitude, but very remote, exiguous and confused; whereas I, to whom God in creating me has given more than to other things, am thereby the more in His image. I am not, however, here taking the word 'image' in its vulgar sense, i.e., as being the portrait or painting of something, but in the larger sense, viz., for whatever has similarity with another. And if I have made use of those words in the *Meditations,* this is because the Holy Scriptures have, here and there, spoken of our being in the image of God."

attentively directed upon myself, not only do I know that I am a thing imperfect, incomplete and dependent on what is other than myself, ever aspiring after something better and greater than myself, but I also know that He on whom I depend possesses in Himself all the great things to which I aspire, and this not indefinitely or potentially only, but really, i.e., actually and infinitely, and that He is thus God. The whole force of this argument, as thus used to prove the existence of God, consists in this, that I recognize that it is not possible that my nature should be what it is, viz., that I should have in me the idea of God, if God did not veritably exist—a God, I say, the idea of whom is in me, who possesses all those high perfections which, however they may transcend my powers of comprehension, I am yet in some fashion able to reach in thought, and who is subject to no defects. And from all this it is sufficiently evident that He cannot be a deceiver, it being manifest by the natural light that all fraud and deception proceed from defect.

But before I examine this conclusion with more care, and before passing to the consideration of other truths which can be obtained by way of it, it seems to me right to linger for a while on the contemplation of this all-perfect God, to ponder at leisure His marvelous attributes, to intuit, to admire, to adore, the incomparable beauty of this inexhaustible light, so far at least as the powers of my mind may permit, dazzled as they are by what they are endeavoring to see. For just as by faith we believe that the supreme felicity of the life to come consists in the contemplation of the Divine majesty, so do we now experience that a similar meditation, though one so much less perfect, can enable us to enjoy the highest contentment of which we are capable in this present life.

MEDITATION IV

Concerning the True and the False

IN these past days I have become so accustomed to detaching my mind from the senses, and have so convincingly noted how very little we can apprehend with certainty regarding things corporeal, how we can know much more regarding the human mind, and even more regarding God, that I shall no longer have difficulty in diverting my thought from things imageable to what, in distinction from all that is material, is purely intelligible. Certainly the idea I have of the human mind, in so far as it is a thinking thing, not extended in length, breadth or depth, and not characterized by anything that appertains to body, is incomparably more distinct than the idea of any corporeal thing. And when I consider that I doubt, that is to say that I am an incomplete and dependent thing, the idea of a being complete and independent, that is to say, of God, then presents itself to my mind with such clearness and distinctness that I can be confident that nothing more evident or more certain can be known by way of our human faculties.[44] I am so confident, owing to this alone, that the idea of God is in me, i.e., that I exist and have the idea, that I can conclude with certainty that God exists, and that my existence depends entirely on Him at every moment of my life. Already, therefore, I here seem to find a path that will lead us from this contemplation of the true God, in whom all the treasures of the sciences and of wisdom are contained, to the knowledge of the other things in the universe.

For, in the first place, I recognize that it is impossible that He should ever deceive me, since in all fraud and deception there is some element of imperfection. The power of decep-

[44] *ab humano ingenio.*

tion may indeed seem to be evidence of subtlety or power; yet unquestionably the will to deceive testifies to malice and feebleness, and accordingly cannot be found in God.

Further, I experience in myself a certain power of judging, which undoubtedly I have received from God along with all the other things I possess; and since He does not will to deceive me, it is certain that this God-given faculty cannot, if I use it aright, ever lead me astray.

As to this, no question would remain, did it not seem to follow that I can never err. For if I hold from God all that I possess, and if He has given me no faculty which is deceitful, it seems that I can never be betrayed into error. It is indeed true that when I think only of God, I am aware of nothing which can cause error or falsity. But on reverting to myself, experience at once shows that I am indeed subject to an infinity of errors, and on examining the cause of these more closely, I note that in addition to the real and positive idea of God, that is, of a Being of sovereign perfection, there is also present to me a certain negative idea, so to speak, of nothing, i.e., of what is infinitely far removed from every kind of perfection, and that I am a something intermediate between God and nothingness, that is to say, placed between sovereign Being and not-being in such fashion that while there is in truth nothing in me, in so far as I have been created by sovereign Being, which can deceive me or lead me into error, yet none the less, in so far as I likewise participate in nothingness, i.e., in not-being, in other words, in so far as I am not myself the sovereign Being, I find myself subject to innumerable imperfections, and ought not therefore to be surprised that I should be liable to error. Thus also I come to know that error, in so far as it is error, is not something real depending on God, but only a defect. To incur an error I have therefore no need of any special power assigned me by God, enabling me to do so. I fall into error because the power which God has given me of distinguishing the true from the false is not in me an infinite power.

This does not, however, entirely satisfy me. Error is not

a pure negation; it is a privation, i.e., the absence of some knowledge that I ought to possess; and on considering the nature of God, it does not seem possible that He should have given me any faculty which is not perfect of its kind, that is to say which is anywise wanting in the perfection proper to it. For if it be true that the more skilled the artisan the more perfectly accomplished is the work of his hands, how can we allow that anything produced by this sovereign Creator of all things can be other than absolutely perfect in all respects. Certainly God could have created me such that I could never be liable to error; and no less certain is it that He invariably wills what is best. Is it then better that I should be liable to error than that I should not?

On considering this more closely, what first occurs to me is that I need not be surprised if I fail to understand why God acts as He does. Nor may I doubt His existence because of my perhaps finding that there are several other things respecting which I can understand neither for what reason nor how He has created them. Already knowing, as I do, that my nature is extremely weak and limited, and that the nature of God is immense, incomprehensible and infinite, I have no difficulty in recognizing that there is an infinity of things in His power, the causes of which transcend my powers of understanding. This consideration is alone sufficient to convince me that the species of cause which we term final is not applicable in respect of physical things; for, as it seems to me, we cannot without foolhardiness inquire into and profess to discover God's inscrutable ends.

I also bethink myself that in inquiring as to whether the works of God are perfect, we should not consider any one creature separately, but the universe of things as a whole. For what, regarded by itself, might perhaps with some semblance of reason appear to be very imperfect, may none the less, when regarded as but a part of the universe, prove to be quite perfect in nature. Thus far, since my resolve has been to doubt of all things, I have as yet known with certainty only my own existence and that of God. But having also thereby come to know the infinite power of God, I am in no position to deny that He may have produced many other things, or at least that He has the power of producing them, so that the existence He has assigned me is no more than that of being a part only in the totality of things.

Consequently, on regarding myself more closely, and on examining what are my errors (for they alone testify to there being imperfection in me), I find that they depend on two concurrent causes, on my power of knowing and on the power of choice, that is, of free will—in other words, on the co-operation of the understanding and the will. For by the understanding alone, I neither affirm nor deny anything, but merely apprehend the ideas of things I can affirm or deny. Viewing the understanding thus precisely, we can say that no error is ever to be found in it. And although there may be an infinity of things in the world of which I have in my understanding no ideas, we cannot on this account say that it is deprived of those ideas as of something which its nature requires, but only that it does not have them, there being indeed no sufficient proof that God ought to have given me a greater power of knowing than He has given me. However skilled an artificer I represent Him to be, I have no reason to think of Him as bound to place in each of His works all the perfections which He can place in some of them. Nor again can I complain that God has not given me a will ample and perfect, that is, a free will. I am conscious of a will so extended as to be subject to no limits. What here, as it seems to me, is truly noteworthy, is that of all the other things which are in me, no one is so perfect and so extensive that I do not recognize it as allowing of being yet greater and more perfect. To take, for example, my faculty of understanding, I at once recognize it as being in me of small extent and extremely limited; and at the same time I frame the idea of another faculty, much more extended and even infinite; and from this alone, that I can represent the latter idea in this way [i.e., as being a faculty that is infinite],[45] I have no difficulty in likewise recognizing that it pertains to the nature of God. If in the same way I examine my memory, my imagination, or any other of my faculties, I do not find any which is not in me small and circumscribed, and in God infinite. Free will alone, that is liberty of choice, do I find to be so great in me that I can entertain no idea of any such power possibly greater, so that it is chiefly my will which enables me to know that I bear a certain image and similitude of God. The power of will is indeed incomparably greater in God than in man; the knowledge and the potency which in God are conjoined with it, render it more constant and more efficacious, and in respect of its object extend it to a greater number of things; nevertheless it does not seem to be greater, considered formally and precisely in itself [i.e., as a faculty]. The power of will consists solely in this, that we have the power to do a thing or not to do it (that is to say, to affirm or to deny, to pursue or to shun it), or rather in this alone, that in affirming or denying, pursuing or shunning, what is proposed to us by the understanding, we so act that we have no feeling of being constrained to it by any external force. For in order to be free it is not necessary that I should be indifferent in the choice between alternatives; on the contrary, the more I am inclined toward one of them, whether because I approve it as evidently good and true, or because God in this inward manner determines my inward thinking, the more freely do I choose and embrace it. Divine grace and natural knowledge, so far from diminishing liberty, augment and confirm it. The indifference of which I am aware when for want of a reason I am not carried to one side rather than to another, is the lowest grade of liberty, testifying to a lack of knowledge, i.e., to a certain negation, not to a perfection in the will. Were the true and the good always clear to me, I should never need to deliberate as to what

[45] Cf. Descartes' Reply to Burman (*A.T.* v, p. 158; Adam's edition, p. 46).

I ought to judge or choose, and I should thus be entirely free, without ever being indifferent.

All this enables me to recognize that the power of will which I have received from God is not of itself the cause of my errors; in its kind it is altogether ample and perfect. Nor is the cause of my errors traceable to my power of understanding or thinking; for since I understand nothing save by the power of understanding which God has given me, undoubtedly all that I apprehend I apprehend rightly, and it is impossible that I should be deceived regarding it. What then is the source of my errors? This alone, that the will is of wider range than the understanding, and that I do not restrain it within the same limits as the understanding, but extend it to things which I do not understand; and as the will is of itself, in respect of such things, indifferent, it is easily deflected from the true and the good, and readily falls into error and sin, choosing the evil in place of the good, or the false in place of the true.

For example, in our recent inquiry as to whether there is any existing world, finding that inasmuch as this inquiry is being made by me it manifestly follows that I myself exist, I could not but judge to be true what I thus clearly apprehend—not that I was forced to do so by any external power, but simply because the strong light of understanding was followed by a strong inclination of the will. My act of belief was thus the more spontaneous and free in proportion as I was the less indifferent in the matter. But not only do I know that I exist inasmuch as I am a thinking thing; there is likewise present to my mind a certain idea of corporeal nature, and I thereupon find myself doubting whether this thinking nature which is in me, or rather by which I am what I am, differs from this corporeal nature, or whether both are not one and the same thing. In so doing I am supposing that I do not as yet know of any reason which should persuade me to give preference to one view over the other. Certainly, in such circumstances, it is a matter of indifference to me which of the two I affirm or deny, or even as to whether I form any judgment at all on this issue.

Moreover this indifference extends not only to things regarding which the understanding has no knowledge, but in general to all those which are not known quite perspicuously[46] at the moment when the will is deliberating upon them; for however probable the conjectures which dispose me to judge in a particular manner, the very awareness that they are only conjectures, and not certain and indubitable reasons, is sufficient to impel me to judge them in the directly opposite manner. I have of late had considerable experience of this, setting aside as false all that I had hitherto unquestioningly held, and doing so for no other reason than that I had come to be aware that they could in some degree be doubted.

Now if I abstain from all judging of a thing which I do not apprehend sufficiently clearly and distinctly, it is evident that I am acting rightly and am not deceived. Should I, on the other hand, decide to deny or affirm, I am not in that case making a right use of my free will, and should I in so deciding choose the wrong alternative, it is evident that I am deceived. Even should I decide for what is true, it is by chance only that I shall be doing so, and still shall not be free from the fault of misusing my freedom. The natural light teaches us that knowledge, by way of the understanding, ought always to precede the determination of the will; and it is in the failure to do so that the privation, which constitutes the form of error, consists. Privation is then, I say, there in the act, in so far as it proceeds from me; it is not to be found in the faculty as I have it from God, nor even in the act in so far as it depends on Him [through His continued upholding of me in existence].

Nor have I any ground for complaint that God has not given me a greater power of understanding or a natural light stronger than that which He has actually given, since it is of the very nature of a finite understanding not to apprehend all things, and of a created understanding to be finite. Hav-

[46] *satis perspicue;* Fr. *avec une parfaite clarté.*

ing every reason to render thanks to God who owes me nothing, and who has yet given me all the perfections I possess, I should be far from thinking Him to have been unjust in depriving me of, or in keeping back, the other perfections which He has not given me.

Nor have I ground to complain in that He has given me a will more ample than my understanding. Since the will consists entire in one single thing, and is, so to speak, indivisible, it would appear that its nature is such that nothing can be taken from it without destroying it; and certainly the more ample it is, the more reason I have to be grateful.

Nor, finally, ought I to complain that God concurs with me in framing those [wrongful] acts of the will, that is to say, the judgments in which I suffer deception. In so far as they depend on God they are entirely true and good and my ability to form them is, in its own way, a greater perfection in me than if I were unable to do so. The privation in which alone the formal [i.e., actual] reason of error or sin consists has no need of concurrence from God since it is not a thing; and if referred to God as to its cause, it ought (in conformity with the usage of the Schools)[47] to be entitled negation, not privation. For it is not in truth an imperfection in God that He has given me the freedom of assenting or not assenting to things of which He has not placed a clear and distinct knowledge in my understanding. On the other hand, unquestionably, it is an imperfection in me that I do not use this freedom aright, rashly passing judgment on things which I apprehend only obscurely and confusedly. I recognize, indeed, that God could easily have so created me that, while still remaining free and while still with only limited knowledge, I should yet not err, viz., by endowing my understanding with a clear and distinct knowledge of all the things upon which I shall ever have to deliberate, or simply by so deeply engraving on my memory the resolution never to pass judgment on anything of which I have no clear and distinct understanding, that I shall never lose hold on that resolution.

[47] Added in French version.

And I easily understand that in so far as I consider myself alone, as if in the world there were only myself, I should have been much more perfect than I now am, had God created me in that fashion. But this does not justify me in refusing to recognize that in respect of the universe as a whole it is a greater perfection that certain of its parts should not be exempt from defect than that they should all be exactly alike. And I have, therefore, no right to complain because God, in placing me in the world, has not willed to assign me the nobler, more perfect rôle. If He has not done so by the first of the means above noted, that which would depend on my having a clear and evident knowledge of all the things upon which I may have to deliberate, at least He has left within my power the other means, viz., that of firmly adhering to the resolution never to pass judgment on things not clearly known to me. For although I am aware of a certain weakness in my nature which prevents me from continuously concentrating my mind on any one thought, I can yet by attentive and oft-repeated meditation so imprint it on my memory that I shall never fail to recall it as often as I have need of it, and so can acquire the habit of not erring.

Inasmuch as it is in this habit that the highest and chief perfection of man consists, I have, I consider, gained not a little by this day's meditation, discovering, as I have done, the cause of error and falsity. Certainly there can be no other cause than that which I have now explained; for so long as I so restrain my will within the limits of my knowledge that it frames no judgment save on things which are clearly and distinctly apprehended by the understanding, I can never be deceived. Since all clear and distinct awareness[48] is undoubtedly something, it cannot owe its origin to nothing, and must of necessity have God as its author— God, I say, who being supremely perfect, cannot be the cause of any error. Consequently, as we have to conclude, all such awareness[49] is true. Nor have I today learned merely

---

[48] *perceptio;* Fr. *conception.* Cf. above, p. 55.
[49] *ou . . . jugement,* added in French version.

what, to escape error, I should avoid, but also what I must do to arrive at knowledge of the truth. Such knowledge is assured to me provided I direct my attention sufficiently to those things which I perfectly understand, separating them from those which I apprehend only confusedly and obscurely. To this task I shall, from now on, give diligent heed.

MEDITATION V

Concerning the Essence of Material Things; and again, concerning God, that He exists

MANY other questions respecting the attributes of God, and respecting my own proper nature, that is to say, respecting my mind, remain for investigation; and perhaps, on some future occasion, I shall return to them. Meanwhile, having discovered what must be done, and what avoided, in order to arrive at the knowledge of truth, what I have now chiefly to do is to endeavor to emerge from the state of doubt into which I fell in the preceding days respecting material things, and to determine whether, with certainty, anything can be known of them.

But before inquiring as to whether any material things exist outside me, I have first to examine the ideas of them in so far as these are in my thought, and to determine which of them are distinct and which confused.

Beyond question, I image distinctly that quantity which philosophers commonly term continuous, the extension in length, breadth and depth that is in this quantity, or rather in the quantified thing to which it is attributed. Further, I can number in it many diverse parts, and attribute to each of them all sorts of sizes, shapes, locations and local motions, and to each of these motions all degrees of duration.

Not only do I know these things distinctly when considering them in general, I can also, on giving attention to them, apprehend innumerable particulars respecting shapes, number, motion and other such things, which are so evidently true and so accordant with my nature, that on beginning to discover them it does not seem to me that I am learning something new, but rather that I am recollecting what I already knew, i.e., that I am for the first time taking note of

things that were already in my mind but to which I had
not hitherto directed my attention.

What here seems to me especially noteworthy is that I
find in my mind innumerable ideas of things which, even
if they do not perhaps exist anywhere outside my thought,
yet cannot be said to be in themselves nothing. Though it
may be in my power to think or not to think them, they are
not framed by me, and possess true and immutable natures
of their own. For instance, when I image a triangle, although
there is not perhaps and never has been anywhere in the
world apart from my thought any such shape, it has yet a
certain determinate nature or essence or form which is immutable and eternal, not framed by me, and in no wise
dependent on my mind, as appears from the fact that diverse
properties can be demonstrated as belonging to the triangle,
viz., that its three angles are equal to two right angles, that
its greatest side is subtended by its greatest angle and the
like, which, whether I will or not, I now clearly recognize as
proper to it, although I had no thought whatsoever of them
when for the first time I imaged a triangle. It cannot, therefore, be said that they have been framed and invented by me.

Nor does the objection hold that perhaps this idea of the
triangle has come into my mind from external things by
way of the sense-organs, through my having seen bodies
triangularly shaped. I am in a position to think of innumerable other shapes which cannot be suspected of ever having
been objects of sense, and of which, no less than of the
triangle, I can demonstrate diverse properties, all of them
clearly apprehended and therefore assuredly true. Each of
these shapes is therefore a something, not a mere nothing; for
it is evident that everything true is something; and as I have
already shown, all those things which I know clearly and
distinctly[50] are true. And even if I had not proved this to be
so, the nature of my mind is such that I cannot but assent
to what I clearly apprehend, at least while I am so apprehending it. Always, as I recall, even while my mind was

[50] *distinctement,* added in French version.

chiefly preoccupied with the objects of sense, I recognized as being the most certain of all truths those which relate to shapes and numbers, and all else that pertains to arithmetic and geometry, and in general to pure and abstract mathematics.

Now if, directly on my being able to find an idea of something in my thought, it at once follows that whatever I clearly and distinctly apprehend as pertaining to the thing does in truth belong to it, may I not derive from this an argument for the existence of God? Certainly the idea of God, that is of a being sovereignly perfect, is no less present to me[51] than is that of any shape or number; and I know that an actual and external existence pertains to His nature no less clearly and distinctly than I know that whatever is demonstrable of a shape or number belongs to the nature of the shape or number. Even, therefore, were it the case that not all of what I have been meditating in these preceding days is true, this at least holds that the existence of God ought not to have for me a lesser degree of certainty than I have hitherto been ascribing to mathematical truths.

This, on first hearing, is not immediately evident, seeming to be a sophism. Being accustomed in all other things to distinguish between existence and essence, I readily believe that existence can also be disjoined from the essence of God, and that God can therefore be conceived as not actually existing. But on closer study, it becomes manifest to me that it is no more possible to separate existence from the essence of God than the equality of its three angles to two right angles from the essence of a triangle or the idea of a mountain from that of a valley; so that to think of God (that is, of a being completely perfect) as without existence (that is, as lacking a certain perfection) is as impossible as to think of a mountain without a valley.

[Here we encounter another objection.] Though I cannot think of God save as existing, any more than I can think of a mountain without a valley, yet just as it does not follow

[51] *apud me.*

that because I cannot think of a mountain without a valley, a mountain exists anywhere in the world, so likewise it does not follow that because I think of God as existing that He does in fact exist. My thinking imposes no necessity on things. I can image a winged horse, though there is no existing horse that has wings. May I not in similar fashion be attributing existence to God although there is no God who is existent?

This objection rests on a fallacy. Because I cannot think of a mountain without a valley, it does not indeed follow that there is any mountain or valley in existence, but only that mountain and valley, be they existent or non-existent, are inseparably conjoined each with the other. In the case of God, however, I cannot think Him save as existing; and it therefore follows that existence is inseparable from Him, and that He therefore really exists. It is not that this necessity is brought about by my thought, or that my thought is imposing any necessity on things; on the contrary, the necessity which lies in the thing itself, that is the necessity of God's existence, determines me to think in this way. It is not in my power to think God as lacking existence (i.e., to think of this sovereignly perfect being as devoid of complete perfection) in the manner in which I am free to image a horse with wings or without wings.

Nor may it be objected that though it is indeed necessary to grant that God exists, provided the supposition has antecedently been made that God possesses all perfections and that existence is itself one of these perfections, the supposition is not in fact itself necessary. If we start by supposing that all quadrilateral shapes are inscribable in the circle, we have to grant that the rhombus can be so inscribed, a conclusion manifestly false. [But the two suppositions are very different in character.] It is not indeed necessary that I should at any time be dwelling on the idea of God. None the less, as often as I may be concerned to entertain the thought of first and sovereign being, summoning this idea from the treasure-house of my mind, I must necessarily attribute all perfections to Him, although I may not then enumerate all of them, nor direct my attention to any one of them separately. And as soon as I take notice that existence is a perfection, I am thereby constrained to conclude that this first sovereign being truly exists—just as while it is not at any time necessary for me to be imaging a triangle, yet whenever I wish to consider a rectilinear figure having only three sides, I have no option save to attribute to it all those properties from which it is rightly concluded that its three angles are not greater than two right angles, even although I may not then be taking note of this particular consequence. Now this does not hold in the case of the rhombus-assumption above cited. For when I consider which shapes are capable of being inscribed in the circle, it is in no wise necessary to hold that all quadrilateral shapes are of this number; on the contrary, I cannot even pretend this to be the case, so long as I decline to accept anything save what I clearly and distinctly apprehend. Consequently there is a great difference between false suppositions of this kind and the true ideas which are born with me,[52] the first and chief of which is the idea of God. For, as I note, there are many respects in which this idea is not fictitious, as depending merely on my thought, but is the image[53] of a true and immutable nature; first, in that I cannot think of anything, save God alone, to the very essence of which existence pertains; secondly, in that I cannot entertain the thought of there being two or more Gods of this kind, and that, granted one such God exists, it is evident to me that He must necessarily have existed from all eternity and will exist to all eternity; and finally, in that I apprehend many other properties in God, no one of which I can either diminish or change.

Thus, whatever proof or mode of argument I may adopt, it always comes back to this, that it is only the things I apprehend clearly and distinctly which have the power to convince me. And although among the things which I apprehend in this manner some are indeed obvious to everyone,

[52] mihi ingenitas; Fr. nées avec moi.
[53] imaginem.

others are manifest only to those who consider them more closely, scrutinizing them earnestly. Once they have been discovered, they are, however, not esteemed any less certain than those others. To take, as an example, the right-angled triangle: that the square of the base is equal to the squares of the other two sides is not at first as manifest to us as that the base lies opposite the greatest angle; yet once it has been apprehended we are not less certain of its truth. As regards God, if my mind were not overlaid by so many prejudices, and beset on all sides by the images of sensible things, I should know nothing prior to knowing Him and nothing more easily. For is there anything more evident than that there is a God, that is to say, a sovereign being, and that of all beings He alone has existence as appertaining to His essence? For a proper grasp of this truth close attention has indeed been required. Now, however, I am as completely assured of it as of all that I hold most certain; and now also I have come to recognize that so absolutely dependent on it are all those other certainties, that save through knowledge of it nothing whatsoever can be perfectly known.

But while my nature is such that I cannot but accept as true all that I apprehend in a really clear and distinct manner, it is also such that I am unable to keep my mind always fixed on one and the same object. Often I have occasion to recall having judged a thing to be true without at the same time being aware of the reasons that determined me in so doing; and it may happen meanwhile that other reasons are presented to me—such as would readily cause me to change my opinion, were I ignorant that there is a God. I should then have no true and certain knowledge of anything; but only vague and vacillating opinions. When for instance I consider the nature of the triangle, instructed, as I have been, in the principles of geometry, it is quite evident to me that its three angles are equal to two right angles; and so long as I attend to the demonstrations I cannot but believe this to be true. None the less, as soon as I cease to attend to the demonstration, and although I may still recollect having had a clear comprehension of it, I may readily come to doubt its truth, if I do not know that there is a God. For I can then persuade myself of being so constituted by nature as to be easily deceived even in those things which I believe myself to apprehend in the most evident manner, especially when I recollect that frequently I have held to be true and certain what afterwards other reasons have constrained me to reckon as false.

But once I have recognized that there is a God, and that all things depend on Him and that He is not a deceiver, and from this, in turn, have inferred that all things which I clearly and distinctly apprehend are of necessity true, then, even although I may no longer be attending to the reasons on account of which I have judged this to be so (provided only I bear in mind that I once recognized them clearly and distinctly), no contrary reason can be brought forward sufficient to lead me to doubt it; and the knowledge I have of it is thus true and certain. Such knowledge extends, in similar fashion, to all the other things I remember as having been at any time demonstrated, the truths of geometry and the like. For what can now be brought against them, to lead me to doubt them? Will it be urged that in the past my nature was such as often to be deceived? But I now know that I cannot be deceived in the things which I know in a perspicuous manner. Will it be said that I have formerly held as true and certain what afterwards I have discovered to be false? But I was then having no clear and distinct apprehension of them, and having as yet no knowledge of the rule by following which I am assured of truth, I readily yielded assent on grounds which I have since discovered to be less strong than I then supposed them to be. What further objection is there? Will it be said that perhaps I am dreaming (an objection I myself raised a little while ago), that is, that all the thoughts I am now entertaining are no more true than those which come to me in dreams? Even so, what difference would that make? For even should I be asleep and dreaming, whatever is present to my understanding in an evident manner is indisputably true.

Thus, in this evident manner, I see that the certainty and truth of all knowledge depends on knowledge of the true God, and that before I knew Him I could have no perfect knowledge of any other thing. And now that I know Him, I have the means of acquiring a perfect knowledge of innumerable things, not only in respect of God Himself and other intelligible things, but also in respect of that corporeal nature which is the object of pure mathematics.

MEDITATION VI

*Concerning the Existence of Material Things and the
Real Distinction between the Mind and Body of Man*

THERE now remains only the inquiry as to whether material
things exist. This at least I already know, that in so far as
they are dealt with by pure mathematics, they are possible
existents, since, as there treated, they are apprehended clearly
and distinctly. Indubitably God possesses the power of producing everything that I am capable of apprehending distinctly; and I have never considered anything to be impossible to Him save what I found to be impossible of distinct
apprehension. Further, the faculty of imagination, of which,
as experience tells me, I make use when I apply myself to the
consideration of material things, is able to persuade me of
their existence; for when I attentively consider what imagination is, I find that it is nothing but a certain application of
the cognitive faculty to a body which is immediately present
to it and therefore existent.

To make this plain, I shall first dwell on the difference
there is between the imagination and pure intellection. For
instance, when I image a triangle I not only apprehend
it to be a shape bounded by three lines, but also by concentrating my attention on these three lines I intuit them as
present, this being what I term imaging. When, however, I
wish to think of a chiliagon, I do indeed apprehend it to be
a shape composed of a thousand sides, and do so just as
easily as in apprehending a triangle to be composed of three
sides only. I cannot, however, image the thousand sides of
a chiliagon as I do the three sides of a triangle, nor intuit
them as present, as it were, with the eyes of the mind.[54]

[54] *tanquam praesentia intueor;* Fr. *les regarder comme présents
avec les yeux de mon esprit.*

And although in accordance with the habit I have of always imaging something when I think of corporeal things, it may happen that I confusedly represent to myself some shape, it is yet evident that this shape is not a chiliagon, since it in no wise differs from what I represent to myself when I think of a myriagon or any other shape of many sides, nor would it be of any use in determining the properties distinguishing a chiliagon from those other polygons. If, however, it be a pentagon which is under question, while I can indeed, as in the case of the chiliagon, apprehend its shape without the aid of the imagination, I am able also to image it, applying my mind attentively to each of its five sides and the area they enclose. Now in thus imaging its shape, I am plainly aware of having to make a certain special effort of the mind, an effort not required in merely thinking of it; and this special effort of the mind makes clear to me the difference there is between imagination and pure intellection.

Therewith I also note that this power of imaging which is in me, in so far as it differs from the power of understanding, is no wise necessary to my essential being, that is to say, to the essence of my mind. For even if I did not have it, I should undoubtedly none the less remain the same as I now am; and from this, it seems, we may conclude that my power of imaging depends on something different from me, i.e., from my mind.[55] And I easily understand that if there exists some body to which the mind is so united that it is able, when it pleases, to apply itself to it, i.e., as it were, to contemplate it,[56] it may in this way be able to image

[55] *a me;* Fr. *de mon esprit.*

[56] *sit ita conjuncta ut ad illud veluti inspiciendum pro arbitrio se applicet.* On Burman's asking in what *inspicere* consists, Descartes replies: "This *inspicere* is a particular mode of thinking, which takes place thus. When external objects act on our senses and trace there an idea or rather an image [*ideam seu potius figuram*] of themselves, and when the mind turns toward [*advertit*] these images [*ad eas imagines*] thus traced in the small gland, it is said to be *sensing.* When these images are traced in the small gland not by the external objects, but by the mind itself, which in the absence of the external objects

corporeal things. If this be so, this mode of thinking differs from pure intellection solely in this, that the mind, in intellection, is turning in some way in upon itself, taking note of some one of the ideas which it possesses in itself, whereas when imaging it is turning itself toward the body and is intuiting in it something conformed to the idea which it has formed for itself or has apprehended by way of the senses. Now if it be the case that body exists, I can, I say, easily understand that the imaging may be carried out in this manner.[57] There is indeed no other way equally convincing of accounting for it; and for this reason I conjecture that body probably does exist. The conjecture [as thus arrived at] is, however, probable only. For however careful and comprehensive my inquiries may be, I nevertheless do not find

represents or forms them in the brain (*eas in cerebro effingit et format*), it is said to be *imaging*. Thus the difference between imagination and sense consists simply in this, that in the one the images are traced [in the pineal gland] by external objects then present to it, while in the other they are traced [in the pineal gland] by the mind in the absence of the external objects, and as it were, with all windows closed" (*A.T.* v, p. 162; Adam's edition, pp. 64-65).

[57] To Gassendi's objection that if the images are to be thus taken as being corporeal, with parts outside of other parts, and therefore as extended, they cannot be received into the self which is unextended, Descartes replies: "Here you ask *how I think that I, an unextended subject, can receive into myself the species or idea of a body which is extended.* I reply that no corporeal species can be received into the mind; in the case of things corporeal no less than in the case of things incorporeal what can alone be received into the mind is a pure intellection [i.e., an act of cognitive awareness, which, even when directed upon the corporeal, is not itself corporeal] without any corporeal species. But as to the imagination, which can be exercised only in respect of corporeal things, there is indeed need of a species which is truly corporeal (*verum corpus*) and to which the mind applies itself, without, however, its being received into the mind. . . . Though the mind is united to the whole body, it does not thence follow that it itself is extended throughout the body, for it is not part of its notion to be extended, but only to think. Neither does it apprehend extension by means of an extended species existing in it, although it images it by applying itself [*convertendo se*] to a corporeal species which is extended, as has already been said" (*A.T.* vii, pp. 387-89; Haldane and Ross, ii, pp. 231-32).

that even from what is distinct in the idea I have of corporeal nature by way of these imagings, any argument can be obtained which justifies my concluding, in a necessary manner, the existence of any body.

Now I am accustomed to image many other things besides that corporeal nature which is the object of pure mathematics, viz., colors, sounds, tastes, pain and the like, though none of them so distinctly. And inasmuch as I apprehend them much better by way of the senses (by the mediation of which and of memory they seem to have reached the imagination), it is proper that, for the more convenient examination of them, I should likewise examine the nature of sense and inquire whether from those ideas which are apprehended by this mode of thinking—the mode which I entitle sensing—I can obtain any certain proof of the existence of corporeal things.

First, I shall recall to mind the things which, as having been sensed, I have hitherto held to be true, and what my grounds were for so regarding them. Secondly, I shall then examine the reasons which afterwards led me to doubt of them. And finally, I shall consider what I ought now to believe in regard to them.

From the start, then, I have sensed myself as having a head, hands, feet and the other members of which this body —a body I considered to be part of myself, and possibly even the whole of myself—is composed. I also sensed this body as being located among other bodies by which it could be affected in many ways, beneficial or harmful, being made aware of what was beneficial by a certain sensation of pleasure and of what was harmful by a sensation of pain. In addition to pleasure and pain, I was aware in myself of hunger, thirst, and other such appetites, as also of certain corporeal inclinations to joy, sorrow, anger, and other such affections. On the other hand, as foreign to myself, I sensed, besides the extension, shapes and movements of bodies, also their hardness, heat and other tactual qualities, and in addition, light, colors, odors, tastes and sounds, the variety of which enabled me to distinguish from one another the sky, the Earth, the sea, and all the other bodies.

Assuredly, since the ideas of all these qualities were claiming my attention, and since it was they alone that I properly and immediately sensed, it was not without reason that I thought I was sensing certain things plainly different from my thinking, namely, bodies from which those ideas proceeded. For as experience showed me, they presented themselves to me without my consent being required, and in such fashion that I could not sense any object, however I might wish to do so, save on its being present to the sense-organ, and was unable not to sense it when it was present.

Further, since the ideas I received by way of the senses were much more lively, better defined, and even in their way more distinct, than any of those which I could deliberately and knowingly frame for myself, it seemed impossible that they could have proceeded from myself; and it followed, therefore, that they must have been caused in me by other things. Having no information regarding these things beyond what these same ideas gave me, the only supposition that could then commend itself to me was that they resemble the ideas. And because I likewise recalled that formerly I had relied more on the senses than on reason, and had observed that the ideas which I framed for myself were not so well defined as those which I apprehended by way of sense, and were for the most part composed of parts of those latter, I was readily persuaded that I had not in my understanding any idea not previously sensed.

Nor was it without reason that I regarded the body, which by a certain special right I called my own, as belonging to me more closely than any other. I could never, indeed, be separated from it as from other bodies; I felt in it, and on account of it, all my passions and all my affections; I was aware of pain and the titillation of pleasure in its parts, and not in the parts of the other bodies located outside it.

When, however, I inquired why from some—I know not

what—sensing of pain a certain sadness of mind follows, and a certain joy on the sensing of pleasure, or why that strange twitching of the stomach which I call hunger should put me in mind of taking food, and dryness of throat of drinking, I could, as in other experiences of this kind, give no reason, save that I am so taught by nature. For assuredly there is no affinity, none at least that I can understand, between this twitching of the stomach and the desire to eat, any more than between the sensing of a thing which causes pain and the thought of sadness which springs from this sensing. And in the same way, it seemed to me, all the other judgments which I was accustomed to pass on the objects of sense had been taught me by nature. For I observed that they were formed in me before I had the leisure to weigh and consider any reasons which might oblige me to make them.

In due course, however, numerous experiences by degrees sapped the faith I had thus reposed in the senses. As I from time to time observed, towers which from afar seemed round on closer view appeared square, colossal statues erected on the summits of these towers appeared small when similarly viewed from below. In innumerable other instances I similarly found the judgments which concerned the things of the external senses to be erroneous: nor indeed only those based on the external senses, but those also which are based on the internal senses. What can be more internal than pain? Yet I have been assured by men whose arm or leg has been amputated, that it still seemed to them that they occasionally felt pain in the limb they had lost—thus giving me ground to think that I could not be quite certain that a pain I endured was indeed due to the limb in which I seemed to feel it.

To these grounds of doubt I have lately added two others of the widest generality. The first of these was that there is nothing of all that I believed myself to be sensing when awake which I cannot think of as being also sometimes sensed during sleep; and since I do not believe that the things I seem to sense in dreams come to me from things located outside me, I no longer found any ground for believing this of the things I seem to sense while awake. Secondly, since I was still ignorant of the Author of my being, or rather was feigning myself to be so, I saw nothing to prevent my being so constituted by nature that I might be deceived even in those things which appeared to me to be unquestionably true.

As to the grounds on which I had before been persuaded of the truth of these things, I had no difficulty in countering them. For inasmuch as I seem to be inclined by nature to many things from which reason was dissuading me, I considered that I ought not to place much confidence in its teaching; and though my sensuous apprehensions do not depend on my will, I did not think that I ought on this ground to conclude that they proceed from things other than myself. There can perhaps exist in me some faculty hitherto unknown to me, which produces them.

Now that I begin to know myself better and to discover the Author of my being, I do not in truth think that I ought rashly to admit all the things which the senses may seem to teach; but neither do I think that they should all be called in doubt.

In the first place, since I know that all the things I clearly and distinctly apprehend can be created by God exactly as I apprehend them, my being able to apprehend one thing apart from another is, in itself, sufficient to make me certain that the one is different from the other, or at least that it is within God's power to posit them separately; and even though I do not comprehend by what power this separation comes about, I shall have no option but to view them as different. Accordingly, simply from knowing that I exist, and that, meantime, I do not observe any other thing as evidently pertaining to my nature, i.e., to my essence, except this only, that I am a thinking thing, I rightly conclude that my essence consists in this alone, that I am a thinking thing (i.e., a substance, the whole nature or essence of which consists in thinking).[58] And although possibly (or rather certainly, as I shall shortly be declaring) I have a body with which I am very closely conjoined, yet since on the one hand I have a clear and distinct idea of myself, in so far as I am only a thinking unextended thing, and on the other hand a distinct idea of the body, in so far as it is only an extended unthinking thing, it is certain that I am truly distinct from my body, and can exist without it.[59]

I further find in myself faculties of thinking which are quite special modes of thinking, distinct from myself, viz., the faculties of imaging and sensing; I can clearly and distinctly apprehend myself as complete without them, but not them without the self, i.e., without an intelligent substance in which they reside. For in the notion we have of them, or (to use the terms of the Schools)[60] in their formal concept, they include some sort of intellection, and I am thereby enabled to recognize that they are at once related to, and distinguished from, the self, as being its modes (just as shapes, movements, and the other modes and accidents of bodies are in respect of the bodies which uphold them).[61]

I am also aware in me[62] of certain faculties, such as the power of changing location, of assuming diverse postures, and the like, which cannot be thought, and cannot therefore exist, any more than can the preceding, apart from some substance in which they reside. But evidently, since the clear and distinct apprehension of these faculties involves the feature of extension, but not any intellection, they must, if they indeed exist, belong to some substance which is corporeal, i.e., extended and unthinking. Now there is, indeed, a certain passive faculty of sense, i.e., of receiving and knowing the ideas of sensible things, but this would be useless to me if there did not also exist in me, or in some other

[58] This explanatory clause added in French version.

[59] I.e., should God so provide.

[60] Added, as required in the French version.

[61] Parenthesis added in French version.

[62] *en moi*, added in French version, the "I" being taken as including the body.

being, an active faculty capable of producing or effecting these ideas. This active faculty cannot, however, be in me —not at least in so far as I am only a thinking thing[63]—since it does not presuppose intellection, and since the ideas present themselves to me without my contributing in any way to their so doing, and often even against my will. This faculty must therefore exist in some substance different from me—a substance that, as already noted, contains, either formally or eminently, all the reality which is objectively [i.e., by way of representation] in the ideas produced by the faculty, and this substance is either body, i.e., corporeal nature, in which there is contained formally, i.e., actually,[64] all that is objectively, i.e., by representation,[65] in those ideas; or it is God Himself, or some creature nobler than body, in which all of it is eminently contained.

But since God is no deceiver, it is evident that He does not of Himself, and immediately, communicate those ideas to me. Nor does He do so by way of some creature in which their objective reality is not contained formally [i.e., actually], but only eminently. For as He has given me no faculty whereby I could discover this to be the case, but on the contrary a very strong inclination to believe that those ideas are conveyed to me by corporeal things, I do not see how He could be defended against the charge of deception, were the ideas produced otherwise than by corporeal things. We have, therefore, no option save to conclude that corporeal things do indeed exist.

Yet they are not perhaps exactly such as we apprehend by way of the senses; in many instances they are apprehended only obscurely and confusedly. But we must at least admit that whatever I there clearly and distinctly apprehend, i.e., generally speaking, everything comprised in the object of pure mathematics, is to be found in them. As re-

[63] Parenthesis added in French version.
[64] *et en effet,* added in French version.
[65] *et par représentation,* added in French version.

gards those other things which are only particular, such as
that the Sun is of this or that magnitude and shape, and
the like, or as regards those things which are apprehended
less clearly,[66] such as light, sound, pain and the like, however dubious and uncertain all of these may be, yet inasmuch
as God is no deceiver and that there cannot therefore, in the
opinions I form, be any falsity for the correction of which
He has not given me some faculty sufficient thereto, I may,
I believe, confidently conclude that in regard to these things
also the means of avoiding error are at my disposal.

Thus there can be no question that all those things in which
I am instructed by nature contain some truth; for by nature,
considered in general, I now understand no other than either
God Himself or the order of created things as instituted by
Him, and by my nature in particular I understand the to-
tality[67] of all those things which God has given me.

Now there is nothing which nature teaches me more
expressly, or more sensibly,[68] than that I have a body which
is adversely affected when I sense pain, and stands in need
of food and drink when I suffer hunger or thirst, etc.; and
consequently I ought not to doubt there being some truth
in all this.

Nature also teaches me by these sensings of pain, hunger,
thirst, etc., that I am not lodged in my body merely as a
pilot in a ship, but so intimately conjoined, and as it were
intermingled with it, that with it I form a unitary whole.[69]
Were not this the case, I should not sense pain when my
body is hurt, being, as I should then be, merely a thinking
thing, but should apprehend the wound in a purely cognitive
manner,[70] just as a sailor apprehends by sight any damage

[66] *et moins distinctement,* added in French version.
[67] *complexionem.*
[68] *ni plus sensiblement,* added in French version.
[69] *illi arctissime esse conjunctum et quasi permixtum adeo ut
unum quid cum illo componam;* Fr. *très étroitement et tellement con-
fondu et mêlé que je compose comme un seul tout avec lui.*
[70] *puro intellectu.*

to his ship; and when my body has need of food and drink I should apprehend this expressly, and not be made aware of it by confused sensings of hunger, thirst, pain, etc. For these sensings of hunger, thirst, pain, etc., are in truth merely confused modes of thinking, arising from and dependent on the union, and, as it were, the intermingling of mind and body.

Besides this, nature teaches me that my body exists as one among other bodies, some of which are to be sought after and others shunned. And certainly on sensing colors, sounds, odors, tastes, heat, hardness and the like, I rightly conclude that in the bodies from which these various sensory apprehensions proceed, there are variations corresponding to them, though not perhaps resembling them; and since among these sense-apprehensions some are pleasing to me, and others displeasing, there can be no doubt that my body, or rather my entire self, inasmuch as I am composed of body and mind, can be variously affected, beneficially or harmfully, by surrounding bodies.

Many other things, however, that may seem to have been taught me by nature, are not learned from her, but have gained a footing in my mind only through a certain habit I have of judging inconsiderately. Consequently, as easily happens, the judgments I pass are erroneous: for example in the judgment that all space in which there is nothing capable of affecting my senses is a vacuum, that in a hot body there is something similar to the idea of heat which is in my mind, that in a white or green body there is the very whiteness or greenness which I am sensing, that in a bitter or sweet body there are these very tastes, and so in other like instances; that the stars, towers and other distant objects are of the sizes and shapes they exhibit to my eyes, etc.

In order, however, that there may in this regard be no lack of distinctness of apprehension, I must define more accurately what I ought to mean, when I speak of being taught by nature. Nature I am here taking in a more re-

stricted[71] sense than when it signifies the totality of all that
God has given me. Many things included in that totality
belong to the mind alone, e.g., the notion I have of the truth
that what has once taken place can no longer not have taken
place, and all those other truths which are known by the
natural light, without the aid of the body;[72] of these latter I
am not here speaking. The term nature likewise extends to
many things which pertain only to body, such as its
having weight, and the like, and with these also I am not
here dealing, but only with what God has given me as a
being composed of body as well as of mind. Nature, taken
in this special [restricted] sense, does indeed teach me to
shun whatever causes me to sense pain, or to pursue what
causes me to sense pleasure, and other things of that sort;
but I do not find that it teaches me, by way of sensory
apprehensions, that we should, without previous careful and
mature mental examination of them, likewise draw conclusions regarding things located in the world outside us; for,
as would seem, it is the task of the mind alone, not of the
composite mind-body, to discern truth in questions of this
kind.

Thus, although the impression a star makes on my eye
is no larger than that made by the flame of a small candle,
there is yet in me no real or positive power determining me
to believe that the star is no larger than the flame; it is
merely that, without reason, I have so judged from my
earliest years. And though on approaching fire I sense heat,
and on approaching it too closely I sense pain, this is no
ground for concluding that something resembling the heat
is in the fire and also something resembling the pain, but
only that in it there is something, whatever it be, which
produces in me these sensations of heat and pain.

71 E.g., than when speaking of the "natural light of reason," which
belongs to mind even apart from the body, i.e., more restricted because referring only to what God has given me in virtue of my being
composed of body as well as of mind.

72 *sans l'aide du corps,* added in French version.

So also, although there are spaces in which I find nothing to affect my senses, it does not follow that in them there is no body, for in this, as in many other matters, I have been accustomed to pervert the order of nature. These sensuous apprehensions have been given me by nature only as testifying to my mind what things are beneficial or harmful to the composite whole of which it is a part. For this they are indeed sufficiently clear and distinct. But what I have done is to use them as rules sufficiently reliable to be employed in the immediate determination of the *essence*[73] of bodies external to me; and, as so employed, their testimony cannot be other than obscure and confused.

I have already sufficiently examined how it happens that, notwithstanding the sovereign goodness of God, falsity has to be recognized as occurring in judgments of this kind. Here, however, a difficulty presents itself respecting the things which I am taught by nature to seek or to avoid, and also respecting the internal sensations in which I seem sometimes to have detected error.[74] Thus, for instance, the agreeable taste of some food into which poison has been introduced may induce me to swallow the poison, and so serve to deceive me. In this instance, however, nature is impelling me to seek only that which is sweet-tasting, not the poison which is unknown to me; and all I can conclude from this is that I am not omniscient—in which there is no reason for surprise. Man's nature is finite, and his knowledge is therefore correspondingly limited.

But even in that to which nature itself directly impels us, we not infrequently err, as when the sick desire to drink and eat what would prove harmful to them. It will perhaps be said that the reason of the error is that their nature has been corrupted. That, however, does not remove the difficulty: the sick man is no less truly God's creature than when in health; and it is therefore no less repugnant to God's

[73] Italics not in text.
[74] *et ainsi que je suis directement trompé par ma nature,* added in French version.

goodness that the sick man's nature should be thus deceptive. A clock composed of wheels and counterweights observes all the laws of nature no less accurately when it is ill-constructed and shows the hours incorrectly, than when it fulfills the purposes of its maker in every respect. In similar fashion, if the body of a man be considered as a kind of machine, so built and composed of bones, nerves, muscles, veins, blood and skin, that even were there in it no mind, it would still have all the motions it now has, with the exception only of those which, as being exercised by order of the will, depend on the mind, I readily recognize that it would be as natural to this body, supposing it to be, for example, dropsical, to suffer that dryness of the throat which is wont to suggest to the mind the sensation of thirst, and so to be disposed by this dryness to move the nerves and other parts in the way that leads to the drinking and thereby to the worsening of its malady, and to do so no less naturally than when, there being no such malady, it is by a similar dryness of the throat moved to drink in furtherance of its well-being. In view of the use for which the clock was designed by its maker, I can indeed say that it is deflected from its proper nature when it thus shows the hours incorrectly; and in the same manner, if I view the machine of the human body as having been framed by God for the motions which ordinarily occur in it, I may recognize that it, too, is departing from its nature when, though the throat be dry, drinking is yet not contributory to its well-being. None the less I recognize that this last manner of understanding the term nature is very different from the other; it is a merely external denomination, depending on my manner of mentally comparing a sick man and an ill-constructed clock with the idea I have of a healthy man and a well-made clock, which signifies nothing to be found in the things of which it speaks; whereas the term nature, according to the other manner of understanding, signifies something veritably found in the things, and which is therefore not without some truth.

But although in respect of a body suffering from dropsy,

it is indeed only in this conventional manner that we can speak of its nature as being corrupt (not being in any need of drink, and the throat being yet parched), none the less in respect of the composite whole, i.e., of the mind in its union with such a body, we have here what is more than merely a manner of speaking; it is a veritable error of [our] nature that it should thus thirst when drink would be harmful to it. And accordingly we have still to inquire why it is that the goodness of God does not prevent [our] nature,[75] i.e., nature as understood in this latter manner, from being deceptive.

In this inquiry, what I first note is the great difference between mind and body, in that body, from its very nature, is always divisible, and mind altogether indivisible. For truly, when I consider the mind, that is to say, my self in so far only as I am a thinking thing, I can distinguish in myself no parts; I apprehend myself to be a thing single and entire. Although the whole mind may seem to be united to the whole body, yet if a foot, an arm, or any other part of the body, is cut off, I know that my mind is not thereby diminished. Nor can its faculties of willing, sensing, understanding, etc., be spoken of as being its parts; it is one and the same mind which wills, which senses, which understands. The opposite holds in respect of a corporeal, i.e., of an extended, thing. I cannot think of it save as readily divisible into parts, and therefore recognize it as being divisible. This, of itself, would suffice to convince me that the mind is altogether different from the body, even if I had not already so decided on other grounds.

In the next place, I take note that the mind is immediately affected, not by all parts of the body, but only by the brain, or rather perhaps only by one small part of it, viz., by that part in which the *sensus communis* is said to be. This part, as often as it is affected in the same way, exhibits always one and the same impression to the mind, although the other parts of the body may meantime have become otherwise

[75] In French version, *la nature de l'homme.*

disposed, as is proved by innumerable experiences on which
there is here no need to dwell.

I further note that the nature of body is such that no one
of its parts can be moved by another a little way distant
from it which cannot be moved in the same manner by
any one of the parts that lie between those two, even though
the more remote part be not then acting. As, for instance,
if the cord, A, B, C, D, be held taut, and its last part, D, be
pulled, its first part will not be moved in a different way from
how it would be were one of the intermediate parts, B or C,
pulled—the last part, D, meanwhile remaining unmoved.
So, too, on my sensing pain in my foot; the science of
physics teaches me that this sensation is generated by way
of nerves dispersed over the foot and extending, like cords,
from it to the brain, and that when they are pulled in the
foot, they pull those inmost parts of the brain in which they
terminate, thereby exciting in them a certain motion which
nature has instituted to enable the mind to sense pain as
if it were in the foot. But since these nerves, in order to
reach from the foot to the brain, have to pass through the
tibia, the leg, the loins, the back and neck, it may happen
that, although their extremities in the foot are not affected,
but only certain of their intermediate parts, in the loins or
neck, the motion excited in the brain will be the same as
would have been caused by an injury to the foot, and the
mind will then necessarily sense pain in the foot just as if
the foot had indeed been hurt. This also holds in respect of
all our other senses.

Finally, I note that each of the motions that occur in
the part of the brain by which the mind is immediately
affected gives rise always to one and the same sensation, and
likewise note that we cannot wish for or imagine any better
arrangement. The sensation which is thus caused is, of all
the sensations which the motion might conceivably cause,
the one best fitted and most generally useful for the conservation of the human body when in full health. Now
experience shows that all our senses are thus constituted;

and in them, therefore, there is nothing which does not testify to the power and goodness of God.

When, for example, the nerves of the foot are violently moved, in an unusual manner, the motion, passing through the medulla of the spine to the innermost parts of the brain, gives a sign to it as to what it should sense, viz., pain as though in the foot, whereby the mind is incited to do all it can to avert what is causing the injury.

God could indeed have so constituted the nature of man that this same motion in the brain should have exhibited to the mind something different; there might, for example, have been exhibited to us the motion itself, in the mode in which it exists in the brain, or in so far as it is in the foot or in some intermediate place between them—in short, something, whatever it be, other than that which we do experience. But of all these [conceivable] alternatives, there is none which would have more effectively contributed to the conservation of the body.

Similarly, when we have need of drink, there is a certain dryness of the throat which moves the nerves of the throat and by way of this the internal parts of the brain, and this motion, in turn, affects the mind with the sensation of thirst, there being nothing in all these happenings which it is more useful for us to know than that we have need of drink for the preservation of our health; and so in other like instances.

In view of these considerations, it is manifest that, notwithstanding the sovereign goodness of God, the nature of man, in so far as it is a composite of mind and body, must sometimes be at fault and deceptive. For should some cause, not in the foot, but in another part of the nerves that extend from the foot to the brain, or even in the brain itself, give rise to the motion ordinarily excited when the foot is injuriously affected, pain will be felt just as though it were in the foot, and thus naturally the sense will be deceived; for since the same motion in the brain cannot but give rise in the mind always to the same sensation, and since this sensation is much more frequently due to a cause that is injurious to the foot than by one acting in another quarter, it is reasonable that it should convey to the mind pain as in the foot, rather than as in any other part. And if it sometimes happens that dryness of the throat is not due to this being required for the health of the body but to a quite different cause, as in the case of the dropsical, it is much better that it should then be deceptive than that it should, while the body is well-disposed, be all the time failing us; and so likewise in other cases.

And certainly, this consideration is of the greatest help in enabling me not only to recognize all the errors to which my nature is subject, but also in making it easier for me to avoid or to amend them. For in knowing that in respect of those things which concern the well-being of the body, all my senses more frequently indicate the true than the false, and being able almost always to avail myself of more than one sense in the examining of any one thing, and being able also to make use of my memory for the connecting of the present with the past, and of my understanding for the reviewing (as already done) of all the causes of error, I ought no longer to fear that the things ordinarily exhibited to me by sense are false. I ought indeed to reject as hyperbolical and ridiculous all the doubts of these past days, more especially that regarding sleep, as being indistinguishable from the waking state. How marked, I now find, is the difference between them! Our memory can never connect our dreams with one another and with the whole course of our lives, in the manner in which we are wont to connect the things which happen to us while awake. If, while I am awake, someone should all of a sudden appear to me, and as suddenly disappear, as happens in dreams, and in such fashion that I could not know whence he came or whither he went, quite certainly it would not be unreasonable to esteem it a specter, that is, a phantom formed in my brain, rather than a real man. When, on the other hand, in apprehending things, I know the place whence they have come, and that in which they are, and the time at which they present themselves to me, and while doing so can connect them, unin-terruptedly, with the course of my life as a whole, I am completely certain that what I thus experience is taking place while I am awake, and not in dreams. And if after having summoned to my aid all my senses, my memory and my understanding, in scrutiny of these occurrences, I find that none of them presents me with what is at variance with any other, I ought no longer to entertain the least doubt as to their truth. God being no deceiver, it cannot be that I am here being misled.

But since the necessities of active living do not always allow of the delay required for so accurate a scrutiny, it must be confessed that the life of man is, in respect of this and that particular, frequently subject to error, and that we have thus to acknowledge the weakness of our nature.

[FINIS]

LETTERS ON THE MIND-BODY PROBLEM,[1] TO REGIUS, TO PRINCESS ELIZABETH, AND TO ARNAULD; AND *REPLIES TO THE SIXTH OBJECTIONS*

[The chief document is the second of the two letters to Princess Elizabeth. But in view of the difficult character of Descartes' teaching and the brevity with which he has expounded it, we cannot afford to ignore his other relevant utterances, and may take first his letter to Regius.]

LETTER TO REGIUS[2]

[Datable as of mid-December, 1641]

YOU could hardly have maintained in your thesis anything harder, or more likely to give great occasion for offense and complaint than this: *quod homo [totus ex corpore et anima]*[3] *sit ens per accidens*: nor do I see how it could be better amended than by your saying that in the ninth thesis you have considered *totum hominem in ordine ad partes ex quibus componitur,* and that in the tenth thesis you have conversely considered *partes in ordine ad totum.* Thus, though in the ninth you have indeed said that *hominem ex corpore et anima fieri per accidens,* you have done so in order that you may signify that in a certain sense the conjunction of the soul with the body can be said to be accidental to the body, and the conjunction of the soul with the body accidental to the

---

[1] Cf. the important passages in *Meditation* VI, above, pp. 231, 234, 239-40.

[2] *A.T.* iii, pp. 460-61.

[3] On Descartes' use of the terms *anima* and *mens, l'âme* and *l'esprit,* cf. above, note to p. 119.

mind, since body can exist without soul and soul without body. For we entitle "accident" everything which can be present or absent without destruction of its subject, although, when regarded in itself, it may be a substance, as in the case of a man's clothing, which is accidental to the man. None the less, you have not thereby said *hominem esse ens per accidens;* and in the tenth thesis you have sufficiently shown that you understand man to be *ens per se.* For there you have said that soul and body, *ratione ipsius,* are incomplete substances; and from this, that they are incomplete, it follows that what they compose is *ens per se.* [My objection holds] that it is not accidental to the human body to be united to the soul, but its very nature; for, since the body has all the dispositions requisite for receiving the soul, and without it is not properly the human body, it could not without a miracle happen that the soul should not be united to it. Also it is not accidental to the soul that it is united to the body; it is accidental to it only after death, on being separated from the body. . . . As I have just said, the union is accidental *quodam modo,* but is not accidental *absolute.*

CORRESPONDENCE WITH PRINCESS ELIZABETH [4]

[In a letter (6/16 May 1643) Princess Elizabeth begs Descartes to help her to a better understanding of the question, how the mind of man, being, as it is, only a thinking substance, can bring about movements in the body.]

For it seems that all determination of movement takes place by the propulsion[5] of the thing moved, by the manner in which it is propelled by that which moves it, and by the qualification and shape of the surface of this latter. Contact[6] is required for the first two conditions, and extension for the

---

[4] *A.T.* iii, p. 661.
[5] *pulsion.*
[6] *l'attouchement.*

third. You yourself entirely exclude extension from the notion you have of mind, and a touching seems to me incompatible with an immaterial thing.

[Descartes, replying on May 31, 1643, writes as follows:][7]

I can truthfully say that this question which your Highness proposes seems to me to be the question which above all others can most reasonably be raised, in sequel to [what I have said in] my published writings. For there are two things in the human soul upon which all the knowledge we can have of its nature depends, on the one hand that it thinks, and on the other that being united to the body it can act and suffer along with the body. I have said [in the *Meditations*] almost nothing of this latter, and have studiously set myself to expound only the former. The reason for my doing so is that inasmuch as my principal design was to prove the distinction subsisting between mind and body, the former could serve in this design, whereas the other, if dwelt on, would have been by no means helpful. But as your Highness is so clear-seeing that there is no concealing anything from her, I shall here endeavor to explain the manner in which I conceive the union of mind and body, and how the mind has the power of moving the body.

First, then, I consider that there are in us certain primary notions,[8] which are, as it were, the originals on the pattern of which we form all the rest of our knowledge. And there are only a very few such notions; for after the most general, those of being, of number, of duration, etc., which apply to everything that we can cognize, we have, for body in particular, no notion save that of extension, from which follow those of shape and movement; and for the soul by itself, we have no notion save that of thought,[9] in which are comprised the cognitions[10] of the understanding and the inclinations of the

[7] *A.T.* iii, pp. 663-68.
[8] *notions primitives.*
[9] *pensée.*
[10] *les perceptions.*

will; finally, for soul and body [operating] together we have no notion save that of their union, and it is on this notion of their union that we have to depend for our notion of the force which the soul has of moving the body, and which the body has of acting on the soul, thereby causing its sentiments and passions.

I consider also that all human science consists simply in distinguishing these notions, and in attributing each of them only to those things to which they pertain. For when we seek to explain any difficulty by means of a notion which does not apply to it, we cannot fail to deceive ourselves, as also when we seek to explain one of these notions by another; being primary, each of them can be understood only by itself. And since our habitual use of the senses has rendered the notions of extension, of shapes and movements, so much more familiar to us than our other notions, the chief cause of our errors is that we ordinarily seek to make use of these notions in explaining things to which they do not apply, as when, in seeking to apprehend the nature of the soul, we look for help to the imagination, or when, in our endeavor to envisage the action of the soul on the body, we view it in the manner of the action of a body on another body.

This is why, in the *Meditations,* which your Highness has condescended to honor me by reading, my [chief] endeavor has been to treat of the notions which pertain to the soul alone. Consequently, in sequel thereto, the question with which I must now deal is our manner of apprehending those notions which pertain to the union of soul and body, as distinguished from those which pertain to body alone or to soul alone. For this purpose, we can, I think, make use of what I have written at the close of my *Replies to the Sixth Objections.*[11] We may not seek for these simple notions otherwise than in our soul, which has them all in itself by its very nature, but which does not always distinguish them

11 Given below, p. 258.

sufficiently from one another, or, it may be, fails to attribute them to the subjects to which they ought to be attributed.

Thus I believe that we have hitherto confounded the notion of the force with which the soul acts on the body with that by which one body acts on another, and that we have attributed both of these notions, not to the soul, since we have not yet come to know it, but to the diverse qualities of bodies, such as weight, heat, etc., which we have imagined to be real, that is to say, to have an existence distinct from that of the body, and consequently to be substances [and, in the case of gravity, to be in effect a self],[12] though we have called them qualities. And in conceiving these qualities we have made use, sometimes of notions which are in us for the knowing of the body, and sometimes those which are in us for the knowing of the soul, according as what we have attributed to them has been material or immaterial. For example, on supposing that weight is a real quality of which we have no other notion save that of its being a force to move the body in which it is toward the center of the earth, we have no difficulty in apprehending how it moves this body nor how it is joined to it; nor do we think that it operates by an actual touching of one surface against another, for we experience in ourselves that we have a particular [i.e., a special, additional] notion for use in apprehending it; and I believe that we are misusing this [additional] notion [i.e., of moving force] in applying it to weight, which is nothing really distinct from body, as I hope to show in my physics. This notion [of moving force] has been given us that we may have an awareness of the fashion in which the soul moves the body. . . .[13]

12 Cf. below, p. 259.

13 *A.T.* iii, p. 668. The over-concise concluding sentence may be expanded as follows: "This [immediately experienced] notion of moving force is what enables us to be aware of the fashion in which the mind [in virtue of its union with the body and therefore in unitary cooperation with the body] moves the body." Cf. below, p. 255: "to apprehend the union of two things is to apprehend them as one single thing."

[The Princess, in her next letter,[14] which, like the first, is brief and pointed, frankly avows that Descartes' reply has failed to remove her doubts and difficulties and that his references to gravity have served only to bewilder her. How, she asks, can the notion of gravity, a notion which, as he points out, he has himself rejected as fallacious, and as not being tenable even in the purely physical sphere, be yet declared helpful in meeting the difficulties she has raised. For her own part, she finds it easier to allow matter and extension to the mind than to attribute to the mind, viewed as an immaterial being, a capacity to move the body and to be moved by it. To this challenge Descartes responds (June 28, 1643) in a manner no less frank and open. Hers is a demand he is eager and ready to meet. Insistent, like himself, on clarity of thought—was she not, just because of this, destined to become his favorite pupil? His previous reply, as he confesses, has been incomplete, and on that account misleading.]

I am very greatly obliged to your Highness, that after having found that I had explained myself badly in my preceding remarks regarding the question you have been pleased to propound to me, you yet deign to have the patience to listen to me further on the same topic, and to give me the opportunity of dwelling on the things I have omitted. Of the omissions the principal seem to me to be these: that after having distinguished three kinds of primary ideas or notions which are known each in its own particular manner, and not by comparison one with another, i.e., the notion we have of the soul, the notion we have of the body, and the notion we have of the union which is between soul and body, I ought to explain the difference there is in these three kinds of notions, and in the operations of the soul by which we have them, and to state the means we have of rendering each of them familiar and easy; and then, in sequence, to explain why I made use of the comparison with weight, and to show that, while we may choose to view the soul as material (for that is what we do in apprehending its union

[14] *A.T.* iii, pp. 690-95.

with the body), we none the less still continue to know that it is separable from the body. These, I take it, are the tasks your Highness would have me discharge.

First, then, I note how very different are the three kinds of notions: the soul apprehends itself solely by means of the pure understanding; body, that is to say extension, shapes and movements, can be known by the understanding acting alone, but much better by the understanding aided by the imagination; and finally the things which pertain to the union of soul and body, can be known only obscurely by the understanding acting alone, or even by the understanding aided by the imagination, but are known very clearly by the senses.[15] Hence it comes about that those who never philosophize, and who make use only of their senses, entertain no doubts that the soul moves the body and that the body acts on the soul. They consider the two as one single thing, that is to say, they apprehend their union; for to apprehend the union of two things is to apprehend them as one single thing. While metaphysical thoughts which bring into exercise the pure understanding serve to render familiar the notion of mind; and while the study of mathematics, which exercises the imagination chiefly in the consideration of shapes and movements, accustoms us to form very distinct notions of body; it is by relying exclusively on the activities and concerns of ordinary life,[16] and by abstaining from metaphysical meditation and concentrating instead on the things which exercise the imagination [in mathematics and physics], that we can learn to apprehend the union of soul and body.

I am almost afraid that your Highness may think that I am not here speaking seriously. But that would be contrary to the respect I owe to her, and I shall never fail to render it to her. I can, indeed, say with truth, that the chief rule which I have always observed in my studies, and which, I am convinced, has been most helpful to me in acquiring

[15] *très clairement par les sens.*
[16] *en usant seulement de la vie et conversations ordinaires.*

knowledge, has been this: that I have never employed myself for more than a very few hours in the day in thoughts which occupy the [understanding aided by the] imagination, and a very few hours in the year in thoughts which occupy the understanding alone; and that I have devoted all the rest of my time to the relaxations of the senses and to the repose of the mind. I have even counted among the exercises of the imagination all serious conversations and everything which calls for the exercise of attention. This is what has made me retire to the country; for though I could still, in the busiest city in the world, have as many hours to myself as I now devote to study, I yet could not employ them so usefully, since my mind would be fatigued by the attention required in the never-ceasing comings and goings of life. And here I take the liberty of writing to your Highness, to express to her how I am indeed filled with wonder that amidst the occupations and cares which are never lacking to those who are at once of great spirit and of high birth, she has been able to find leisure for the meditations which are required for right understanding of the distinction which exists between mind and body.

But I have judged that it has been these very meditations which have caused her to find obscurity in the notion we have of their union. The human mind, as it seems to me, is not capable of conceiving distinctly at one and the same moment both the distinction between soul and body and their union. To do so, we should have to conceive them as one single thing, and at the same time to conceive them as two; and this cannot be done. And in dwelling on this (assuming that your Highness would still have the reasons which prove the distinction of soul and body strongly present to her mind, and not wishing to suggest that they must be set aside in representing the notion of the union which each one of us, without philosophizing, constantly experiences in himself, viz., that he is a single person, having at once a body and a thought[17] of such a nature that this thought can

17 *une pensée.*

move the body and can sense the accidents which befall it),
I made use in my previous letter of the comparison with
weight and with those other qualities which we commonly
imagine to be united to certain bodies in the manner in
which thought is united to our body. The fact that these
qualities are not indeed real in the manner in which they
are being supposed to be real, and that the comparison is
in that respect defective, did not prevent me from using the
comparison, since I was assured that your Highness would
not thereby be misled, already fully persuaded as you are
that the soul is a substance distinct from the body.

But since your Highness declares that it is much easier to
attribute matter and extension to the soul than to attribute
to it the capacity to move a body and to be moved by it
[i.e., to be sensuously affected] without being itself material,
I beg her to feel quite free to attribute to the soul this matter
and this extension; for that is precisely what we do in apprehending it as united to the body. And after having viewed
them in this way, and having experienced the union in her-
self, it will be easy for her to recognize that the matter she
will have thus attributed to this thought[18] is not the same
as thought [i.e., not the same as the soul] and that the extension of this matter is of a different nature from any
extension that can be attributed to thought. For whereas the
extension of matter is determined to a certain location from
which it excludes all other corporeal extension, this does not
hold of the extension appropriate to thought.[19] And thus
your Highness will still be entirely free to fall back on the

[18] à cette pensée.

[19] This is a somewhat free translation; the original reads: "Et
après avoir bien conceu cela, et l'avoir éprouvé en soi-même, il lui
sera aisé de considérer que la matière qu'elle aura attribuée à cette
pensée n'est pas la pensée même, et que l'extension de cette matière
est d'autre nature que l'extension de cette pensée, en ce que la
première est déterminée à certain lieu, duquel elle exclut toute autre
extension de corps, ce que ne fait pas la deuxième." Descartes has
expressed himself on this point much more explicitly in the passage
quoted below from his Replies to the Sixth Objections.

knowledge of the distinction of soul and body, notwithstanding that she has conceived their union.

Finally, while I believe that it is very necessary to have
thoroughly comprehended, once in one's life, the principles
of metaphysics, since it is they which give us the knowledge
of God and of our soul, I also believe that it would be very
injurious to occupy the understanding frequently in dwelling
upon them, since we cannot to any good purpose neglect
the functions of the imagination and the senses; and that
we had best be content to retain in memory and belief the
conclusions once we have drawn them, employing all the
remaining time we have in study of those thoughts in which
understanding acts together with the imagination and the
senses. . . .

RELEVANT PASSAGES FROM DESCARTES' REPLIES TO THE SIXTH OBJECTIONS AND FROM HIS LETTER TO ARNAULD

[The passage in Descartes' *Replies to the Sixth Objections* to
which he has, in his first letter, directed Princess Elizabeth's attention, amplifies and helps us to clarify what he has been intending to signify by his "gravity" illustration. But before passing to it, the following considerations should be borne in mind.
Holding, as Descartes does, that the mind is incapable of in-
venting a single new simple idea, all complex notions, even
those which are, as we say, "fictitious," must allow of being resolved without remainder into natures which we have genuinely experienced; and this is the criterion on which he relies
in his examination of the "substantial forms," i.e., of the occult properties, family and powers, appealed to in the Aristotelian physics. "Gravity" conceived as a property or force in
bodies, carrying them toward the Earth's center, is, Descartes
declares, a typical substantial form; and is the example which
he almost invariably chooses in his discussion and criticism of
them. What, he asks, are the experienced data which have been
presumed to justify the notion of gravitation? They are, in the

first place, the movements of falling bodies, and what we choose to call their weight when at rest. Secondly, there is our inner awareness, no less immediate, and therefore no less clear, of the mind's active agency when willing movements of the limbs. It is this latter experience of which we are making use when we fabricate the notion of gravity as an active agency in *bodies*. But when apprehended distinctly, and not merely clearly, it has to be recognized as being possible of existence only in some mind.

This general line of criticism, which in principle is applicable in the case of all the other substantial forms and faculties, Descartes supplements, in the special case of gravity, in a twofold manner. First, by proof that the movements, to explain which it is postulated, can, like all other physical occurrences, be accounted for mechanistically. And secondly, by drawing attention to the ambiguous manner in which gravity, considered as a *physical* entity, is being conceived. Though entitled "a real quality indwelling in solid bodies," it is, in truth, as the epithet "real" implies, being regarded as a substance, i.e., on the pattern of a self or soul indwelling in bodies and acting as the originating source of their movements.

On taking due account of all these considerations, and distinguishing, clearly and distinctly, our ideas of mind from our ideas of body, we thus discover that all the current notions of substantial forms and powers have been composed or manufactured (*conflatas effictasve*) by a surreptitious combining of the two, and as such are confused and misleading.

The relevant passage in Descartes' *Replies to the Sixth Objections* is as follows. Asking how the unphilosophical mind, lacking in true understanding of the distinction between mind and matter, judges of body, he proceeds:]

From infancy . . . the mind has been conscious of its own proper nature and has had present to it the idea of thought as well as of extension; but since in thinking of things purely intellectual it has always at the same time engaged in imagining something corporeal, it has taken the two ideas to be one and the same, and has referred all the notions it has of intellectual things to the body. And not having yet freed myself from these prejudices, there was nothing which I knew with sufficient distinctness, and nothing which I did not suppose to be corporeal, even though the ideas of those things which I was supposing to be corporeal were often formed in ways that concerned minds rather than bodies.

For since I was apprehending gravity, for example, in the guise of a real quality indwelling in solid bodies, and although I called it a quality, yet since in referring it to the bodies in which it dwelt, I added the epithet real, I was in truth thinking it to be a substance—just as clothing regarded by itself is a substance, although when referred to the man whom it clothes it is a quality. Similarly the mind, though certainly a substance, can be styled the quality of the body to which it is conjoined. And although I have been viewing gravity as diffused throughout the whole of the heavy body, none the less I have not been ascribing to it that very extension which constitutes the nature of the body. (For true bodily extension is an extension that rules out all inter-penetration of parts.) I have been of the opinion that there was as much gravity in a mass of gold or of some other metal a foot long, as in a piece of wood ten feet long; nay, I believed it could all be contracted within a mathematical point. Indeed I also saw that even while remaining co-extensive with the heavy body, it could exercise its force at any point of the body, because whatever the part might be to which a rope was attached, it pulled the rope with all its weight, exactly as if the gravity resided in the point alone which the rope touches, and was not diffused through its other parts. Certainly it is in no other way that I now understand mind to be co-extensive with the body, the whole in the whole, and the whole in any of its parts. But what most decisively shows that this idea of gravity has been derived from that which I had been holding in regard to mind is, that I have been thinking of gravity as that which carries bodies toward the center of the Earth as if it had within itself some knowledge of this center. For it could not act as it did without knowledge, nor can there be any knowledge save in mind. Nevertheless, I was also ascribing

to gravity certain other things which cannot be understood
to apply to mind in the same sense; as e.g., that it was divisible, measurable, etc.

But after I had noted these things with sufficient care,
and had accurately distinguished the idea of mind from the
ideas of body and of corporeal movement, and had discovered that all the other ideas which I previously had of
real qualities and of substantial forms had been composed
or manufactured by me out of these ideas of mind and body,
I easily released myself from all the doubts here advanced.[20]

LETTER TO ARNAULD [21]

(July 29, 1648)

[Another passage, no less helpful in understanding why Descartes has so persistently dwelt on the notion of gravity,
occurs in one of his letters to Arnauld. Arnauld had written
him asking how it can be that the mind has power to control
movements of the animal spirits in the brain and nerves,
though, as Descartes has himself emphasized, our mind has no
awareness of them. (And, as Arnauld might also have pointed
out, Descartes, in his *Replies to the Sixth Objections,* had
argued that gravity, to be capable of carrying bodies toward
the center of the Earth, would have to have knowledge of that
center.) Descartes replies in the following manner:]

It is true that we are not aware of the way in which our
mind discharges the animal spirits into this or that nerve;
for this does not depend on the mind alone, but on the
mind's union with the body. Yet we do have knowledge of
all the action by which the mind moves the nerves, in so far
as such action is in the mind, since it is no other than the

[20] *A.T.* vii, pp. 441-43 and ix, pp. 240-41. Cf. *Meditation* VI,
above, p. 244: "When I consider the mind, that is to say, my self in
so far only as I am a thinking thing (*res cogitans*), I can distinguish
in myself no parts; I apprehend myself to be a thing single and
entire."

[21] *A.T.* v, pp. 221-23.

inclination of the will to this or that movement of the limbs; and this inclination of the will is followed by the flow of the animal spirits into the nerves, and by all that is requisite for the movement—all this being due to the appropriate disposition of the body, of which the mind can be ignorant, and to the mind's union with the body, of which the mind is certainly aware; otherwise the mind could never incline its will to the moving of the limbs.[22]

Accordingly, though we are not in a position to understand, either by reasoning or by any comparison drawn from other things, how the mind, which is incorporeal, can move the body, none the less we cannot doubt that it can, since experiences the most certain and the most evident make us at all times immediately aware of its doing so.[23] This is one of those things which are known in and by themselves and which we obscure if we seek to explain them by way of other things. Nevertheless [having thus forewarned you], I shall here make use of a comparison. The majority of philosophers, believing that the weight of a stone is a real quality, distinct from the stone, believe themselves to understand sufficiently well in what manner this quality can move a stone toward the center of the Earth, and they do so because

[22] This is a free interpretation of the difficult, over-concise text: *atque hanc voluntatis inclinationem sequuntur spirituum in nervos inflexus, et reliqua, quae ad istum motum, requiruntur; hocque propter aptam corporis configurationem quam mens potest ignorare, ac etiam propter mentis cum corpore unionem, cuius sane mens conscia est; aliquin enim ad membra movenda voluntatem suam non inclinaret.*

[23] Here Descartes is again stating his argument elliptically. Since the union of mind and body is known only by way of sense, not of understanding, it is abidingly incomprehensible to us; and the union of mind and body being thus incomprehensible, so likewise are the modes of their interaction, whether in the moving of the limbs or in the generation of sensations and other passions. This, too, Descartes proceeds to argue, is why the notion of the union has to be acknowledged as being for us primary and ultimate, i.e., as being interpretable only in terms of itself. All voluntary movements, all sensations and passions, rest on the union; neither mind by itself nor body by itself can suffice to account for their occurrence. The movements, as being willed, are foreign to the body; the sensations and passions, as being sensuous, are foreign to mind as well as to body.

they think they have a manifest experience of it. For myself, persuaded as I am that there is no such quality in nature, and that there can therefore be no true idea of it in the human understanding, I judge that in representing this idea to themselves they are making use of the idea they have in themselves of incorporeal substance, and that their manner of doing so is such that it is no more difficult for us to apprehend how the mind moves the body than it is for them to apprehend how such a quality carries the stone downwards. That they do not declare this weight to be a substance makes no difference; for they do, in effect, view it as a substance, since they think of it as being real, and as capable in virtue of some power, that is to say, by way of Divine Power, of existing apart from the stone.[24] Nor does their declaring it to be corporeal make any difference; for if by the corporeal we mean that it pertains to body even while being of a different nature from body, the mind can also be said to be corporeal in that it is suited to union with the body. But if by corporeal we mean that which partakes of the nature of body, weight, as above viewed, is as different from the corporeal as is the human mind.

[24] Descartes is here intent on making complete the analogy which he is suggesting between the relation in which gravity stands to body and the relation in which soul stands to body.

THE PASSIONS OF THE SOUL[1]
[SELECTIONS]

PART I

OF THE PASSIONS IN GENERAL, AND INCIDENTALLY THE WHOLE NATURE OF MAN

Article 1. *What in respect of a subject[2] is passion,*
is in some other regard always action

IN nothing do the sciences we have inherited from the ancients appear more defective than in what they have written on the passions. This is a topic which has at all times been much studied, and would not appear to be of any quite special difficulty. Does not everyone on experiencing the passions within himself have no need, in the discovery of what they are, of observing anything outside himself? None the less, what the ancients have taught regarding them is so slight and for the most part so far from credible, that I cannot hope to get within sight of the truth save by departing from the paths they have followed. In other words, I feel myself obliged to write as if I were treating of a matter to which no one before me had ever paid due attention. On proceeding to do so, I observe that whatever occurs in the way of novelty or change, is by the philosophers ordinarily termed a passion[3] in respect of the subject to which it hap-

---

[1] Begun in 1645, later revised and extended, and published in 1649. Cf. *A.T.* iv, p. 309 ff.; xi, p. 293 ff.

[2] Cf. above, p. 81 n.

[3] The wide general sense in which Descartes is here using the term "passions" is explained below, in Articles 7, 25 and 27-29.

pens and an action in respect of what causes it to happen. Though agent and patient are often very different, the action and the passion are thus always one and the same thing. We are allowing it these two names because of the two diverse subjects to which we can refer it.

Article 2. *That to understand the passions of the soul we have to distinguish its functions from those of the body*

I note that we are not aware of any subject which acts upon our soul more immediately than does the body with which it is conjoined, and that consequently we ought to recognize that what in the soul is a passion is in the body usually an action. There is therefore no better way of gaining an understanding of the passions than to examine the difference there is between mind and body, with a view to knowing to which of the two we should attribute each one of the functions that are in us.

Article 3. *What rule we should follow in so doing*

We shall not find much difficulty in doing this, if we take note that whatever we experience as being in us, and which, we find, can also exist in completely inanimate bodies, has to be attributed to our body, and on the other hand that all which is in us, and which we cannot anywise view as appertaining to a body, has to be attributed to the soul.

Article 4. *That the heat and movement of the limbs proceed from the body, the thoughts from the soul*

Thus, because we cannot view the body as in any fashion thinking, we are right in believing that all the various kinds of thoughts which are in us appertain to the soul; and because we do not doubt that there are inanimate bodies which can move in as many or more diverse ways than can our limbs, and which have as much heat or more (as experience shows us in the case of flame, which has in itself more heat and movement than any of our members), we ought to recognize that all the heat and movements which are in us, in so far as they do not anywise depend on thought, appertain exclusively to the body.

Article 5. *That it is an error to believe that the soul gives the body its movement and heat*

Proceeding on these lines, we shall avoid a very serious error into which many have fallen, and which indeed I esteem to be the primary cause of our failure hitherto to explain the passions and other matters pertaining to the soul. The error is that, from observing how all dead bodies are devoid of heat, and consequently of movement, it has been thought that it is the absence of the soul which has caused these movements and this heat to cease; and thereby, without reason we have come to believe that our natural heat and all the movements of our body depend on the soul. What, on the contrary, we ought to hold is that the reason why soul absents itself on death is that this heat ceases and that the organs which operate in moving the limbs disintegrate.

Article 6. *The difference there is between a living and a dead body*

That we may avoid this error, let us recognize that death never comes through failure of soul, but solely because some one of the principal parts of the body disintegrates. Let us hold that the body of a living man differs from that of a dead man just as any machine that moves of itself (e.g., a watch or other automaton when it is wound up and thereby has in itself the corporeal principle of those movements for which it is designed, together with all else that is required for its action) differs from itself when it is broken and the principle of its movement ceases to act.

. . . . .

Article 17. *Concerning the functions of the soul*

After having thus considered all the functions which appertain to the body alone, we easily recognize that there remains in us nothing which we should attribute to our soul save only our thoughts. These are of two principal kinds, the actions of the soul and its passions. All our volitions I name actions, because we experience them as proceeding directly from our soul and as seeming to depend on it alone: while, on the other hand, we can give the general title passions to all those modes of awareness which often arise in us without our soul making them to be what they are, and which in all cases it receives from the things which they [stand for and] represent.

Article 18. *Concerning the will*

Our volitions, in turn, are also of two kinds. Some actions of the soul terminate in the soul itself, as when we will to love God, or in general apply our thought to some non-material object. Our other actions terminate in our body, as when from our merely willing to walk, it follows that our legs are moved and that we walk.

Article 19. *Concerning cognizing*[4] [*i.e., awareness*]

Our cognizings are likewise of two kinds. Some have the soul

4 *De la perception.* Cf. Article 28.

as their cause, others the body. Those which have the soul
as their cause are the cognizings of our volitions and of all
the imagings[5] and other things which depend on these volitions. For it is certain that we cannot will anything without
cognizing by the same means that we will it; and although
in respect of our soul it is an action to will something, we
can say that to be aware that it wills is likewise a passion.
Yet because such cognizing and such volition are really one
and the same thing, it is always named from what is the
more noble, and accordingly it is not customary to call it a
passion but always to view it as an action.

Article 20. *Concerning the imagings and other thoughts which are formed by the soul*

When our soul applies itself to image something which does
not exist, as in representing to itself an enchanted palace or
a chimera, and also when it applies itself to think of something which is purely intelligible and not imageable, e.g., to
think of its own nature, the awareness it has of these things
depends chiefly [for its initiation] on the act of will which
causes us to think of them. This is why we are wont to view
them as actions rather than as passions.

Article 21. *Concerning the imagings which have the body alone as their cause*

As to the cognizings which are caused by the body, they
for the most part depend on the nerves. But there are also
some which do not, and which though entitled, like those
above referred to, imagings, yet differ from them in that our
will plays no part in forming them. Acordingly they cannot
be numbered among the actions of the soul; they come about

5 *imaginationes.* Cf. *New Studies,* p. 142 ff.

owing to the manner in which the spirits (variously agitated and coming upon traces of diverse impressions which have preceded them in the brain) take their course fortuitously by certain pores rather than by others. Such are the illusions of our dreams and the daydreams we often have when awake —our thinking wandering carelessly without directing itself to any of them. Some of these imagings are passions of the soul taking the term passion in its most proper and exact meaning, and they may all be so named if we take it in a more general sense. Since, however, they do not have so notable and so determinate a cause as the cognizings the mind receives by intervention of the nerves, and appear to be only their shadows and pictures, we must, to distinguish them properly, first of all consider the [two-fold] difference exhibited by these others.

Article 22. *How the other cognizings differ from one another*

The cognizings which I have not yet considered all come to the soul by intervention of the nerves; and between them there are these differences: that some of them we relate to outside objects which strike our senses, others to our body or to some of its parts, and others to our soul.

Article 23. *Concerning the cognizings we relate to objects external to us*

The cognizings we relate to things external to us, viz., to the objects of our senses, are caused (at least when we are not mistaken in our opinion) by those objects which, in exciting certain movements in the organs of the external senses, also excite, by way of the nerves, movements in the brain, which then cause the soul to sense them. Thus when we see the light of a torch, and hear the sound of a bell, this light and this sound are two different actions which, simply by exciting two different movements in certain of our nerves, and thereby in the brain, give the soul two different sensations, which we so relate to the subjects we are supposing to be their causes that we think we see the torch itself and hear the bell, and not that we are merely sensing the movements which proceed from them.

Article 24. *Concerning the cognizings we refer to our body*

The cognizings we refer to our body, or to certain of its parts, are those we have of hunger, thirst, and of our other natural appetites—to which may be added pain, heat and the other affections which we sense as in our limbs, not as in external objects. Thus we can sense at one and the same time, and by way of the same nerves, the cold of our hand and the heat of the flame which it approaches; or contrariwise the heat of the hand and the cold of the air to which it is exposed, without there being any difference between the actions that cause us to feel the heat or the cold of our hand and the actions which cause us to feel what is external to us, excepting only that inasmuch as one of these actions follows upon the other, we judge the first to be already in us, and what supervenes upon it as not yet so, but as in the object which causes it.

Article 25. *Concerning the cognizings we refer to our soul*

The cognizings which we refer exclusively to the soul are those whose effects we feel as in the soul itself, and in respect of which we do not usually know any proximate cause to which we can relate them. Such are the feelings of joy, anger and the like, excited in us sometimes by the objects that move our nerves and sometimes by other causes. All our cognizings, both those we refer to objects external to us and those we refer to the various affections of our body, are indeed passions in respect of our soul, when we use the term passion in its most general meaning. We are, however, wont to restrict the term to signify only those which are related to the soul itself; and it is these alone that I have here undertaken to explain under the title, passions of the soul.

Article 26. *That the imagings which depend solely on the fortuitous movement of the spirits may be passions just as truly as the cognizings which depend on the nerves*

We have still to note that whatever the soul is aware of by intervention of the nerves can also be represented by the fortuitous course of the [animal] spirits, without there being any other difference save only that the impressions which come into the brain by way of the nerves are usually more lively and more definite than those excited there by the spirits. This is what led me to say in Article 21 that the latter are, as it were, the shadows or the pictures of the former. We must also note that it sometimes happens that the picture is so similar to the thing it represents that while we can be deceived regarding the cognizings which refer to objects outside us, or at least regarding those which refer to certain parts of our body, we cannot be thus deceived regarding the passions. So close, so interior, to our soul are the passions, that it is impossible it should sense them unless they veritably are what it senses them as being. Often when asleep, and sometimes even when awake, we image certain things so vividly that we think we see them before us or sense them in our body, although they have yet no such existence there. But whether asleep or day-dreaming, we cannot be sad, or be stirred by any other passion, save in so far as the soul does have the passion veritably in itself.

Article 27. *The definition of passions of the soul*

Having thus considered how the passions of the soul differ from all its other thoughts, we may, it seems to me, define them, in general terms, as being those cognizings, or feelings,[6] or emotions of the soul, which we thus view as specially pertaining to it, and which are caused, upheld and fortified by some movement of the [animal] spirits.

Article 28. *Explanation of the first part of this definition*

We can entitle them cognizings[7] when we use this word in a general manner to signify all the thoughts which are not actions, i.e., not volitions, of the soul, but not when using it to signify only evident cognitions.[8] For experience shows us that those who are the most excited by their passions are not those who know them best, and that their passions are to be counted as belonging to that group of cognizings which the close alliance of mind and body renders confused and obscure. We may also entitle them feelings,[9] as being received into the soul in the same fashion as the objects of the external senses, and otherwise not known by it. But it is better to name them emotions of the soul,[10] not only because this name can be given to all the changes which take place in it,[11] i.e., to all the various thoughts which the soul can know, but especially because, of all the various kinds of thoughts it can have, there are no others which agitate and unsettle it so powerfully as do these passions.

[6] *perceptions, ou sentiments.*
[7] *perceptions.*
[8] *des connaissances évidentes.*
[9] *sentiments.*
[10] *émotions de l'âme.*
[11] Cf. Article 41.

Article 29. *Explanation of the other part of the definition*

I add that they quite specially refer to the soul, in order to distinguish them from the other feelings which are not so referred—some, such as odors, sounds, colors, referred to external objects, others, such as hunger, thirst, pain, referring to our body. I also add that they are caused, upheld and fortified by some movement of the [animal] spirits, in order to distinguish them from those of our volitions which can also be entitled emotions of the soul, but which besides being referred to the soul are also caused by it; and also in order to explain their nearest, most proximate cause, which again distinguishes them from the other feelings.

Article 30. *That the soul is united to all parts of the body conjointly*

But for the more perfect understanding of all these things, we must know that the soul is really joined to the whole body, and that we cannot, properly speaking, say that it is in any one of its parts to the exclusion of the others—the body being unitary, i.e., in some fashion indivisible, in virtue of the disposition of its organs which are so related each to the others, that when any one of them is removed, the whole body is rendered defective. Again, the soul is of such a nature that it has no relation to extension, nor to the dimensions or other properties of the matter composing the body, but only to the whole assemblage of its organs, as appears from our inability to think of the half or the third of a soul, or of its occupying a space. It does not become smaller on the removal of a part of the body. When, however, the assemblage of the bodily organs disintegrates, it itself, in its entirety, withdraws from the body.

Article 31. *That there is a small gland in the brain in which the soul exercises its function more specifically than in its other parts*

We have also to bear in mind that although the soul is joined to the whole body, there is yet in the body a certain part in which it exercises its functions more specifically than in all the others. It is a matter of common belief that this part is the brain, or possibly the heart—the brain because of its relation to the senses, the heart because it is there we feel the passions. But on carefully examining the matter I seem to find evidence that the part of the body in which the soul exercises its functions immediately is in no wise the heart, nor the brain as a whole, but solely the innermost part of the brain, viz., a certain very small gland, situated in a midway position, and suspended over the passage by which the animal spirits of the anterior cavities communicate with those of the posterior cavities, in such fashion that its slightest movements can greatly alter the course of those spirits; and reciprocally that any change, however slight, taking place in the course of the spirits can greatly change the movements of this gland.

Article 32. *How we know this to be the chief seat of the soul*

The reason which persuades me that the soul cannot have anywhere in the body any other location for the immediate exercise of its functions is that I observe all the other parts of the brain to be double, just as we have two eyes, two hands, two ears, and indeed, all the organs of our external senses double; and that since of any one thing at any one time we have only one single and simple thought, there must be some place where the two images which come from the two eyes, and where the two impressions which come from one single object by way of the double organs of the other senses, can unite before reaching the soul, and so prevent their representing to it two objects in place of one. We can easily think of these images or other impressions as being united in this gland by mediation of the spirits which fill the cavities of the brain. There is no other place in the brain save only this gland, where they can be thus united.

Article 33. *That the seat of the passions is not in the heart*

As to the opinion of those who think that the soul receives its passions in the heart, it is not of any weight. Its sole foundation is the feeling we have of the changes brought about in the heart by the passions, and it is easy to show that this alteration is felt in the heart solely owing to the intervention of a small nerve which descends to it from the brain, just as pain is felt in the foot owing to the intervention of the nerves of the foot, and just as the stars are apprehended as in the heavens owing to the intervention of their light and of the optic nerves. Thus it is no more necessary that our soul should exercise its functions immediately in the heart, in order that its passions be felt there, than it is necessary for the soul to be in the heavens in order that the stars be seen there.

Article 34. *How the soul and the body act on one another*

Let us then allow that the soul has its chief seat in the small gland which is in mid-brain, and that from there it radiates through all the rest of the body owing to the intervention of the [animal] spirits, the nerves and even the blood, which, participating in the impressions of the spirits, can carry them by way of the arteries to all its members. . . .

Article 35. *An example of the manner in which impressions from objects unite in the gland which is in mid-brain*

If we see some animal approach us, the light reflected from its body depicts two images of it, one in each of our eyes. The two images, by way of the optic nerves, form two others in the interior surface of the brain which faces its cavities. From these, by way of the spirits which fill these cavities, the images then radiate toward the small gland which the spirits encircle, and do so in such fashion that the movement which constitutes each point of one of the images tends toward the same point of the gland as does the movement constituting that point in the other image which represents the same part of the animal; and in this way the two brain-images form but one image on the gland, which, acting immediately on the soul, causes it to see the shape of the animal.

Article 36. *An example of the manner in which the passions are excited in the soul*

Moreover, if this shape is very startling and terrifying, i.e., if it is closely related to things which have previously been hurtful to the body, it excites in the soul the passion of anxious apprehension,[12] and thereupon either of courage, or it may be of fear or terror,[13] according to the varying temperament of the body or the strength of the soul, and according as it has been by defense or by flight that we have hitherto secured ourselves against the harmful things to which the impression stands related. Such past actions so predispose the brain, in certain men,[14] that the spirits reflected from the image thus formed on the gland then proceed to take their

---

[12] *de la crainte.*
[13] *de la peur ou de l'épouvante.*
[14] Cf. Article 39.

course, partly in the nerves which serve in turning the back and in moving the legs for flight, partly in those which enlarge or contract the heart, partly in those which so enlarge or contract the orifices of the heart, or which so agitate the other parts whence the blood is sent to the heart, that this blood, being there [through the heat of the heart] rarefied in some unusual manner, conveys to the brain [animal] spirits suited to the maintenance and fortifying of the passion of fear, suited, that is to say, to the holding open, or to the re-opening, of those pores of the brain which conduct them to those same nerves. And since the pores, by which they pass, mainly operate through the small nerves which serve to contract or enlarge the orifices of the heart, this causes the soul to feel the pain chiefly in the heart.

Article 37. *How it seems that all passions are caused by some movement of the [animal] spirits*

This is also true of all the other passions; they are one and all chiefly caused by the spirits which are contained in the cavities of the brain, in so far as these operate by way of the nerves which serve to enlarge or contract the orifices of the heart. . . . From this it can be clearly understood why in my definition I have declared each of them to be caused by some one particular movement of the spirits.

Article 38. *An example of the movements of the body which accompany the passions but which [unlike them] do not in any wise depend on the soul*[15]

For the rest, just as the course which these spirits take to-

---

[15] These movements, though, like the passions, not *initiated* by the soul, yet differ from the passions in that they occur in the body, not in the soul.

ward the nerves of the heart suffices to give that [precise] movement to the gland through which fear is placed in the soul, so, too, this same course by which at the same instant certain spirits proceed toward the nerves which serve to move the legs for flight suffices to cause yet another movement in the gland, thereby enabling the soul to sense and apprehend this flight—the flight being thus excited in the body exclusively by the disposition of the [bodily] organs, and without any co-operation on the part of the soul.

Article 39. *How one and the same cause may excite different passions in different men*

The impressions which the presence of a terrifying object makes on the gland causes fear in certain men, and yet in other men can excite courage and confidence. The reason of this is that all brains are not constituted in the same manner, and that one and the same movement of the gland which in some excites fear, in others causes the spirits to enter partly into those brain-pores which serve to move the hands for self-defense and partly into those which agitate the blood and drive it toward the heart in the manner required to provide the spirits proper for the continuing of the defense and for the persistence in the will to do so.

Article 40. *The chief effect of the passions*

For it is all-important to note that the principal effect of all the passions in men is to incite and dispose the soul to will those things for which they [the passions] are preparing the body. Thus the feeling of fear incites in it the will to flee, that of courage the will to resist attack; and similarly with the others.

Article 41. *The power of the soul in respect of the body*

But the will is in its nature so free that it can never be constrained; and of the two kinds of thoughts which I have distinguished in the soul (on the one hand its actions, i.e., its volitions, and on the other its passions, taking this word in its most general sense as covering cognizings[16] of every sort), the former are absolutely in its power and cannot be changed by the body save indirectly, whereas the latter are absolutely dependent on the actions which produce them, and (except when it is itself their cause) cannot be changed by the soul save indirectly. Now the action of the soul consists entirely in this, that simply by willing it makes the small gland to which it is closely united move in the way requisite for producing the effect aimed at in the volition.

Article 42. *How we find in the memory the things we wish to remember*

Thus when the soul wills to recall something, this volition, by causing the gland to bend successively now to one side and now to another, impels the spirits toward this and that region of the brain, until they come upon the part where the traces left by the object we will to recall are found. These traces consist in the manner in which the spirits, owing to the paths they have taken on the presence of that object, have so modified the pores of the brain that these have thereby acquired a greater facility than the others of being opened in that same fashion when the spirits again come toward them. The spirits on meeting these pores therefore enter into them more easily than into the others, and thereby excite that special movement in the gland which represents that same object to the soul, and so enable it to know what it has willed to remember.

16 *perceptions.* Cf. Article 28.

Article 43. *How the soul can image, be attentive, and move the body*

When we wish to image something we have never seen, this volition has the power of causing the gland to move in the manner required in driving the spirits toward the brain-pores on the openings of which the thing can be represented. Thus, too, when we wish to hold our attention fixed for some little time on some one object, this volition keeps the gland bent in this direction. And lastly, when we will to walk or to move the body in any manner, this volition causes the gland to impel the spirits toward the muscles which bring about this effect.

Article 44. *That each volition is naturally connected with some movement of the gland, but that by practice or by habituation it may be connected with others*

Yet it is not always the will to excite in us some movement or some other effect which itself enables us to excite it; for that depends on how nature or habit has, in this or that case, connected each movement of the gland with some one particular thought. Thus, for instance, if we wish to adjust our eyes for the apprehension of a far-distant object, this volition causes the pupil to enlarge; and if we wish to look at a very near object, this volition causes it to contract. Should we, however, think only of enlarging the pupil, we may indeed so will, but we do not thereby enlarge it. For it is not with the volition to enlarge or contract the pupil that nature has connected the movement of the gland which serves to impel the spirits toward the optic nerve in the manner requisite for this enlarging or contracting of the pupil, but instead with that of looking at objects distant or near. When in speaking we think only of what we wish to say, this makes us move the tongue and lips much more promptly and much more effectively than if we thought of all the various actions they must go through in pronouncing the words that express this meaning. The habits we have acquired in learning to speak have connected the action of the soul, which by way of the gland can move the tongue and lips, with the meaning of the words that follow upon these movements rather than with the movements themselves.

Article 45. *What the power of the soul is in respect of the passions*

This also holds in respect of the passions. They cannot be directly excited or suppressed by the action of our will, but only indirectly through representation of the things which are customarily conjoined with the passions we wish to have, and contrary to those we wish to suppress. Thus, in order to excite courage and to suppress fear, the will to do so is not sufficient; we have to bring to mind the reasons, the signs, which suggest to us that the danger is not great, that there is more security in defense than in flight, that we shall have the glory and joy of having conquered, whereas we can expect nothing but regret and shame from having fled, etc.

Article 46. *What prevents the soul from having complete control over the passions*

There is one special reason why the soul is unable to change or suppress its passions in an effortless manner, and this reason is what has led me, in defining them, to say that they are not merely caused, but also upheld and fortified by some particular movement of the [animal] spirits. They are almost all accompanied by some commotion[17] taking place in the heart, and consequently also in all the blood and [animal]

---

[17] *de quelque émotion.*

spirits, so that until this commotion has subsided, the passions remain present to our thought in the same manner as sensible objects are present to us in thought during the time they act on our sense-organs. Just as the soul, in making itself closely attentive to some other thing, can prevent itself from hearing a slight noise or feeling a slight pain, but cannot in the same way escape hearing thunder or feeling fire burning the hand, it is similarly easy to overcome the lesser passions, but not those that are more violent and powerful; we have to await the abating of the commotion in the blood and spirits. The most the will can do while this commotion is in its full strength, is to refuse consent to its effects, and to restrain several of the movements to which it disposes the body. For instance if anger causes the hand to be upraised for striking, the will can usually arrest it [from further action]; if fear incites the legs to flight, the will can restrain them, and so in all other like cases.

Article 47. *In what consists the contests we are wont to suppose as taking place between the lower and the higher parts of the soul*

All the contests we are wont to conceive as taking place between the inferior part of the soul which we call the sensuous and the superior which is rational, or, as we say, between the natural appetites and the will, consist solely in the repugnance there is between the two movements in the pineal gland—the movement excited by the spirits and the contrary movement excited by the will. For there is in us but one soul, a soul that has no diversity of parts, i.e., it is at once sensuous and rational, and all its appetites are volitions. The error committed in representing it as displaying diverse personalities that ordinarily are at variance with one another, arises from our failure to distinguish its functions from those of the body, to which alone we must attribute whatever in us is observed to be repugnant to our reason. There is, therefore, no contest save that which takes place in the small gland which is in the center of the brain, when it is impelled to one side by the soul, and to another by the animal spirits which, as above said,[18] are entirely corporeal; often the two impacts are contrary to one another; and the stronger holds the other in check. We can, indeed, in respect of movements excited in the gland by the spirits, distinguish two sorts of movement. Some of them represent to the soul the objects which are moving the senses, or, it may be, the impressions by which it is faced in the brain; and these have no influence on the will. The others do have an influence on the will, viz., those which cause the passions and the bodily movements which accompany the passions. Though the former often prevent the soul from acting, or are themselves hindered by its actions, they are yet not directly contrary to those actions; and we notice no conflict. This we observe as taking place only in respect of the latter sort of movements, i.e., between them and the volitions which are repugnant to them, e.g., between the force by which the spirits impel the gland in causing the soul to desire something and the force through which the soul, by way of the will, impels the gland in a contrary direction, to shun this something. What gives prominence to this conflict is that, as already noted,[19] the will, not having the power to excite the passions directly, is constrained to address itself to the task of considering in succession a number of different things. One of these, it may be, has the power to change for a moment the course taken by the spirits; but the thing next considered may have no such power, and the spirits revert to their previous condition, owing to the unchanged, but still continuing and contrary disposition in the nerves, heart and blood. This is how it comes about that the soul feels itself, almost at one

[18] In Article 10: *Car ce que je nomme ici des esprits, ne sont que des corps.*

[19] Article 43.

and the same time, impelled to desire and not to desire one and the same thing; and this is what has occasioned us to picture the soul as having in it two conflicting powers. There is nothing, however, to prevent our recognizing the frequent occurrence of conflict [provided we do so rightly], namely, when the cause exciting a certain passion in the soul also excites, quite independently of the soul, certain movements in the body, and when the soul immediately on apprehending the movements arrests or strives to arrest them, as happens in the case of fear. What is then exciting the fear [in the soul] is also causing the spirits to enter the muscles which serve to predispose the limbs for flight, and the resolve to be brave then counters this predisposition.

Article 48. *How we come to know the strength or weakness of souls, and what the evil is in those who are weakest*

It is by the outcome of these conflicts that each individual can come to know the force or weakness of his soul. Those whose nature is such that the will can easily conquer the passions and arrest the bodily movements which accompany them have without doubt the strongest souls. But there are those who cannot gain knowledge of their strength, owing to their never equipping the will with its proper weapons, but only with those which certain passions provide in the resisting of other [contrary] passions. What I call its proper arms are the firm and determinate judgments bearing on the good and the evil, in accordance with which it has resolved to regulate the actions of its life. The weakest of all souls are those whose will does not determine itself to follow its assured judgments, but continually allows itself to be carried away by present passions which, as being contrary to one another, draw the will now in one direction and now in another. Being thus made to battle against itself, the soul is reduced to a condition than which none can be more deplorable. Thus while fear represents death as an extreme evil, and as one that can be avoided only by flight, ambition on the other hand represents the infamy of this flight as an evil worse than death. The two passions agitate the will in opposite ways; yielding now to the one and now to the other, it is in continual opposition to itself, and the soul is thus rendered enslaved and unhappy.

Article 49. *That when knowledge of the truth is lacking, the strength of the soul does not suffice*

Few men are indeed so weak and irresolute as to desire only what their passions dictate to them. Most men have determinate judgments in accordance with which they regulate a part of their actions; and although their judgments are often false, and often indeed founded on the passions by which they have previously allowed their will to be overcome or attracted, none the less, inasmuch as the will continues to conform to the judgments, the passion that has caused their actions being absent, they may be considered its proper weapons; and we may esteem souls to be stronger or weaker according as they are able to follow those judgments more or less constantly in resisting the present passions that are at variance with them. There is, however, a great difference between resolutions which proceed from some false opinion and those which rest on knowledge of the truth. In following the latter we are assured that we shall never have ground for regret and repentance; in following the former we are no less assured of inevitably incurring regret and repentance, on discovery of our error.

Article 50. *That there is no soul so feeble as not to be able, if rightly directed, to acquire an absolute power over its passions*

Here it is helpful to know, that although, as already said,[20]

[20] Article 44.

each movement of the gland seems to have been naturally joined from our earliest years to some one of our thoughts, we can none the less by habituation join it with another, as experience shows in the case of words. These excite in the gland movements which, as instituted by nature, represent to the soul only their sound as pronounced by the voice, or, when they are written, the shape of their letters. Nevertheless, by the habit we have acquired in thinking what they mean when their sound has been thus heard and their letters thus seen, they have accustomed us to think this meaning rather than the shape of their letters or the sound of their syllables. It is also helpful to know that although the movements, alike of the gland and of the spirits and brain, which represent certain objects to the soul, are naturally connected with those which excite in it certain passions, they can, by habituation, be separated from them and joined with other very different passions; and to know that this new habit can be established by one single action independently of long usage. Thus when we are unexpectedly met by something very foul in food which we are eating with relish, the shock this gives us so changes the disposition of our brain that we can no longer see such food without abhorrence, food in which we previously took pleasure. The same thing is to be observed in animals. For although they lack reason, and perhaps thought of any kind, all the movements of the spirits of the gland, which in us excite the passions, are none the less in them, and serve to maintain and fortify not, as in us, the passions, but the movements of the nerves and muscles which customarily accompany them. Thus when a dog sees a partridge, he is naturally disposed to run toward it; and on his hearing a gun fired, the noise naturally incites him to flight. None the less setters are usually so trained that the sight of a partridge causes them to stop, and that the noise which they afterwards hear when the partridge is shot causes them to run to it. These considerations are helpful to us, as encouraging us to practice watchfulness in respect of our passions. For since we can with some little address and skill change the movements of the brain in animals devoid of reason, manifestly we can do so still more effectively in the case of men. Even those who have the weakest souls can acquire a very absolute empire over all their passions, provided they employ sufficient skill in the management and guidance of them.

PART II

THE NUMBER AND ORDER OF THE PASSIONS, AND EXPOSITION OF THE SIX PRIMITIVE PASSIONS

[Articles 52-53, 69-78]

Article 52. *Their manner of operation, and how they may be enumerated*

THE objects which move the senses do not excite diverse passions in us corresponding to all the diversities which are in them, but only in accordance with the diverse ways in which they can injure or profit us, i.e., only in so far as they are, to use a general term, of concern to us. The manner of operation of the passions, one and all, consists in this, that they dispose the soul to will the things which nature tells us are of concern to us, and to persist in so willing. The agitations of the [animal] spirits which customarily generate this and that passion also at the same time dispose the body to the movements required in our reaction to the things thus acting on the sense-organs. This is why, in order to enumerate the passions, all we have to do is to examine, in an orderly manner, in how many diverse ways—ways that are of concern to us—our senses can be moved by their objects.

Article 53. *Wonder*

[*L'Admiration*. There is no quite satisfactory English equivalent; the only possible alternatives to "wonder" are such terms as "surprise," "interest," "concern." As Descartes points out, the passion, starting as a shock of surprise, endures as a mode of wondering concern. This in turn influences the soul in two very different ways. As an *inquiring* wonder, at once question-

289

ing and open-minded, it favors those habits of mind which have made possible the sciences and philosophy. When, on the other hand, it takes the form of interest in the novel *quâ* novel, in what is "extraordinary" and "mysterious," it tends to generate, alike in the vulgar and in the bookishly learned, a positive distaste for what is the sole proper food of our finite minds, the simple and evident, the clear and distinct.]

When a first encounter with an object surprises us and we judge it to be new, or very different from what we have hitherto known or from what we have supposed it ought to be, this causes us to wonder and to be surprised. And since this can happen prior to our knowing at all whether this object is or is not serviceable to us, it seems to me that wonder is the first [i.e., in the sense of being the first to be awakened] of all the passions . . .

["Wonder" serves to illustrate in an admirably typical manner all the main distinctive features in Descartes' exposition of the nature and functions of the passions; and the sections dealing in corresponding fashion with the other passions may therefore be here omitted. Each passion, as already stated,[21] is the mental counterpart of some bodily commotion. As he now proceeds to show, what differentiates the passion of wondering surprise from the other passions is that the bodily commotion in which it originates is exclusively cerebral. Until we have learned whether the novelty engaging our wonder is beneficial or harmful—and this can come only later, as the outcome of our wondering—no other passion can be aroused, and there is therefore no call for the wider bodily commotions required in pursuit of the good and in defense against evil. This should not, however, mislead us into thinking that in the case of wonder the bodily commotion, as being exclusively cerebral, accounts for no more than merely the passion *quâ* mental. Like all the other bodily commotions, it has a two-fold effect. In addition to generating the passion in the mind, it also leads in an instinctive automatic manner to certain quite specific, adap-

[21] Article 46.

tive moments in the body. In the case of wonder the movements so generated—independently of the mental passion and
simultaneously with it—are the movements required for the
securing of an adequately attentive and sufficiently prolonged
scrutiny of the object or occurrence arousing the wonder, i.e.,
for the appropriate steadying and adjusting of the sense-
organs, all of which are centralized in and controlled by the
brain. But what is true of the other passions still applies, in
some corresponding fashion, in the case of wonder. To take
them in their more strictly mental aspect: since, as Descartes
argues, they one and all have as their specific *mental* function
the fortifying of the soul in the entertaining of those ideas
which are at the moment of special concern to it, enabling it to
accord to them such steady and prolonged attention as they
may require, any evil effects this or that passion may have must
consist either in the fortifying and conserving of ideas beyond
what is needful, or in the fortifying and conserving of others
which are harmful. Wonder, as he proceeds to show, shares,
with all the other passions, this ambiguous two-fold power;
and therefore stands, as they do, in need of regulation and
control.]

Article 69. *That there are only six primitive passions*

. . . There are only six which are simple and primitive,
viz., wonder, love, hatred, desire, joy and sadness. All
others are composed of some of these six, or are species of
them. . . . (I know well that in adopting this enumeration
of the passions I am at variance with all who have written
on the subject. But it is for a very weighty reason that I
do so. They base their enumeration on a distinction they
draw, within what they entitle the sensible part of the soul,
between two appetites which they name the *concupiscent*
and the *irascible*. As already said, I do not recognize in the
soul any distinction of parts, and the alleged distinction
seems to amount to no more than saying that the soul has
two faculties, one of desire and one of anger; and since it

has also in the same manner the faculties of wonder, love, hope, fear, and of thereby receiving into itself every other passion, and of executing the actions to which the passions impel it, I do not see why they have chosen to refer them all to concupiscence and anger.)[22]

Article 70. *Concerning wonder: its definition and its cause*

Wonder is a sudden surprise of the soul causing it to consider with attention those objects which seem to it novel and unexpected. Primarily it is caused by an impression we have in the brain, an impression which represents the object as unusual, and calling therefore for special attention. It is also conditioned by the movement of the [animal] spirits which, owing to this same brain-impression, and in sequence upon it, are made to flow with great force to the part of the brain where the impression is located, for the fortifying and conserving of it there, and for the passing of the spirits thence into the muscles which serve to hold the sense-organs steadily fixed, so that what is novel—if it is by those sense-organs that the novely has been presented to us—may be kept under observation.

Article 71. *That in this passion there occurs no change in the heart or in the blood*

This passion has the special feature, that we do not find it to be accompanied by any such change in the heart and blood as occurs in the other passions. The reason of this is that, not having good or evil as its object, but only knowledge of the things about which we are wondering, it stands in no relation with the heart or blood on which all the good

[22] This passage is from the preceding Article 68, here omitted.

of the body depends, but only with the brain which contains the sense-organs mediating the knowledge.

Article 72. *In what the strength of wonder consists*

This does not prevent its having considerable strength because of the element of surprise, i.e., the sudden and unexpected arrival of the impression, changing the movements of the spirits. This feature of surprise is at once proper and peculiar to this passion. So that whenever surprise is met with in the other passions (as it usually is in almost all of them), what we then have is wonder conjoined with them and augmenting them. The strength of any given passion depends on two things, viz., on the novelty, and on the movement it causes being from the start in full force. For certainly such a movement has more effect than those which, being feeble in the beginning and increasing only little by little, can easily be turned aside. It is also certain that sense-objects which are novel affect the brain in parts not ordinarily affected, and that since those parts are more responsive or less resistant than those which a frequent agitation has hardened, the effects of the movements they excite are thereby augmented. We shall be the more readily persuaded of this, if we consider how in similar fashion the soles of our feet, accustomed to a contact somewhat hard, proportioned as it is to the weight of the body they support, are yet in walking but little aware of the contact, whereas on their being tickled the slight and gentle contact is almost insufferable, the reason being that it violates the routine of our ordinary experience.

Article 73. *What astonishment is*

This [feature of] surprise has so much power in causing the [animal] spirits which are in the cavities of the brain to flow toward the place where the impression of the object of our wonder is located, that sometimes it draws them all there, and causes them to be so completely engaged in conserving this impression that none pass thence into the muscles, and indeed that none depart at all from the tracks they have antecedently been following in the brain. In this way the whole body is caused to stay as immobile as a statue, disabling us from apprehending the object otherwise than as initially presented, and so from acquiring a more particular knowledge of it. This is what we commonly entitle being astounded. It is an excess of wonder, and can never be other than harmful.

Article 74. *The function of the passions and how they can be harmful*

We can easily understand, from what has been above said, that the utility of all the passions wholly consists in their manner of fortifying and prolonging in the soul the thoughts which it is good it should conserve, and which, lacking their support, might readily have been effaced from it. On the other hand, all the harm they can cause consists in their fortifying and conserving these thoughts beyond what is required, or in their fortifying and conserving others on which it is not good to dwell.

Article 75. *The special function of wonder*

We can, in a quite special degree, say of wonder that it is serviceable in that it causes us to apprehend, and to retain in our memory, things of which we were previously ignorant. For we wonder only over what appears new and unusual, and nothing can so appear to us unless we have not previously known it, or perhaps because it is different from the things we have known—this being the difference which has made us regard it as unusual. Now although a thing previously unknown to us presents itself in all its novelty to our understanding and our senses, it is not merely on that account retained in our memory. We so retain it only if its idea has been fortified in our brain by some passion, or alternatively, by our understanding, should our will have determined us to a quite special attention, and to reflection upon it. The other passions may serve to make us take note of the things which are beneficial or harmful; wonder alone has the function of leading us to take note of those which appear only rarely. Hence, as we see, those who have no natural inclination to this passion are usually very ignorant.

Article 76. *In what ways wonder can be harmful, and how we can make good its deficiency and curb its excess*

But we are much more apt to wonder too much than too little. We allow ourselves to be astonished by things that merit little or no consideration; and this may entirely prevent or pervert the use of reason. This is why, good as it is to be born with some inclination to the passion, qualifying us as it does for the acquisition of the sciences, we must none the less, and precisely by way of these sciences, endeavor to emancipate ourselves from it as much as possible. For its deficiency is easily made good by special reflection (to which our will can always oblige our understanding) in respect of those things we judge to be worth the trouble. There is, however, no remedy that will cure us of excessive [mistaken] wonder other than that of acquiring the requisite amount of knowledge, and by the light of this knowledge passing to the consideration of all those things which can [rightly] seem very rare and very strange.

Article 77. *That it is neither the most stupid nor the cleverest who are most carried away by wonder*

For the rest, though only the dull and stupid are in no wise naturally disposed to wonder, this is not to say that those with the highest mental equipment are always the most disposed to it. Those so disposed are those who, although they have a fairly good supply of common sense, are yet diffident as to their abilities.

Article 78. *That excessive indulgence in wonder may become a habit, unless we fail to correct it*

This passion seems to diminish with use, since the more numerous the unusual things we find to wonder at, the more we accustom ourselves to them. Ceasing to wonder, we regard all we subsequently discover as being common. So long, however, as the passion is in excess, it causes us to give all our attention to the first [surprising] image of some object, without proceeding to any other knowledge of it, and thus induces a habit which disposes the soul to stop short in this same fashion in respect of all the other objects presenting themselves to it—so long, that is, as they appear to it to be novel, however trifling the novelty be. This is what causes the continuance of the malady in those who suffer from a blind curiosity; they seek out rarities only in order to wonder over them, and not in order to get knowledge of them. For little by little they become so given over to wonder, that things of no importance monopolize their attention to the exclusion of those which might more usefully be studied.

THE SEARCH AFTER TRUTH[1]

[The following passage, taken from the beginning of the dialogue (*A.T.* x, pp. 499-506), is a helpful commentary on the argument of Articles 74-78. Eudoxus is here Descartes' mouthpiece.]

Poliander. You are, I consider, indeed happy in having learned all these wonderful things from the Greek and Latin books. Had I studied as you have done I should, it seems to me, have been as different from what I am as the angels are from you. . . .

Epistemon. The best you could have learned, in such matters, is that the desire for knowledge, a desire common to all men, is a malady which cannot be cured. For curiosity increases as we indulge it; and since deficiencies in our souls trouble us only in so far as we become aware of them, you have an advantage over us, in that you do not see, as we do, that so many things are lacking to you.

Eudoxus. Can it be, Epistemon, that you, who are so well instructed, can be of the opinion that there is in nature so universal a malady, and that it is a malady for which nature yet produces no remedy? As for me, just as I believe that in every country fruits and rivers suffice to appease the hunger and thirst of men, so too, I am convinced, there are in plenty ascertainable truths which satisfy in quite ample fashion the curiosity of well-regulated minds. The body of a person suffering from dropsy is not further removed from its proper condition than the minds of those who are perpetually at the mercy of an insatiable curiosity.

[1] *Recherche de la Vérité*, begun, presumably, at some date subsequent to the completion of the *Meditations*, left unfinished, and published posthumously in 1701. Cf. *New Studies*, p. 28.

Epistemon. . . . I cannot believe that anyone ever knows so much that he has not still sound reasons for desiring to know more.

Eudoxus. What then will you say of me if I assure you that I no longer feel a passion to learn something more and that I am as content with the little knowledge I have as Diogenes was with his tub, and this without my having any need of his philosophy? For the science possessed by my neighbors does not set any limits to mine, not in any such manner as their fields do in surrounding my own small property. My mind, disposing as seems appropriate to it all the truths it is encountering, does not dream of there being others to discover, and thus enjoys the same repose as would the king of an isolated country, were his kingdom so completely cut off from all others that he has no thought of there being beyond his frontiers anything save infertile deserts and uninhabitable mountains.

Epistemon. If any other but you spoke to me thus, I should regard him as either vain or lacking in curiosity. This solitude, however, to which you have retired, and the little concern you have had to become known, removes from you the charge of vanity. The time you have devoted to travel, consorting with learned men, and inquiring into all that is most recondite in the existing sciences, no less assures me of your not lacking curiosity. I cannot therefore but confess that I consider you to be indeed happy, and that I am convinced that you must be in possession of a science much more perfect than that of others.

[Here, and in what follows, the reader should bear in mind what, in Descartes' view, is the outstanding merit of his new physical teaching. Having demonstrated, as he professes to have done, that all physical processes are sheerly mechanical, and that the only causes operative on the Earth and in the heavens are impact and pressure, he is in position to claim that *in principle* we already know the answer to all the questions which can be asked regarding them. In other words, his thesis is that nature is non-mysterious, and that it is not through a more detailed knowledge of physical happenings, but only through a metaphysical understanding (no less demonstratively established, and no less final in respect of its principles) of the Creative Source of physical happenings and of the self, that we can alone hope to find what is truly worthy of wonder, awe and veneration. Questions of detail, if eventually found to be of *practical* importance, can then on the lines of the established physical and metaphysical principles be fruitfully dealt with as need arises.]

Eudoxus. I thank you for your good opinion of me. But I should not so abuse your courtesy as to require you to believe what I have just said, solely on my own testimony. I should be wrong in advancing opinions so far removed from common belief, were I not at the same time in a position to supply evidence in their support. This is why I beg you both to stay on here, while this delightful weather lasts, that I may at leisure show you some part of the things I know. . . .

To make you more distinctly understand the nature of the teaching I am going to expound to you, I would have you note the difference there is between the sciences and those simple modes of knowledge which can be acquired independently of any appeal to reason, such as languages, history, geography, and in general all that rests on experience. For I readily grant that one man's experience of life would not suffice to acquire experience of all the things that are in the world; and I am no less convinced that it would be folly to desire all that. It is no more the duty of a self-respecting man to know Greek and Latin than to know the language of Switzerland or Brittany, or the history of the Romano-Germanic Empire than that of the smallest State in Europe. . . . As to the sciences . . . it is, I confess, impossible for us to treat of them in all their detail; to do so, we should have had to examine all the herbs and stones brought to us from the Indies, to have beheld the phoenix, and in short to be in ignorance of nothing in nature, however rare and strange. None the less, I shall, I believe, have effectively fulfilled my promises if, in explaining to you the truths which can be deduced from things so ordinary as to be known to all of us, I succeed in showing how you are thereby enabled to discover all the others, should you be concerned to put yourself to the trouble of inquiring into them. . . .

After drawing your attention to the works of men in things corporeal, after having stirred wonder in you by exhibiting to you machines, extremely powerful, very strange and rare automata, visual appearances seemingly real, and impostures the subtlest that artifice can devise, I shall proceed to uncover the secret devices on which they rest; and these are so simple, that you will no longer be tempted to feel wonder regarding any product of human devising. I shall then pass to nature's own products, and after showing you the cause of all their changes, the diversities of their qualities, and how the soul of plants and of animals differs from ours, I shall submit for your consideration the structural composition of all sensible things. . . . All this having been done, your passion for knowledge will, I trust, no longer be so violent, and what I have said will seem to you so well established that you will then, I hope, agree that a man of sound mind, were he nurtured in a desert, and were he illumined solely by the light of nature, could not, if he rightly pondered all the above reasons, have sentiments at variance with ours.

MODERN LIBRARY GIANTS

A series of full-sized library editions of books that formerly were available only in cumbersome and expensive sets.
THE MODERN LIBRARY GIANTS REPRESENT A SELECTION OF THE WORLD'S GREATEST BOOKS

These volumes contain from 600 to 1,400 pages each